Even
the Rat
Was
White

Even the Rat Was White:
A Historical View of Psychology

Robert V. Guthrie

Psychological Sciences Division
Office of Naval Research

Harper & Row, Publishers
New York   Hagerstown   San Francisco   London

Sponsoring Editor: George A. Middendorf
Project Editor: Karla Billups Philip
Designer: Andrea Clark
Production Supervisor: Francis X. Giordano
Compositor: Monotype Composition Company, Inc.

Art Studio: Vantage Art, Inc.

Even The Rat Was White: A Historical View of Psychology

Library of Congress Cataloging in Publication Data
Guthrie, Robert V.
     Even the rat was white.
     Bibliography: p.
     Includes index.
     1. Psychology—History.   2. Afro-American psychologists.
3. Ethnopsychology—History.   4. Anthropometry—History.
5. Blacks—Psychology.
I. Title.   [DNLM: 1. Psychology—History—U.S.
2. Ethnopsychology—History—U.S.   3. Negroes—History—U.S.
4. Race Relations—History—U.S.
E185.625 G984e]
BF105.G87   155.8   75-26520
ISBN 0-06-042561-X

To the memory of
Edward J. Barnes, 1929–1975
—a scholar, a colleague, and a friend.

Contents

Preface

This book is an attempt to present, document, and analyze vignettes in the study of man as viewed from one historical perspective. The book is divided into three parts: Part One, Psychology and Racial Differences; Part Two, Psychology and Psychologists; and Part Three, Conclusion. Part One seeks to establish some social antecedents of psychology by outlining the relationship between psychology and anthropology. Growing from this discussion are historical analyses of early psychological testing and eugenic philosophies. Chapter 1, Brass Instruments and Dark Skins, presents methodologies used to collect and measure human physical characteristics. There are discussions of the investigations of skin color, hair texture, and other characteristics. Various schemata of black-white racial combinations are evaluated and discussed. In Chapter 2, Psychology and Race, the union between psychology and anthropology is explored with emphases on early research patterns and speculations between black-white differences. Events which reinforced the nativistic themes of individual differences are explored. Chapter 3, Psychometric Scientism, is a historical analysis of the background of mental testing, with emphasis on the concept of the "mulatto hypotheses" of the 1920s. Documentary evidence illustrates the obsession of early white American psychologists with the testing of black people. Lewis Terman, of Stanford-Binet test fame, is discussed in regard to his philosophies. The ill-fated attempt by black and brown scholars during the 1930s to prevent mass IQ testing, their arguments, and their precautions against the use of psychological testing are related. Chapter 4, Psychology and Eugenics, is devoted to a discussion of the relationship between the race-betterment movement in America and the role psychologists played in supporting this concept.

Part Two discusses the development of psychology as an independent field of study and its impact on formal education in black colleges and universities. A history of those black Americans who earned doctorates in psychology and educational psychology is found in this section. Chapter 5, Psychology and Education in Black Colleges and Universities, traces the involvement of psychology in the growth and development of higher education for blacks. Early staffing and research patterns are outlined and the importance of psychology in teacher training programs is stressed. Chapter 6, Early Black Psychologists, deals with black Americans awarded the doctorate in psychology and educational psychology from 1920 to 1950 and lists dissertation titles and granting institutions. Biographical sketches outline the interests and accomplishments of most of these scholars. Chapter 7 is devoted to the first black American to be awarded the doctorate degree in psychology, Francis Cecil Sumner. A man of profound talent, Sumner's vitae warrants his recognition as the Father of Black American Psychologists.

The final section, Part Three, Conclusion, is a backward look into the material presented and a brief glance into contemporary occurrences.

In many ways, writing this book was an exciting adventure. Because much of the material was not readily available, there was a good deal of painstaking research in which I had the satisfaction of uncovering information that had appeared lost through the passage of time. There were moments of despair and frustration; yet, what seemed to be dead-end roads often led to new vistas. Tracing the black Ph.D. recipients in psychology did not offer the difficulties encountered in discovering the names of the educational psychologists. The educators were harder to locate because in most cases their degrees had been awarded by schools of education without speciality specifications. I tried to include as much information as possible in the biographical sketches in order to fill this void in our history.

Germination for this book came in 1969 with the opening sentence of an American Psychological Association journal article, "The Negro Psychologist": "Little is known about the origins, education and training of Negro psychologists."[1] This declaration of void stimulated my appetite for more information and, as a result, I formally began researching the origins and training of early black psychologists in 1972. That research resulted in Part Two of this book.

Years ago, during my own undergraduate and early graduate training in psychology, it became obvious, at least to me, that the profession of psychology had maintained an unhealthy alliance with several racist themes. The similarities in attitude, approach, and interest between psychology and anthropology appeared to be highly interrelated. In order to document these alliances, I began a formal study of this area in 1973. The resulting data led to Part One of this book.

I owe a particular debt to the research facilities of the University of Pittsburgh, Howard University's Moorland-Spingarn Research Center, and the Archives of Clark University. In addition, the libraries of the National Institute of Education, Smithsonian Institution, University of Maryland, Morehouse College, George Washington University, Tillotson College, Stanford University, University of Washington, and the Library of Congress were valuable sources of information.

Special acknowledgments are extended to Max Meenes, James Bayton, Oran Eagleson, S. O. Roberts, Martin Jenkins, Frederick Watts, Mae Claytor, James Morton, Miriam Kyle, Carlton Goodlett, Montraville Claiborne, Ruth Howard, Alberta Turner, Katharine Beverly, J. Henry Alston, Charles Thompson, Mamie Clark, Julia Bond, Lorraine Morton, Lily Brunschwig, Howard Wright, Julia Canady, Roger Williams, and Kenneth Clark—all of whom provided valuable information.

During various phases of my research and writing, discussions

1. L. Wispe, P. Ash, J. Awkard, L. Hicks, M. Hoffman, and J. Porter, "The Negro Psychologist in America," *American Psychologist* 24:2 (1969), pp. 142–150.

with Pittsburgh colleagues Edward Barnes, George Fahey, Michael Gladis, Norman Dixon, and Raymond Hummel were especially stimulating. Appreciation is extended to a Washington colleague, Eunice Turk, who read the entire manuscript with helpful suggestions. Tribute is given to Joyce Harris who did a most thorough job of typing the manuscript. Finally, unestimable credit is given to my wife, Elodia, whose encouragement from the beginning insured that this book had to be written.

R.V.G.

one
Psychology and Racial Differences

1
Brass instruments and dark skins

Long before the dawn of literary history, great African states of civilization emerged and flourished.[1] The Bantu and Hottentot tribes were engaged in large-scale cattle, goat, and sheep raising activities; Pygmies manufactured bark cloth and fiber baskets; and the Ashantis wove rugs and carpets and produced glazed pottery. Black Africans manufactured and used iron while Europeans were still in the stone age.[2] The Kingdom of Songhay produced learning centers—at Sankore, Gao, Walata, Timbuktu, and Jenne—that flourished at about the same time Spanish explorers were busy plundering the Americas and Portuguese and English voyagers were searching the shores of West Africa for ivory and gold.

The Europeans knew little about the peoples of Africa, and

their ignorance undoubtedly nourished feelings of apprehension. The Spanish spoke of "moreno" savages with temples of gold and the English reported "blacke soules" with mounds of glistening ivory. The English transmitted their perceptions of the African inhabitants in clear and often poetic detail:

> And entering in [a river], we see
> a number of blacke soules,
> Whose likelinesse seem'd men to be,
> Their Captaine comes to me
> as naked as my naile,
> Not having witte or honestie
> to cover once his taile.[3]

According to W. D. Jordan (1968), descriptions of the African's skin color as *black* was ". . . an exaggerated term in itself for it suggests that the Negro's complexion had powerful impact upon their perception."[4] It is debatable whether this impact was based upon the suddenness of contact or as a mere visual misperception, but *black* was used to describe all the inhabitants of Africa regardless of their varying degrees of darkness. It is also important to realize that the English language had placed extreme negative connotations on the concept of blackness; this helps to explain the immediate fears and eventual disdain of English-speaking people for the African. As an outgrowth of the negative notion of blackness, the Caucasian standard of beauty was frequently foisted upon the African, who was variously described as ugly, disfigured, or cursed from this frame of reference.

Religious Views

Since Europeans believed that "original" man was white, attempts to explain the presence of blacks in foreign lands often came from interpretations of religious writings. One view held that the African's dark skin and his consequent enslavement by other men had been a proclamation from God. As one story from the Old Testament was interpreted, Ham had looked at his father's drunken and naked body while his other brothers, Shem and Japheth, had covered their father, Noah, without looking at him (Genesis 9:20–25). When Noah sobered up and awoke, he blessed and rewarded Shem and Japheth for their tolerance; for Ham's ridicule, he made Canaan, Ham's son, a servant to his brothers. With Canaan now designated a "servant of servants," his descendents were doomed to a role of subjugation by supreme authority. The verses said nothing of skin color, but various interpretations held that

since the descendents were to be enslaved, it was logical they
had to be black. In the Old Testament, the Canaanites were described as a debased people, and by the time of Solomon, most
were reduced to human servitude.[5]

On the other hand, in the oral tradition of the Jews, as presented in the Babylonian Talmud (200–600, A.D.), Ham is cursed
for another reason. As this story goes, God forbade anyone to
have sexual relations while on the Ark, and Ham disobeyed the
proclamation. Thus Ham was condemned to blackness and his
descendents to perpetual servitude. In each religious explanation
Ham was accused of wrongdoings, and blackness was the direct
punishment, along with the curse of slavery.[6]

Philosophical and Scientific Views

Ancient white philosophers held that the African's blackness and
woolly hair were caused by exposure to the hot sun, while the
inhabitants of northern areas were white as a result of the colder
climate and those in warm, temperate areas were intermediate in
color. Later philosophical views also proposed similar relation-
ships between the climate and skin color. Blumenbach, the
founder of physical anthropology, held that blackness was caused
by a tendency in the tropics for carbon to become embedded in
the skin. Schweinfurth, in *Heart of Africa,* wrote that "the dark
skin is based on the ferruginous nature of the laterite soil."[7] Waitz
felt that "hot and damp countries favour the darkening of the
skin and that within the same race the skin tends to be much
darker in low marshy districts than on the neighbouring up-
lands."[8] As a result, these theories advanced the concept that the
darkness of skin color increased in proportion to the nearness of
the equator and that the geographical latitude of one's home
could be inferred from his skin color. However, as explorers
began to encounter people of dark skin in many corners of the
globe, the equatorial hypothesis was shattered.

It is interesting to note that while the ancient Egyptians recognized skin color differences, they made little effort to explain
such differences. The Egyptians decorated the walls of royal
tombs with representations of the four races of mankind whom
they believed to populate the world. They painted the Egyptians
red, the Asiatics or Semites yellow, the southerners or Negroes
black, and the westerners or northerners white with blue eyes
and fair beards (Figure 1.1).

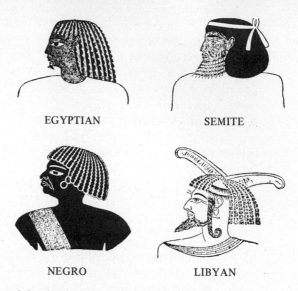

EGYPTIAN   SEMITE

NEGRO   LIBYAN

Figure 1.1 Ancient Egyptian Race Portraiture. (*Source:* Alfred C. Haddon, *History of Anthropology* [London: Watts, 1934], p. 4. Reprinted by permission of C. A. Watts & Company.)

Anthropometric Classifications

At the turn of the century, the Smithsonian Institution (Washington, D. C.) vigorously proceeded to increase data collection of human physical characteristics. Having recently acquired an anthropological collection from the Army Medical Museum, the Smithsonian showed a growing concern with the educational possibilities of the study of man. To this end, a Division of Physical Anthropology was established at the Smithsonian with Ales Hrdlicka as assistant curator-in-charge. In short order, Hrdlicka undertook the task of publishing instructions for standardization in measurement and observation of human characteristics. His "Directions for Collecting Information and Specimens for Physical Anthropology" joined the table of contents of the impressive Smithsonian Institution *Bulletin*. Previous sections of the *Bulletin* had given directions for collecting birds, insects, rocks, and minerals; Hrdlicka's contribution humanized the listing. His instructions included collection techniques in physical anthropology, involving crania, brains, and skeletons, and general observations. He called for the necessity of utilizing appropriate aids and instruments to measure "the special senses; the pressure or traction force; to make, on healthy individuals valuable observations on pulse, respiration, and temperature; to test for swiftness or endurance in running; to observe the capacity for carrying burdens, enduring hunger and thirst, and capacity for excess in food."[9]

Skin Color Measurement

Hrdlicka's technique for reporting skin color differences was presented in precise instruction to his pupils:

> In this particular [skin color], it is first of all necessary to choose for comparison the same parts of the skin, and among those who wear the clothes, preferably those parts that are usually covered. The upper part of the arm or the back is especially suitable for this purpose. In this case the color should invariably be compared with and recorded by some well-known standard, and the observation should be extended to both sexes and numerous individuals. It was largely a lack of precision in reporting the color of the skin that made a red man of our brown Indian, and other similar examples.[10]

Hrdlicka's preference for skin color standards designed by Broca (1879) was evidenced by his reference to them in several of his publications. Essentially, Broca's technique was a matter of comparison. A set of pattern colors resembling the color selection cards seen in many of today's paint stores was used to match the skin hue of the subjects. A numbering system accompanied the color standards, allowing subjective observation to be converted into statistical objectivity.[11] While Broca's standards were designed to measure only skins of color (those normally outside the Caucasian groupings of man), his technique was praised for its accuracy. "Broca's set of pattern colors, records the colour of any tribe he is observing with the accuracy of a mercer matching a piece of silk,"[12] was one statement typical of the praise.

Following the spirit of these color standards, various other attempts were made at skin color assessment utilizing paints, oils, lithography, and other tools. All met with general failure. The more interesting methods utilized devices called the *tintometer* (Gray, 1908); the *color top* (Davenport, 1912); *color blocks* (von Luschan, 1918); *color standards* (Fritsch, 1916); and the *photometer* (Shaxby and Bonnell, 1928; Dice, 1930).

Tintometer

John Gray's tintometer (Figure 1.2) was designed for measuring the amount of pigmentation in hair and eyes, as well as the skin:

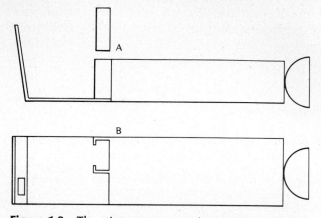

Figure 1.2 The tintometer or pigmentation meter: A, side view; B, top view. (*Source:* J. Gray, "A New Instrument for Determining the Colour of the Hair, Eyes, and Skin," *Man* 8:27[1908]:54. Reprinted by permission of the Royal Anthropological Institute of Great Britain and Ireland.)

It consists of a single tube of rectangular section (1 inch by 1 1/4 inch) and 4 inches in length. At one end of the tube is an eye-piece with a lens, and in the other end are 2 rectangular apertures, side-by-side. Surrounding one of the apertures is a sheath or pocket into which one of the standard-coloured glasses is dropped. The bottom of the rectangular tube is extended about 2 inches beyond the end of the one, where it is turned up nearly at right angles. On one side of this upwardly projecting piece is pasted a strip of white paper to form the white surface opposite the coloured glass; and on the other side is a rectangular opening which is placed over the hair, eye, or skin whose pigment is to be measured.[13]

The tintometer failed to show much promise in spite of its technically interesting properties. One of the chief reasons for its lack of popularity was due to an increasing interest shown in a toy originally manufactured to show school-age children the properties of color mixture.

Color Top

The color top, made at the turn of the century by the Milton Bradley Company in Springfield, Massachusetts, was a little device designed for expressing color quantitatively (Figure 1.3). The toy, later called "The Pupil's Color Top, No. 8109," had disks of standard black, red, yellow, and white colors arranged so that varying proportions of each were exposed as sectors of a circle. (The four color variables were labeled: Nigrum (N), Red (R), White (W), and Yellow (Y).) When the top was spun, the colors blended. By varying the proportions of the sectors (with small dissecting forceps) the color of the blend was altered. When this hue matched the color of an individual's skin, percentages were recorded. Careful instructions called for comparisons to be made with that part of the skin that was not exposed to sunlight; the deltoid region of the upper arm was often used. Specifics of this operation followed much the same procedure previously outlined by Hrdlicka:

> Skin color is to be taken on an unexposed and an exposed portion of the skin. The underside of the upper arm, which is not usually exposed is a good place to record skin color unexposed to light and wind. If this part has been exposed, the chest will serve. The cheek is usually studied for the effects of light and wind in pigment. Both are important . . . If a color top is employed, hold the spinning top as near the skin surface as possible, adjusting the disks until an approximate match results. Then record by letters and percentages the portions of each disk exposed.[14]

Even with these precise instructions, technical complaints began to be sounded in two respects: the problem of producing the desirable color and individual variances in interpreting the match between the color of the top and the color of the skin. As early as 1921, Todd and Van Gorder warned that "If the Bradley color top is to be used in the estimation it is essential to make necessary correction for the occurrence of a considerable amount of black in the red disc."[15] Later, Todd and others reiterated,

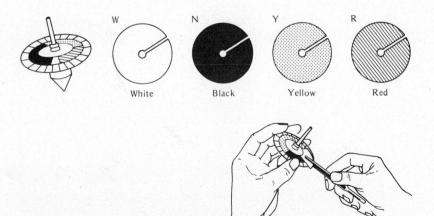

White   Black   Yellow   Red

Figure 1.3 The color top and method of adjusting the color disks. (*Source:* Louis R. Sullivan, *Essentials of Anthropometry. A Handbook for Explorers and Museum Collectors,* revised by H. L. Shapiro. [New York: American Museum of Natural History, 1928], p. 21.)

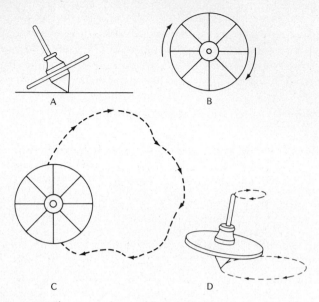

Figure 1.4 The several possible movements of a spinning color top: B always occurs, C is usually present, A and D generally occur. (*Source:* H. A. Bowman, "The Color-Top Method of Estimating Skin Pigmentation," *American Journal of Physical Anthropology* 14:1[1930]. Reprinted by permission of the publisher, Wistar Press.)

". . . there is one problem which must be faced before we can proceed . . . namely the amount of black (N) in the red disc."[16] In 1930, Bowman declared the situation hopeless: "We cannot therefore hope for uniformity in the red disc of the color top . . ."[17] Herskovits (1926) also recognized similar problems in his use of the top.[18] Nevertheless, before the top's popularity began to diminish, researchers had thoroughly overworked its usefulness. From movements of the spinning top (Figure 1.4) to the effects of lighting (Figure 1.5) to the possibilities of uniformity in speed and movement (Figure 1.6), the top was researched into oblivion.

Color Blocks

Felix von Luschan's porcelain scale of skin color standards was internationally acclaimed by virtue of his stature and esteem in the field of anthropology.[19] (His classic treatise, *Voelker Rassen Sprachen,* was a popular textbook for many early anthropologists.) The technique for using this scale was simple: the color blocks were held next to the skin until the match was made. Each block was numbered similarly to Broca's plates and the results were recorded in much the same manner. Bowman's (1930) criticism was typical; he found that the test raised resentment in the subject who became aware that his color was being matched against a European or white standard.[20]

Color Standards

Gustav Fritsch (1916) attempted to quantify skin color variations on racial grounds using seven subdivisions, each of which contained variations of seven shades.[21] He duplicated these shades with oil colors painted on strips of special paper. In order to high-

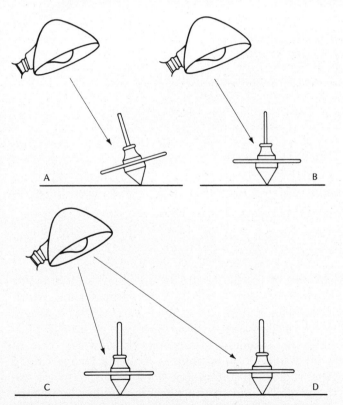

Figure 1.5 Effect of incidence of light on the color top: Tops A and C register a lighter shade than tops B and D because the latter are more obliquely illuminated. (Source: H. A. Bowman, "The Color-Top Method of Estimating Skin Pigmentation," *American Journal of Physical Anthropology* 14:1[1930]. Reprinted by permission of the publisher, Wistar Press.)

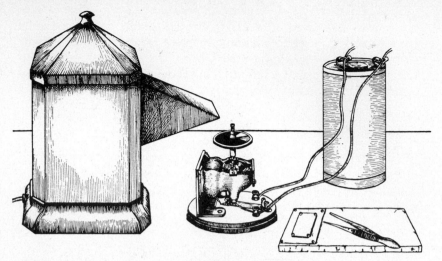

Figure 1.6 Color top mounted on Ajax motor with dry-cell connection, a forerunner to the modern color wheel apparatus.
(*Source:* H. A. Bowman, "The Color-Top Method of Estimating Skin Pigmentation," *American Journal of Physical Anthropology* 14:1[1930]. Reprinted by permission of the publisher, Wistar Press.)

light these colors to improve the color recognition, the strips were surrounded by a dark field. A total of forty-nine strips were formed into a small case that was easily carried. Fritsch's oil colors received scant acceptance even though they were used for many research endeavors.

Photometer

J. H. Shaxby and H. E. Bonnell (1928) proposed an interesting method for quantifying the luminance of various skin colors. Utilizing a photometer (Figure 1.7), the researchers took a light source, such as a candle, and set it a foot away from the photometer. The arm of a subject was then moved until the color of the subject's skin matched the brightness reflected by the candle onto the screen inside the photometer. Then after measuring the distance of the subject's arm to the photometer, the luminance of the skin was calculated with the equation $I_1/D_1^2 = I_2/D_2^2$.

In spite of the mathematical aspect of this technique, research into the photometer's ability to measure skin color differences met with consistent failure. The reflecting degrees of various skin colors were miniscule, thus providing no significant differences between races of people.

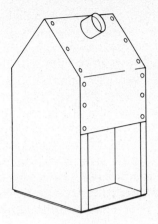

Figure 1.7 The photometer was used for measuring the luminating power of a stimulus. This photometer dates back to the 1800s. (*Source:* A. M. Granda Collection, University of Delaware. Reprinted by permission.)

Finally, in the waning days of skin color measurement, these instructions were written by Ales Hrdlicka (1939):

> On the pectoral parts of the chest may also be made certain tests developed by the writer which in many instances of doubtful mixtures between Whites and Indians or other Yellow-browns, and between Whites and other colored races, will help us to arrive at a conclusion. They are tests for the blood reaction of the skin. In a full-blood individual of the Yellow-brown or other dark races, if the chest is exposed and the observer makes three or four vertical lines over the pectoral parts by drawing his finger nail over the skin with a certain amount of pressure, there will be little or no visible reaction; but if there is any mixture with Whites the lines will show as fairly broad red marks, and the flush will be of some duration—both features being the more marked the more white blood is present in the individual under examination, provided he is in the ordinary state of health.[22]

Beyond the many attempts to measure skin color variations, other human physical attributes were subjected to measurement: hair color and texture and the thickness of lips became of particular importance.

Hair Texture Measurements

Scientific discussions relative to hair texture differences date to the nineteenth century. Pruner Bey (1863) maintained that hair constituted the best means of race identification: "A single hair representing the average form characteristic of the race might serve to define it."[23] J. C. Prichard (1855) claimed that the hair of the black man was decidedly different from that of any of the other races of man. He felt that the hair of the black man was wool, not hair. He later expounded the difference between sheep's wool and "Negro" hair as the degree of "crispation."[24] For a long time it was felt that "tufted" hair grew in separate bunches that, while scattered evenly over the scalp, were isolated tufts with intervening bald spaces. Rudolf Virchow (1895) added to the debate by stating that "between these peppercorns there occur apparently bald spaces which gives the impression that all the hair forming each grain grows from a single spot."[25]

Bey classified hair in three categories:[26]

1. Short, crisp, or fleecy, usually called "woolly," almost invariably jet black; characteristic of all black races.
2. Long, lank, or cylindrical, horse-mane type, mostly black; characteristic of all American and Mongoloid peoples.
3. Intermediate, wavy, curly, or smooth, every shade; characteristic of Caucasian people.

Paul Broca (1879) classified hair in three similar categories, which he then further subdivided according to length and color:[27]

1. Straight-Haired.
   Dolicho (long): Eskimo.
   Brachy (short): (red) Prairie Indians; (olivaster) Mexican, Peruvian; (yellow) Guarani, Samoyede, Mongol, Malay.
2. Wavy- or Curly-Haired.
   Dolicho: (blonde) Cimmerian, Scandinavian, Anglo-Saxon; (brown) Mediterranean (Basque, Corsican, Berber), Semite; (black) Australian, Indo-Abyssinian; (red) Fulah, Red Barabra (Nubian).
   Brachy: (blonde) Finn; (chestnut) Kelt, Slav; (brown) Iranian, Galcha.
3. Woolly-Haired.
   Dolicho: (yellowish) Bushman; (black) Oceanic, Papuan; African, Kafir.
   Brachy: Negrito.

Much later, Sullivan (1928) considered straight hair "natural" hair and attempted to calibrate other types using special measurement techniques. He first described three degrees of "waviness" (Figure 1.8):

Following straight hair three degrees of waviness are recognized. While they are described in terms of depth only as low, medium, or deep waves, the degree is really determined by the depth in relation to the width of the wave. The width of a wave is the distance from the apex of one wave to the apex of the next wave. The depth is the distance from a line tangent to these two points to the greatest depth between the two waves. When the deph is from 1/12 to 1/10 of the width, the hair is described as low waved. When the depth fluctuates above or below 1/6 of the width, it is described as a medium or moderate wave. When the depth fluctuates above and below 1/2 of the width it is described as deeply waved.[28]

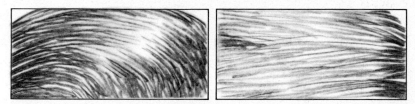

Straight

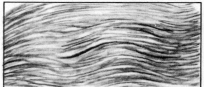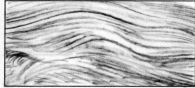

Low waves

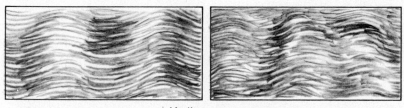

Medium waves

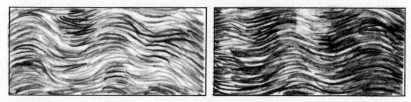

Deep waves

Figure 1.8   Degrees of hair waviness. (*Source:* Louis Sullivan, *Essentials of Anthropometry,* [New York: American Museum of Natural History, 1928], p. 47.)

Sullivan also described three *forms* of hair (curly, frizzly, and woolly) and went into further detail concerning measurement (Figure 1.9):

> Real curly hair is rare. . . . Before a hair can be called curly it should form at least three-fourths or more of a circle. . . . It is not to be mistaken for the matted woolly hair of Negroes. It is easily distinguished from this by the diameter of the curl or spiral which fluctuates around 2 centimeters near the head and dwindles gradually as the spiral continues. Frizzly hair is hair with a very short deep wave, but it does not form a curl or a spiral. It is distinguished by the small dimensions of the wave. A low wave is frequently about 5 centimeters wide and about .5 centimeter deep; a medium wave is about 3.5 or 4 centimeters wide and 6 or 7 millimeters deep; a deep wave is about 2.5 centimeters wide and about 12 millimeters deep, but frizzly hair has a wave only about 5 millimeters wide, and about the same depth or slightly less. Woolly hair is the familiar negro hair consisting of more or less closely coiled spirals linked together forming a matted mass. . . . One frequently sees very closely coiled hair grouped together in tufts which are more or less isolated from each other. The scalp is clearly visible between the tufts.[29]

Other speculations in hair texture research included Berstein and Robertson's (1927) conclusion that "negroid hair . . . weighs less than that of the average Caucasoid . . . the hair of negroids contains numerous air bubbles of large sizes not evident in the hair of Mongoloids and Caucasoids."[30] Because of differences in hair classification proposed by these and other researchers, Sullivan warned his readers to use the standards that he outlined and study them until they were firmly fixed in the mind: "Keep them constantly with you in the field since one easily loses the perspective in the new racial environment."[31]

Hexa, Penta, Tria, etc.

Browne's (1895) speculation that the hair of the white man would not felt while the "wool" of the black man would felt led to some complicated terminologies. Essentially, Browne suggested that two distinct species of man existed. When racial crossings occurred, the question of hybridization was complicated:

> Browne found that the hair from the heads of "hybrids" formed by the crossing of any two "species" of man consisted of filaments characteristic of each of the parent species. That is, the hair of a mulatto born of a "pure" Negro and a "pure" white are both eccentrically elliptical and oval. By close observation he could determine the "degree of hybridity" of any given individual, and he prepared

an elaborate set of tables which gave the nomenclature of human hybridity, of hybrids both "simple" (the offspring of two species only) and "compound" (the offspring of the crossing of all three species). Using the term "mulattin" to denote all crosses of the

Figure 1.9 A standard to aid in describing the form of the hair: (A) straight, (B) low wave, (C) medium wave, (D) deep wave, (E) and (F) curly, (G) frizzly, (H) and (I) woolly, (J) coiled or spiral tufts. (*Source:* Louis Sullivan, *Essentials of Anthropometry*, p. 47.)

black and white species (or mixtures of oval and eccentrically ellipti-
cal types of hair) he found that the simple crossing of black and
white could produce seven degrees of hybridity: "Helpta Mullatin"
(14 parts white to 2 parts black), or [14:2], "Hexa Mullatin" [12:4]
"Penta Mullattin" [10:6], "Tetra Mullattin" [8:8], "Tria Mullattin"
[6:10], "Di Mulattin" [4:12], and "Mono Mulattin" [2:14]. Applying
the same prefixes to the terms "costin" and "Mestisen," he gave the
degrees of "simple hybridity" between the black and Indian and
white and Indian, respectively. Compound hybrids led to such lin-
guistics feats as "Hypta-hypo-mono-mullatin" and "Penta-hyper-
mono-mullatin."[32]

Measuring Hair Color

Far more emphasis was placed on the measurement of hair texture than of hair color. Nevertheless, techniques were developed
for measuring the degree of variances in hair color, and one of
them used the color wheel for that purpose. Bellamy (1930) proposed a method of matching cuttings of hair to existing color
charts from which percentages of color mixtures were calculated
(for example: 85 percent black, 12 percent red, and 3 percent
yellow).[33] Bellamy went so far as to suggest that the prevalence of
blondness or brunetness should be indicated on regional maps
for the purpose of further research.

Measuring Thickness of Lips

Davenport's *Guide to Physical Anthropometry and Anthroposcopy* (1927) delineates no less than 35 "observations" of the
human body. Among these "observations" is a discussion concerning the measurement and classification of lip sizes.

> When lightly closed, height measured at the maximum to one side
> of median; width to angles; then lips may be classified by height
> divided by width ratio as:
>
> | | |
> |---|---|
> | Thin | below 0.20 millimeters |
> | Medium | 0.20–0.29 mm |
> | Thick | 0.30–0.44 mm |
> | Very Thick | 0.45 mm and over[34] |

Another technique for estimating sizes of lips was offered by
Sullivan in a similar guidebook, *Essentials of Anthropometry*. This
procedure called for the matching of the subject's lips to a set of
illustrated drawings (Figure 1.10).

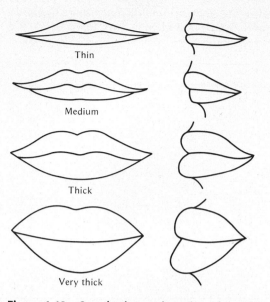

Figure 1.10 Standard to aid in describing the thickness of the lips. (*Source:* Louis Sullivan, *Essentials of Anthropometry*, p. 58.)

Anthropometry and Blacks

The previous review of attempts to categorize hair texture, skin color differences, and lip sizes suggests the significance that many researchers placed on anthropometric measurements. The American black was more often than not targeted as a subject for investigation. Melville Herskovits, one of the leading authorities in anthropology, summed up the state of affairs in the opening chapter of his book, *The Anthropometry of the American Negro* (1930):

> The American Negro has long been recognized as constituting one of the major social and economic problems of the United States. Although there have been numerous studies resulting from this recognition most of these deal with the more imperative phases of the problem of the association of Negroes and Whites. Nor is this strange, for the presence of a considerable body of individuals among a large population from whom they differ in physical type, and particularly in such an easily recognized trait as skin color, must inevitably bring on a body of taboos, repressions, conflicts, and social and economic complications of more or less grave import.[35]

Table 1 Form Used For Collecting Anthropometric and Genealogical Information (Howard University and New York City)

Anthropometric information

Form H 1   *No.*

NAME
ADDRESS   CLASS

Length of Head: Width of Head: Index
Height of Nose: Width of Nose:
                                                                                al-al
                                                                                sp-tip
                                                                                cr-tip
Thickness of Lips: Width of Mouth:
                    center
                    right
Height of Face: Bizygomatic Width:
            n-a
            n-gn
Height of Ear: Width of Ear:
Metacarpale laterale to M. mediale   Phal. III to Dak. III
Skin-color:
            Inner Upper Arm   N   R   Y   W

            Outer Upper Arm   N   R   Y   W
Minimum Width of Forehead: Angle of Eyes:
Distance between Inner Corners of Eyes: Outer:
                                                        Interpupillary Distance:
Height of Head:
Acromial Width: Width of Hip:
Weight: Height: Height sitting:

Date _____

Genealogical information

NOTE: This information is strictly confidential. No reference will be made to it in
      any way other than by number.
By *Negro* is meant *all* Negro, that is, African or descent from African, with *no*
      mixture of White or Indian blood.
By *Mixed* is meant mixed Negro and White, that is, neither all White nor all Negro.
By *White* is meant *all* White, without any mixture of Negro blood.
If you have Indian blood, indicate this in the proper place by the initial (I).

NAME	ADDRESS	CLASS
DATE OF BIRTH	PLACE OF BIRTH	
Are you Mixed?	Negro?	White?
What is your father's name?		
When was he born?	Where?	
Is he Mixed?	Negro?	White?
What is your mother's name?		
When was she born?	Where?	
Is she Mixed?	Negro?	White?
What was your father's father's name?		
Where was he born?		
Was he Mixed?	Negro?	White?
What was your father's mother's name?		
Where was she born?		
Was she Mixed?	Negro?	White?
What was your mother's father's name?		
Where was he born?		
Was he Mixed?	Negro?	White?

Table 1 (Continued)

What was your mother's mother's name?
Where was she born?
Was she Mixed?   Negro?   White?

If you know the names and racial make-up of ancestors farther back than your grandparents,
  will you give this information about them on the back of this sheet?

(Anthro. data _____)

SOURCE: M. J. Herskovits, *The Anthropometry of the American Negro*, Columbia University Press, 1930,
p. 11. Reprinted by permission of the publisher.

Using a long, detailed form (Table 1) to insure uniformity in his
collection of data, Herskovits made an extensive study of the
physical measurements of black students at Howard University.
His study, for its scope and coverage, proved to be the single
most important of its kind. (Ten other anthropometric studies of
blacks, made in the United States from 1925 to 1930, are listed in
Table 2).

Brass Instruments Used
for Anthropomorphic Investigations

Herskovits utilized the primary tools for measuring skeletal dimensions—the anthropometer, the sliding caliper and the spreading caliper. The anthropometer (Figure 1.11) was a graduated rod
with a horizontal arm that moved up and down. It was used for

Table 2 Anthropometric Studies Conducted in the United States,
1925–1930

Location	Subjects	Researcher
New York City	Native Born Blacks	Herskovits
New York City	Native Born Blacks	King
New York City	West Indian Born	Herskovits
New York City	West Indian Born	King
New York City	Native Born, Upper Class Blacks	Hurston
West Virginia	Native Born Blacks	King
Howard University	Black Students	Herskovits
Fisk University	Black Students	Blackwood
Tennessee A & I College	Black Students	Blackwood
St. Louis	Blacks	Von Luschan
Tuskegee Institute	Black Females	Blackwood

SOURCE: M. J. Herskovits, *The Anthropometry of the American Negro*, Columbia University Press, 1930,
p. 12. Reprinted by permission of the publisher.

the measurement of stature or sitting height. The spreading cali-per (Figure 1.12A) was used to measure distances between two points separated by a protruding shape, cranial dimensions, for instance; the sliding caliper (Figure 1.12B) was used to measure any relatively small linear dimension, such as the size of lips. All of these tools were graduated in millimeters.

Defining Racial Differences

Differences between the physical measurements of blacks and whites led to a number of discussions of racial classification. Such questions as by what criteria is an individual classified as white? or black? or whatever? became increasingly difficult to answer. It was obvious that visual observations were confusing; large num-bers of blacks with mixed ancestry complicated the matter of identification. While Herskovits felt that the number of blacks who claimed Indian ancestry, for example, was inaccurate be-cause "indian ancestry has distinct prestige value among Ameri-can Negroes," it was obvious to the most casual observer that significant numbers of persons of mixed ancestry existed.

White researchers became leery of visual techniques for the identification of races and called for warnings of being misled by the effects of skin bleaching, hair dyeing, hair straightening, and the use of wigs, hair pieces, etc. To help avoid the potential errors inherent in casual observation, Sullivan (1928) called for the so-licitation of hearsay information. He encouraged the recording of such evidence as "looks part white" or "neighbor says he is part Negro" for anthropological data gathering. The United States Census Bureau, while recording only black-white mixtures (Table 3), called for the classification of "Negro" if even one relative could be traced to African descent. Not allowed the wide vari-ances permitted whites, which disregarded ethnic subdivisions, the Negro was placed in a single category, regardless of his lan-guage or point of origin.

In 1910, the Sixty-first Congress accepted from the Immigration Commission a unique book, the *Dictionary of Races or Peoples*, prepared by Daniel and Elnora Folkmar.[36] The Folkmars, follow-ing Blumenbach's broad racial classifications of black, white, red, yellow, and brown, implemented a Comparative Classification of Immigrant Races or Peoples for their research (Table 4). While the dictionary treated more than 600 subjects in its classification system, black people were placed in a single, narrow category. The dictionary stated that the Negro belonged to ". . . that grand

Figure 1.11 Anthropometer. (*Source:* C. B. Davenport, *Anthropometry and Anthroposcopy,* 1927.)

Figure 1.12 Anthropometric measuring devices. A, spreading caliper; B, sliding caliper.

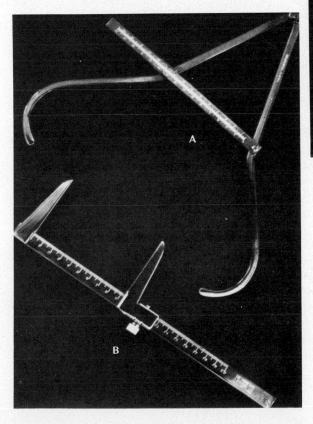

Table 3 Population Figures for Black and Mulatto U.S. Citizens (1850–1920)

Year	Total Negro	Black	Mulatto	% Black	% Mulatto
1920	10,463,131	8,802,577	1,660,554	84.1	15.9
1910	9,827,763	7,777,077	2,050,686	79.1	20.9
1890	7,488,676	6,337,980	1,132,060	84.8	15.2
1870	4,880,009	4,295,960	584,049	88.0	12.0
1860	4,441,830	3,853,467	588,363	86.8	13.2
1850	3,683,808	3,233,057	405,751	88.8	11.2

SOURCE: M. J. Herskovits, *The Anthropometry of the American Negro,* Columbia University Press, 1930, p. 19. Reprinted by permission of the publisher.

division of mankind distinguished by its black color and, generally speaking, by its woolly hair."[37] This classification included "aliens whose appearance indicates an admixture of Negro blood, whether coming from Cuba or other islands of the West Indies, North or South America, Europe, or Africa."[38]

Classification of Black-White Mixtures

In order to classify those blacks of mixed racial background, specific terminology was created by academicians. *Mulatto* described the offspring of the union of a pure white with a pure black person. The term appears to have been derived from the Latin word, *mula,* meaning mule. This offers an interesting parallel, for the mule is a hybrid animal, resulting from the union of a horse and a jackass, which is destined not only to be a creature of burden, but which genetically cannot reproduce its own kind. For many years, in fact, it was argued that blacks and whites were unable to interbreed successfully and produce fertile offspring; while children could be produced from a black-white combination of parents, it was believed that two mulatto offspring could not reproduce.

Other fractionated divisions in racial makeup were designated *quadroon,* the child of a mulatto and a white, three-fourths white and one-fourth black, and *octoroon,* the child of a white and a quadroon, seven-eighths white and one-eighth black.[39] While there was no commonly agreed upon term for the child of a pure black and a mulatto (three-fourths black and one-fourth white), Ferguson (1916) suggested the ridiculous term *Sambo.*[40]

In some instances, psychologists utilized far less complicated systems of identification. Ferguson (1916) classified black children into four groups—"pure," "three-fourths," "mulatto," and "quadroon"—based on skin color, hair texture, and general facial and

Table 4 Comparative Classification of Immigrant Races or Peoples

BASED ON BRINTON (cf. KEANE)

Race	Stock	Group	People	Ripley's races with other corresponding terms
Caucasian ..	Aryan	Teutonic...	Scandanavian: Danish, Norwegian ...., Swedish ...., German (N. part) ...., Dutch ...., English (part) ...., Flemish.............	I. TEUTONIC; H. Europæus (Lapouge).; Nordic (Deniker); Dolicho-leptorhine (Kohlmann).; Germanic (English writers).; Reihengräber (German writers).
		Lettic......	Lithuanian	Kymric (French writers).
		Celtic	Scotch (part) ...., Irish (part) ...., Welsh	Part Alpine.
		Slavonic ...	Russian ...., Polish ...., Czech: Bohemian ...., Moravian ...., Servian ...., Croatian ...., Montenegrin ...., Slovak ...., Slovenian ...., Ruthenian ...., Dalmatian ...., Herzegovinian ...., Bosnian	II. ALPINE (OR CELTIC); H. Alpinus (Lapouge).; Occidental (Deniker).; Disentis (German writers).; Celto-Slavic (French writers).; Lappanoid (Pruner-Bey).; Sarmatian (von Höider).; Arvernian (Beddoe).
		Illyric......	Albanian.............	
		Armenic ...	Armenian	
		Italic	French ...., Italian (part) ...., Roumanian ...., Spanish ...., Spanish-American ......, Mexican, etc. ...., Portuguese	Part Alpine.; Part Mediterranean.; III. MEDITERRANEAN; H. Meridionalis (Lapouge).; Atlantic-Mediterranean and Ibero-Insular (Deniker).; Iberian (English writers).
		Hellenic ...	Greek	Ligurian (Italian writers).
		Iranic	Hindu ...., Gypsy	Part Mediterranean.; Part Teutonic.
	Semitic	Arabic.....	Arabian.............., Hebrew ...., Syrian	Part Mediterranean.
		Chaldaic ..		
	Caucasic		Caucasus peoples	Doubtful.
	Euskaric		Basque	
Mongolian..	Sibiric	Finnic	Finnish ...., Lappish............., Magyar ...., Bulgarian (part)	
		Tataric......	Turkish, Cossack, etc....	
		Japanese ...	Japanese, Korean	
		Mongolic...	Kalmuk	
	Sinitic	Chinese ...	Chinese ...., East Indian (part, i.e., Indo-Chinese)........	
Malay			Pacific Islander (part)...., East Indian (part)	
Ethiopian			Negro	
American (Indian)..				American Indian ....

SOURCE: D. Folkmar and E. Folkmar, *Dictionary of Races or Peoples*, Document No. 662 (Washington, D.C.: Immigration Commission, 1911).

cranial data. Strong (1913) labeled blacks as "dark," "medium," or "light." Crane (1923) devised the following scale: (1) *So light* as to be possibly mistaken for a white person at first glance; (2) *Very light,* but instantly recognizable as a colored person; (3) *Medium dark;* (4) *Very dark;* and (5) *Pitch black,* African in appearance.

"No Scientific Basis for Discrimination"

The heavy emphasis placed upon the categorization of races and the subsequent psychological testing of various groups of people often led to conclusions of racial superiority and inferiority. The brewing anti-Semitism in Europe led to a realization, among some American scholars, that erroneous conclusions had been made of its "scientific" data. In 1928, at its annual meeting, the American Anthropological Association adopted a resolution which declared in part: "Anthropology provides no scientific basis for discrimination against any people on the ground of racial inferiority, religious affiliation, or linguistic heritage."[41] This proclamation came about not because the scientists were convinced of the black man's racial equality, but because of the European situation. Psychologists, too, issued a similar disclaimer in an attempt to erase the interpretations made from psychological testing data (see Chapter 3 for further discussion).

Notes

1. C. B. Davenport, *Guide to Physical Anthropology and Anthroposcopy* (Cold Spring Harbor, New York: Eugenics Research Association, 1927).
2. L. R. Sullivan, *Essentials of Anthropometry, A Handbook for Explorers and Museum Collectors,* rev. ed., H. L. Shapiro (New York: American Museum of Natural History, 1928).
3. R. Hakluyt, "The First Voyage of Robert Baker to Guinie" in *Principall Navigations, Voiges and Discoveries of the English Nation* (London, 1589), p. 132.
4. W. D. Jordon, *White Over Black* (Chapel Hill, N.C.: University of North Carolina Press, 1968) p. 5.
5. Much of this indictment was based on the Canaanite religious rites, which deeply shocked the Hebrews. It is interesting to note that the Canaanites invented three different alphabets, one of which (the Phoenician) became the ancestor of practically all those of the Western world.
6. F. Welsing, as quoted by Genevieve E. Kaete in "Soul: The Sixth Sense," *New Directions,* 1:3 (Spring 1974), pp. 12–17. An interesting reversal of the

"black-skin-deficit" philosophy can be viewed in a recent interpretation by black psychiatrist Frances Welsing (1974). She advances the notion that Adam and Eve were the first albino children of black parents in the Garden of Eden (Africa) who were ashamed of their skin's whiteness. Welsing further explains that Africa's first albinos then wandered ". . . into Europe into a climate where there was less sun and their pigmentation could function in the environment."

7. J. Schwinfurth, *Heart of Africa* (Berlin: Junker and Dunnhaupt, 1938).

8. T. Waitz, *Introduction to Anthropology* (London: Longmans, 1863).

9. A. Hrdlicka, "Directions for Collecting Information and Specimens for Physical Anthropology," (Part R, No. 39), Washington, D.C., United States National Museum, 1904, p. 25.

10. Ibid.

11. P. Broca, "Instructions generales pour les recherches anthropologiques a faire sur le vivant," 2nd ed., Paris, 1879.

12. J. Deniker, *The Races of Man: An Outline of Anthropology and Ethnography* (Freeport, New York: Books for Library Press, 1900) p. 47.

13. J. Gray, "A New Instrument for Determining the Colour of the Hair, Eyes, and Skin," *Man*, 8:27 (1908), pp. 54–58.

14. L. R. Sullivan, *op. cit.*, p. 43.

15. T. W. Todd and L. Van Gorder, "The Quantitative Determination of Black Pigmentation in the Skin of the American Negro," *American Journal of Physical Anthropology*, 4:3 (1921), pp. 239–260.

16. T. W. Todd, B. Blackwood, and H. Beecher, "Skin Pigmentation," *American Journal of Physical Anthropology*, 11:2 (January–March 1928), pp. 187–205.

17. H. A. Bowman, "The Color-Top Method of Estimating Skin Pigmentation," *American Journal of Physical Anthropology*, 14:1 (January–March 1930), pp. 59–70.

18. M. J. Herskovits, "Age Changes in Pigmentation of American Negroes," *American Journal of Physical Anthropology*, 9:3 (1926), p. 323.

19. F. von Luschan, *Voelker Rassen Sprachen*, (Berlin: Welt Verlag, 1922).

20. Bowman, *op. cit.*, p. 59.

21. G. Fritsch, "Bermerkungen zu der Hautfarbentafel," *Mitt Anthrop Ges Wien*, 16:H, Berlin (1916), pp. 183–185.

22. Ales Hrdlicka, *Anthropometry* (Philadelphia: Wistar Institute of Anatomy and Biology, 1939).

23. P. Bey, as quoted by J. C. Prichard in *Natural History of Man*, E. Norris, ed. (London: Wilson and Ogilvy, 1855).

24. Ibid.

25. R. Virchow, *Zeitschrift fur Ethnologie* (Berlin: Heft 11, 1895) p. 152.

26. Bey, *op. cit.* p. 79.

27. P. Broca, *Atlas d'anatomie Descriptive du Corps Humain* (Paris: G. Masson, 1879) p. 37. Other recognized schema were interestingly prepared by Muller (1900), Deniker (1900), and Haeckel (1866). Deniker's scheme was based on a fusion of two, three, or more "races" which set forth "thirty types" based on the different textures of the skin.

28. Sullivan, *op. cit.*, pp. 44–48.

29. Ibid., pp. 48–49.

30. M. Berstein and S. Robertson, "Racial and Sexual Differences in Hair Weight," *Journal of Physical Anthropology*, 10:3 (July 1927), pp. 379–385.

31. Sullivan, *op. cit.*, p. 50.

32. W. Stanton, *The Leopard's Spots, Scientific Attitudes Toward Race in America 1815–1859* (Chicago: University of Chicago Press, 1960) p. 152.

33. R. Bellamy, "Measuring Hair Color," *American Journal of Physical Anthropology*, 14:1 (January–March 1930), pp. 75–77.

34. B. Davenport, *Guide to Physical Anthropometry and Anthroposcopy* (Cold Spring Harbor, N.Y.: Eugenics Research Association, 1925), p. 42.

35. M. J. Herskovits, *The Anthropometry of the American Negro* (New York: Columbia University Press, 1930).

36. D. Folkmar and E. C. Folkmar, "Dictionary of Races or Peoples" (Document No. 662) (Washington, D.C.: The Immigration Commission, 1911) p. 150.

37. Ibid., p. 100.

38. Ibid., p. 101.

39. During antebellum days in New Orleans, female octoroon parties were fairly common events for the entertainment of white men.

40. G. O. Ferguson, Jr., *The Psychology of the Negro: An Experimental Study* (New York: The Science Press, 1916).

41. "The New York Meeting of the American Anthropological Association," *Science* (New Series), 89 (1939), pp. 29–30.

2
Psychology and race

Something of an academic coup occurred late in the nineteenth century in the emergence of the new science of psychology. The established sciences of biology and physics looked to the new discipline with great expectation and excitement. Both new adherents and older scientists watched with the hope that psychology would be a deliverance from the scientific doldrums and fads of the eighteenth and nineteenth centuries. By declaring itself the study of the *mind,* psychology claimed ownership of all that dealt with animal and human behavior. The new discipline cut a wide swath through the ivy halls of academia at a time when the Western *Weltanschauung* was infected by racism and social Darwinism, and psychology eventually became an important contributor to the era.

Ethnical Psychology

Psychology and anthropology were bedfellows during this golden age of racism; both searched for, and consequently magnified, the existence of racial differences, mental abilities, and character traits among the peoples of the world. Their zest and zeal reinforced prevailing western mythologies of racial superiority and the resultant exploitation of non-white peoples.

The initial union between psychology and anthropology took place in Germany when P. W. A. Bastain (1871) insisted on the essential connection between psychology and ethnology. (Ethnology was that subbranch of anthropology concerned with the study of race; it was a field of study so significant that David Wechsler [1939] saw fit to include the word in a section of his IQ test designed to measure an individual's knowledge of general information.) While Bastain was not especially concerned with studying black people, his interest in ethnical psychology negated earlier views which held, "it is not worthwhile to look into the soul of the negro. It is a judgment of God which is being executed that, at the approach of civilization, the savage man must perish."[1] However, at the turn of the century, increased interest in racial studies began to appear accompanying the concept of Negritude. Dennett's (1906) statement was typical of this view:

> I cannot help feeling that one who has acquired a kind of way of thinking black, should be listened to on the off-chance that a secondary instinct, developed by long contact with the people he is writing about, may have driven him to a right, or nearly right, conclusion.[2]

In 1910, Haddon expanded on the term *ethnical psychology* to include the "uncivilized," defining it as "the study of the minds of other races and peoples, of which, among the more backward races, glimpses can be obtained only by living among them and endeavoring to reach their point of view by means of observation and experiment."[3] Haddon's definition was a milestone because it not only cemented the connection between the two disciplines but suggested a methodological stance as well. Psychology's concern with race was thus legitimized by direction and purpose.

Robert S. Woodworth, then chairman of anthropology and psychology of the American Association for the Advancement of Science and later (1914) president of the American Psychological Association, illustrated psychology's concern and interest in studying the comparative nature of men:

> One of the most agreeable and satisfying experiences afforded by intellectual pursuits comes from the discovery of a clean-cut dis-

tinction between things which are superficially much alike. The aesthetic value of such distinctions may even outweigh their intellectual value and lead to sharp lines and antithesis where the only difference that exists is one of degree.[4]

Anthropologists, sensing the conflict of shared interest and losing their battle for complete ownership of the study of the races, relinquished a portion of the field to psychologists who would study the behavior of individuals in carefully defined laboratory or experimental situations. This move consequently justified anthropology's continued research on small communities by means of observation and interview at a face-to-face level. And the arrangement was appealing to psychologists, for they viewed themselves as experimental scientists with the accouterments of a laboratory milieu.

An early cooperative research effort between psychologists and anthropologists began when the Cambridge Anthropological Society sent an expedition in 1889 to study the mental life of the inhabitants of the Torres Straits:

> For the first time trained experimental psychologists investigated, by means of an adequate laboratory equipment, a people in a low state of culture under their ordinary conditions of life. The foundations of ethnical experimental psychology were thus laid.[5]

Among the "brass instrument Tarzans" who made this historic trip to the Torres Straits and the Fly River district of British New Guinea were W. H. R. Rivers, C. S. Myers, and William McDougall. McDougall went on to promulgate, among other racist views, the dogma of "instincts" in man. (The instinct theory asserted that inborn and unlearned response tendencies determined social behavior.) The Torres Straits studies were made in the best tradition of Wundtian psychophysics. Hearing, vision, taste, tactile acuity, pain, motor speed and accuracy, fatigue, and memory tests were performed on the unsuspecting, cooperative, sepia-skinned villagers. Unsurprisingly, the voices of science concluded that the "wild" natives of the South Pacific did not surpass western man in any trait; rather, the inhabitants were found to be far less intelligent than their examiners. This adventure by the Cambridge Anthropological Society provided an important impetus for American psychologists to seek and study racial variances in man.

Racial Designations

Among other things, anthropology provided psychology with the racial systems needed to justify intellectually the existence of differences among human beings. Where early classifications had

stemmed from theologically derived doctrines and divided mankind into descendants of Shem, Ham, and Japhet, Carl von Linnaeus (1738) made racial distinctions based on color of skin, temperament, customs, and habits (Table 5) This scheme, which
designated psychological as well as physical characteristics of the
different races, assigned the qualities of capriciousness, negli-
gence, and slowness to black people. The biblical explanation for
mankind's groupings had presented a major problem of congru-
ence: As the white man explored and plundered new worlds, he
claimed that the "discovered" savages were not descendents of
Adam and therefore were outside the grace of God. Linnaeus'
racial distinctions, therefore, proved advantageous for those seek-
ing to justify the inferiority of the colored races.

Following Linnaeus, a number of racial classifications were
made, all of which placed the black man at the bottom of the
human family hierarchy. The relative question of race categorization reached such ridiculous proportions in this country that the
U.S. Senate commissioned Daniel and Elnora Folkmar to prepare,
for the Immigration Commission, a *Dictionary of Races or Peoples* (see Chapter 1). Under the entry "Negro," this official government document described the black man as "belonging to the
lowest division of mankind from an evolutionary standpoint."
The definition of Negro embraced ". . . Negro, or African (black)
whose appearance indicates any admixture of Negro blood . . .
whether coming from Cuba, or other islands of the West Indies,
North or South America, Europe, or Africa."[6] The term *Negro* was
thus considered a racial designation without regard to place of
origin, which removed from consideration any ethnic characteristics within the race. From this framework, the role of inferiority
was clearly assigned to all black peoples of the world.

In support of racial classifications, anthropologists contributed
many other interesting—and ridiculous—methods for judging

**Table 5 Eighteenth Century Racial Distinctions and Habits Based on
Skin Color**

Racial Groups	Descriptions
Homo Americanus	Reddish, choleric, erect, tenacious, contented, free; ruled by custom
Homo Europaeus	White, ruddy, muscular, stern, haughty, stingy; ruled by opinion
Homo Asiaticus	Yellow, melancholic, inflexible, light, inventive; ruled by rites
Homo Afer	Black, phlegmatic, indulgent, cunning, slow, negligent; ruled by caprice

SOURCE: Carl von Linnaeus, *Systema Naturae*, 1735.

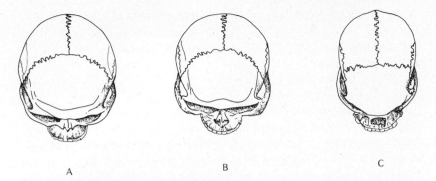

A   B   C

Figure 2.1 Norma verticalis or Blumenbach's View for Racial Identification: (A) Caucasian, (B) Mongol, (C) Negro.

variations within Homo sapiens. John Friedrich Blumenbach (1824) developed a method for visually judging cranium variation (Figure 2.1). The *norma verticalis,* or Blumenbach's View, was regarded as an accurate technique by scientists and was performed in the following manner: ". . . the skull was placed between the feet of the observer and after examination from above, classed as oblong, round, and so forth, for the purpose of determining the race to which it belonged."[7] Blumenbach's procedures were also used as a technique for distinguishing those skulls whose previous owners were designated as "civilized" or "uncivilized." Several years later similar claims declared that the posterior balance of the skull—its ability to rest on the posterior edge of the occipital hole and the inferior edge of the orbits—was a distinctive sign of the Negro race.[8]

Among the theoreticians who speculated from these views and spun similar webs were F. J. Gall and G. Spurzheim. Their six volume *Anatomy and Physiology of the Nervous System* (1817) laid the basis for phrenology by asserting that the brain was the organ of the mind. While Gall and Spurzheim accurately speculated that different kinds of behavior were controlled by separate parts of the brain, they mistakenly declared that the external shape of the skull reflected the shape of the brain underneath. Since whites were generally judged to be more intelligent than blacks, the Gall and Spurzheim line of reasoning eventually led early psychologists to conclude that the skull capacities of whites were greater than the skull capacities of blacks:

. . . the skull capacity of modern European whites is 1560 cc. and that of European whites of the neolithic period is the same; the skull capacity of the mongoloid is 1510 cc., that of the negroes of the Pacific Ocean is 1460 cc., and that of African negroes is 1405 cc.[9]

Henry Garrett, as late as 1963, still supported this theory when he wrote that the black man's brain "on the average is smaller, lighter, less fissured, and more primitive in many respects than the White's brain."[10]

The alleged skull-capacity differences among humans were also matched with studies concerning the shape of the face (Figure 2.2). Isadore Saint-Hilaire (1847) divided human facial structures into *orthognathic* (oval face with vertical jaws), *eurygnathic* (high cheekbones) and *prognathic* (projecting jaws). From these models it was concluded that the black race was prognathous (forward jawed), the Asian eurygnathic (vertical jawed), and the white race orthognathous (upright jawed). In short, the African was considered more apelike, and therefore inferior, in comparison to whites. In this regard, anthropologist Franz Boas, who later became a leading spokesman for racial equality, wrote:

> We find that the face of the negro as compared to the skull is larger than that of the American, whose face is in turn larger than that of the white. The lower portion of the face assumes larger dimensions. The alveolar arch is pushed forward and thus gains an appearance which reminds us of the higher apes.[11]

It was not long before the inferior physical status assigned to blacks was joined by similar attributes along psychological dimensions. An early contention held that "primitive races" could not abstract, inhibit impulses, or choose according to standards of value. Tylor (1916) set a bias for educational psychologists with this observation:

> In measuring the minds of lower races, a good test is how far their children are able to take a civilized education. The account generally given by European teachers who have had the children of lower

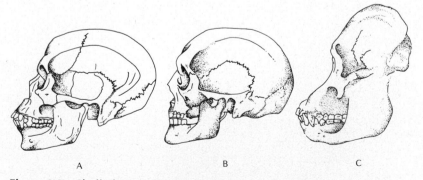

A B C

Figure 2.2 Skull shapes: (A) Prognathous skull of Negro, (B) Orthognathous skull of Caucasian, (C) Skull of Orang. (*Source:* A. H. Keane, *Ethnology* [London: Cambridge University Press, 1916], p. 183.)

races in their schools is that, though they often learn as well as the white children up to 12 years old, they often fall off, and are left behind by the children of the ruling race.[12]

This view was similar to early animal studies which held that anthropoids also developed physically and mentally at a rate comparable to humans, but ceased to do so beyond the infancy period in humans. Tylor's observations—which were widely accepted during his time—are interesting in that fifty years later the reverse of his philosophy was espoused under the banner of "cultural deprivation."

Literary and Philosophical Biases

Poets like Rudyard Kipling ("The White Man's Burden", 1899) provided romanticism and justification for racist themes with reference to "those ye better" and the "half-devil and half-child" natives of non-European countries. Philosophers such as Count Arthur Joseph de Gobineau provided the important discourse to "prove" white racial superiority over other groups. Gobineau (1915), whose racism was distinctly a class concept, annunciated:

> The negroid variety is the lowest, and stands at the foot of the ladder. The animal character that appears in the shape of the pelvis, is stamped on the negro from birth, and foreshadows his destiny. His intellect will always move within a very narrow circle . . . The very strength of his sensations is the most striking proof of his inferiority.[13]

Gobineau's attempt to intellectually justify French colonial rule over North Africa concluded with this analysis: "The black race represents passion and is the source of lyricism and artistic temperament; the yellow man represents utility, order and mediocrity; the white race is the expression of reason and honor."[14]

It is interesting to note that Gobineau felt that civilization occurred when "races" intermarried. He did not suggest intermarriage between white and black, however, but the union between various types within the white race (as Aryan with Mediterranean). He felt that the rise and fall of so-called great civilizations occurred with the mixing of "inferior blood" with "superior blood," thereby causing "bastardization" and "decadence." Several decades later, this view served as a philosophical basis for Nazi Germany's race-betterment policy and the subsequent mass extermination of Jews.

The Count's deliverances were joined by overwhelming and amazing scientific attempts to "prove" white superiority. Professional discussions and scholarly papers appeared with the needed consensual validation for white superiority; literally hundreds of research projects were initiated and results were published. The nineteenth century was a time which scholars of later years would come to view with embarrassment for its unbelievable conclusions drawn from calibrating brains, skeletons, nerves, limbs, torsos, skulls, and even fetuses of black people.

Nativism: Themes of Race Differences

The question of the relative capacities of the races was almost wholly anthropological and philosophical in character; as such, it held center stage until four separate historical events provided the linkage to psychological theory. These events reinforced nativistic themes by declaring that human differences resulted from innate causes within people rather than stemming from environmental forces in society. In order to understand these influences, let us briefly review each event.

1. Darwin's Origin of Species

In 1859, Englishman Charles Darwin's *On the Origin of Species by Means of Natural Selection* was published. Darwin's theory of evolution "influenced the development of modern psychology as much as any other single event in the nineteenth century. It would be impossible to understand what psychologists today are trying to accomplish or why they go about it as they do unless one first understood something of the importance of evolutionary theory for our contemporary vision of man and his destiny."[15] The *survival of the fittest* shibboleth maintained that only the strongest and most intelligent individuals would survive the struggles between man and man and between man and environment. Darwin underscored the appeal for recognizing the importance of individual differences by placing the onus of man's plight on man himself, rather than on the ills of his society. This line of reasoning led many psychologists to turn their research energies to investigations of sensory and intellectual differences between individuals in order to solve the puzzle of man's successes and failures. Darwin's writings also led psychologists to question anew the relationship of man to the "lower" animals and to reexamine the gospel of early philosophers, notably Descartes. The comparative aspect of psychology nurtured the "white coat" obsession of psychologists in emulating the biological sciences in their study of lower animals via instrumentation, e.g., Yerkes: anthropoids; Thorndike and Guthrie: cats; and the standard of traditional psychologists: the rat; yes, even the rat was white!

2. Galton's Eugenics

Sir Francis Galton, an Englishman and interestingly, a cousin of Darwin, provided the linkage between scientific naturalism and psychology.[16] Galton's *Hereditary Genius: Its Laws and Consequences* (1869) attempted to illustrate that genius and greatness followed family lines; *English Men of Science* (1874) and *Natural Inheritance* (1899) were written to substantiate this claim. (He was not an unduly modest man—his own family was included in his great sons of England compilations.) Galton tried to show that "great" men inherited not only intellectual ability but specific types of talents (for literature, medicine, music, etc.). His intense concern about the importance of inheritance led him to propose a science of heredity, eugenics, which promoted the idea of racial improvement through selective mating and sterilization of the "unfit." Galton stated that:

> . . . No more than there is equality between man and man of the same nation is there equality between race and race. This differentiation of men in physique and mentality has led to the slow but still imperfect development of occupational castes within all civilized communities. We may not admit these castes, but they exist nevertheless; probably in a perfectly efficient society, there would always be castes suited to specialized careers—the engineer, the ploughman, the mathematician, the navyman, the statesman, the actor and the craftsman. Even now we are progressing slowly towards tests for occupational fitness, and eventually that fitness should be intensified by marriage within the caste. . . .[17]

To some psychologists Galton's eugenic doctrine meant the genetic control of the feebleminded; to others, it meant the genetic control of social undesirables, but each perspective found its own dangerous interpretation (see Chapter 4 for further discussion).

3. German Psychophysics

While England and France favored a deductive and mathematical approach to science, Germany placed its emphasis on classification and the inductive approach, and it was in Germany that the initial application of experimental method to psychology was made. Leaders included Ernst Weber, Gustav Fechner, Hermann von Helmholtz, and Wilhelm Wundt. The times seemed to favor Germany as the place of origin for experimental psychology because for nearly a hundred years German intellectual history had created a scientific temperament better suited to taxonomic description than that of France or England.[18]

Psychophysics—the study of the effect of physical processes on the mental processes—was the outgrowth of the German contribution to psychological history. Stimulated specifically by the work of Wundt (1879), psychological laboratories began to appear in Europe (most notably in Leipzig) and later in America (most notably at Cornell University). Nineteenth century psychology was a product of the union of philosophy and physiology which focused on discovering the "structure," or anatomy of individual conscious processes. Its methodology was called *introspection* and its problem was to describe the content or structure of the mind in terms of psychological elements and their combinations. This concept, called *structuralism,* greatly influenced early American psychology and created an enthusiastic interest in the teasing apart of the mind with the "brass instruments" of physiology.

Brass instruments of psychological research were used to quantitatively measure human responses to various sensory stimuli (Figure 2.3). Early methods for producing sound made use of small whistles or metal bars. The Galton whistle (a) was activated by squeezing a rubber bulb and was closed by a piston. As the piston was adjusted, the tone of the sound varied. The tuning forks (b), when struck, were designed to sound in unison when an adjustable weight was raised or lowered on one of the forks. In addition to auditory measurements, the sensory modalities of smell, taste, and skin sensitivity and reaction were subjected to psychological experimentation.

The olfactometer (c) was designed to measure the greatest distance that a blindfolded subject could detect the odor from an opened bottle. A valve releasing degrees of the odor was located on one end of the rubber tubing.

A forerunner of what was later called the aesthesiometer was the temperature stimulator (d) which was designed to measure both skin tactual sensitivity and the awareness of temperature differences. Hot and cold water were released through two copper tubes that culminated in a metal tip, and this tip was lightly pressed to the skin of a blindfolded subject.

Measurements of taste sensitivity were frequently performed. The taste sensor (e) was a glass applicator whose aperture was placed on the subject's tongue. The inlet, connected to a system

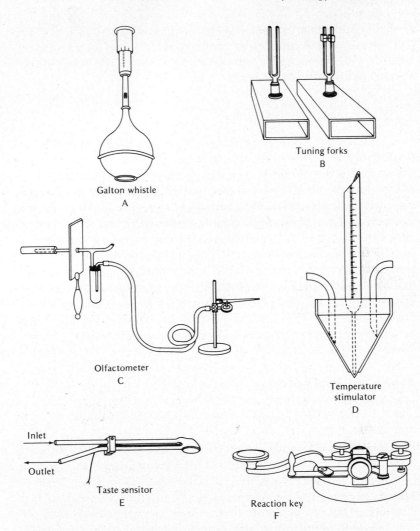

Galton whistle
A

Tuning forks
B

Olfactometer
C

Temperature
stimulator
D

Inlet

Outlet

Taste sensitor
E

Reaction key
F

Figure 2.3 Brass instruments used for early psychological investigations. (*Source* [a–d, f]: E. B. Titchener, *Experimental Psychology* [New York: Macmillan Co., 1905]. Reprinted by permission of the publisher. *Source* [e]: T. G. Andrews, *Methods of Psychology* [New York: John Wiley, 1948]. Reprinted by permission of the publisher.)

of tubes, allowed various solutions to be directed through the apparatus.

The reaction key (f) was used to measure individual differences in responding to various sound or light stimuli. This simplistic device was the forerunner of complex reaction timers currently in use in many psychological laboratories.

Later, American psychologists showed a growing interest in the more practical application of the study of conscious processes, thereby placing significant emphasis on child psychology, mental testing, and educational psychology.

4. Mendelian Genetics

Though the Austrian monk Gregor Mendel published his scientific inquiry into the genetic differences of garden peas in 1866, it was not until 1900 that the dust was blown off his research and the disturbing parallel was made between agricultural and human inheritance. Mendel's discovery was of major importance because it helped to establish the fact that genetic traits come to the individual in units rather than through a blending of qualities from one's ancestors. While Mendel's work was valid for *physical* differences, it led many researchers to make quick, unsubstantiated parallels to psychological and other nonphysical aspects of human behavior, without regard for environmental conditions. It was this framework that encouraged the growth of hereditary-environmental issues in psychological theory.

American Psychology and Racial Investigation

The events led by Darwin, Galton, Wundt, and Mendel, combined with earlier anthropomorphic research, brought about a tremendous interest in measuring human attributes through experimental research in psychology. The popular notion of darker-race inferiority frequently provided grounds for comparing psychological and physical attributes among human beings.

The earliest recorded attempt by American researchers to measure psychological capacities in different races was made in 1881 when C. S. Meyers tested Japanese subjects and proved that the Asians were slower in reaction time than Europeans. Shortly afterwards, utilizing a popular reaction time device, Bache (1895) tested American Indians and Negroes and concluded that these "primitive peoples" were highly developed in physiological tasks and attributes while higher human forms ". . . tended less to quickness of response in the automatic sphere; the reflective man is the slower being."[19] Bache's results are summarized in Table 6.

In 1898 the Cambridge Anthropological Society launched its expedition to New Guinea, thus inspiring research efforts by psychologists to measure psychological attributes of various races.

Table 6 Group Differences in Reaction Time, 1895

Group	Number of cases	Auditory R.T.	Visual R.T.	Electrical R.T.
Whites	12	146.9	164.8	136.3
Indians	11	116.3	135.7	114.6
Negroes	11	130.0	152.9	122.9

SOURCE: R. M. Bache, "Reaction Time with Reference to Race," *Psychological Review*, 2 (1895), pp. 475–486.

Large numbers of individual sensory investigations occurred during the early 1900s as a result of the New Guinea expedition; however, none reached the magnitude and fanfare of the St. Louis World's Fair experiments.

A unique convention was held in 1904, in conjunction with the Louisiana Purchase Exposition (St. Louis), during which studies were conducted on 1100 individuals, including 300 so-called primitive peoples of the world. The World's Congress of Races convened with prominent psychologists in attendance. Leading the group were R. S. Woodworth, later president of the American Psychological Association, and F. G. Bruner, a graduate student in psychology. In what has been described as a carnival atmosphere, psychologists at the World's Fair tested Igorots and Negritos from the Phillipine Islands, Malayans, Singhalese, Pygmies, and American Indians. The scientists' investigations were many and varied, dealing with the participants' abilities to detect sounds, withstand pain, and react to buzzers. Since these were pre-Binet days, tests of intelligence were relegated to the manipulation of simple form board puzzles. Results were tallied after each racial group was given from one week to one month to flex its intellectual and sensory muscles for these mental olympics.

Without surprise, the general conclusions reached by interpreting the testing data were that the darker-skinned participants (such as the Negritos and Pygmies) rated lower in intelligence. Literally reams of data were accumulated and stored away for later analyses. Bruner used a portion of the findings for his dissertation, but very little further evaluation resulted from the remaining data. Woodworth, in a speech to an American Association for the Advancement of Science meeting in Boston (1909), reported vague reactions to the massive data. Clues to the final disposition of the voluminous data can be detected in an autobiographical statement by Woodworth:

> When the Fair was over, we promptly worked over our data, and reported some of the results of the auditory tests . . . and I gave a general summary of our results and their bearing on the question

of racial differences in mental traits. Further than that, the results have never been published, not from any doubt on our part as to their value, but partly because of the unlimited number of fascinating correlations which still remained to be worked out. . . .[20]

Two years later, an interesting psychological analysis appeared in an Atlanta University publication under the title "Some Psychological Considerations on the Race Problem" (1911). This report was one of the earliest writings in America to criticize specifically the accuracy of psychological research and the interpretation of accumulated data. The author, Herbert Miller, met the heredity-environment issue head-on and criticized the paucity of psychological training of those who performed the research. Miller underlined heavily the need for recognizing the importance of social conditions and environmental factors when interpreting data pertaining to oppressed minority groups. He presented an interesting quotation from W. E. B. DuBois:

> [Negroes] must perpetually discuss the Negro problem, must live, move and have their being in it, and interpret all else in its light or darkness. From the double life that every American Negro must live as a Negro and American, as swept on by the current of the Nineteenth Century while struggling in the eddies of the Fifteenth . . . from this must arise a powerful self-consciousness and a moral hesitance which is almost fatal to self-confidence. Today the young Negro of the South who would succeed cannot be frank and outspoken, but rather is daily tempted to be silent and wary, politic and shy. His real thoughts, his real aspirations, must be guarded in whispers; he must not criticize, he must not complain. Patience and adroitness must in these growing black youth, replace impulse, manliness, and courage. . . . At the same time, through books and periodical discussions and lectures he is intellectually awakened. In the conflict some sink, some rise.[21]

Citing this quotation, Miller stressed the inappropriateness of drawing conclusions from unequal environments. Miller's evaluation of earlier studies dealing with quickness and accuracy of perception, disconnected memory, rational instinct and suggestibility, and color preference found no significant differences in these respects between blacks and whites. Little, if any, recognition of Miller's article came from the traditional psychological establishment.

Archives of Psychology and Racial Studies

Over the next dozen years, a number of psychologists made a series of rapid-fire studies utilizing sensory measurement devices, producing a vast array of impressive statistical tables, curves, ranges, and distributions which gave credibility to the "inferiority" myth for black Americans. The prestigous *Archives of Psychology,* edited by R. S. Woodworth, included three notable publications which exemplified the obsession of some early psychologists with the study of black people.

M. J. Mayo's *The Mental Capacity of the American Negro* (1913), based on the grades of 150 white and 150 black pupils in the schools of New York City, concluded that "there seem to be statistical grounds for holding to the view of substantial racial equality" between black and white youngsters.[22] Mayo introduced his study by stating a clear bias: "Among Europeans and their descendants in all parts of the globe there has always existed a feeling of the superiority of the white race. It is a feeling bred in the bone and so strong that it can hardly be eradicated." A few paragraphs later, he continued: "White Europeans always regarded their type as ideal—or at least the most nearly human type—and they have not hesitated to consider wide departures therefrom as evidence of inferiority."[23]

Three years later, G. O. Ferguson published *The Psychology of the Negro: An Experimental Study* (1916). This study was considered a classic, by whites, in the study of the American black man. Ferguson's study predicted:

> Without great ability in the processes of abstract thought, the negro is yet very capable in the sensory and motor powers which are involved in manual work. An economy would indicate that training should be concentrated upon these capacities which promise the best return for the educative effort expended.[24]

In accord with the mulatto hypothesis, he, too, felt that mental ability in the black was proportionate to the amount of "white blood" he possessed. As far as emotions were concerned, Ferguson concluded that blacks were strong and volatile and that "instability of character . . . involving a lack of foresight, an improvidence, a lack of persistence, small power of serious initiative, a tendency to be content with immediate satisfactions, and deficient ambitions" characterized the personality traits of blacks. He also expressed the theory that "defective morality is a negro characteristic."[25] His statement undoubtedly laid the foundation for other research in the measurement of morality attributes in minority groups.

Race Differences in Inhibition (1923) explored the racist theme: "What is the psychological explanation of the immorality which the negro everywhere manifests?"[26] Unfortunately, the author, Albert Loyal Crane, chose not to recognize Miller's study of 1906, for nowhere in Crane's literature is there a hint of Miller's conclusion:

. . . from the manifestations of immorality among the Negroes, or from their failure to recognize certain social conventions, that the Negro is incapable of morality or of adaptation to the social demand, is a conclusion based upon inadequate evidence. Morality and social adaptation are the result of the interpretation of the value of a situation, and not a necessary development of inherent capacity.[27]

Crane sought only to substantiate what he was predisposed to prove, that immorality was due to defective inhibition in the American black. To test his hypothesis, Crane devised a guillotine-like device. A heavy block of wood was dropped from a height above the subject's hand, which rested on a platform. The subject was told that the block would stop before it hit him, and he was told not to move his hand. The subject did not know that a slight shock would be administered to create the illusion that the block had hit him. The hand movements were electrically recorded. Crane concluded from his findings that:

It does not seem improbable that, in those vocational pursuits which involve great sensory shocks and strains not unaccompanied by danger, the black man should prove more efficient than the white . . . true, considerable persuasion might frequently be necessary to induce the colored man to undertake a dangerous pursuit, but, from the results of this experiment, it appears that it would frequently prove to have been very much worthwhile.[28]

In what must have been acceptable behavior for psychologists during this era, Crane shared his feelings with colleagues in this bit of folksy information:

Only the fellow scientist who has attempted to induce 100 Southern darkies to offer themselves as subject in an experiment of this sort can have any conception of the difficulties involved in actually getting the subjects into the laboratory . . . during the course of the four months in which the writer was attempting to entice negroes into his laboratory, he gladly provided vocal solos for negro churches, harangued Thanksgiving meetings, and delivered formal graduation addresses at negro commencements.[29]

Crane's unprofessional attitude and behavior, mixed with racist condescension, were apparent throughout the study: "It was a never-to-be-forgotten experience, the humor and zest whereof, however, more than compensated for the many weary and discouraging hours which it cost to witness a subject fleeing over the hill in fright. . . ."[30] Crane's assistants contributed remarks such as: "Why you can lead some of those darkies right through the switch room (apparatus) and they'll follow you blindly without ever seeming to think about what the switches might be for."[31]

It was unfortunate that studies such as those by Mayo, Ferguson, and Crane were representative of psychology's investigations into racial differences; they not only provided inaccurate data that led to racist conclusions, but they also called into question the intentions of psychological researchers.

Notes

1. H. Burmeister, *The Black Man: The Comparative Anatomy and Psychology of the African Negro* (New York: W. C. Bryant, 1853).

2. R. E. Dennett, *At the Back of the Black Man's Mind* (London: Macmillan, 1906).

3. A. C. Haddon, *History of Anthropology* (New York: Putnam, 1910) p. 6.

4 R. S. Woodworth, "Racial Difference in Mental Traits," *Science* (February 1910), p. 171.

5. Haddon, *op. cit.*, p. 104.

6. D. Folkmar and E. Folkmar, "Dictionary of Races or Peoples" (Document No. 662) (Washington, D.C.: The Immigration Commission, 1911) p. 150.

7. J. Barzun, *A Study in Superstition: Race* (New York: Harper and Row, 1935) pp. 35–36.

8. Ibid., p. 36.

9. G. O. Ferguson, Jr., *The Psychology of the Negro: An Experimental Study* (New York: The Science Press, 1916) p. 27.

10. H. E. Garrett, *How Classroom Desegregation Will Work* (Richmond, Virginia: Patrick Henry Press, 1967) p. 21.

11. F. Boas, *The Mind of Primitive Man* (New York: Macmillan, 1922) p. 73.

12. E. B. Tylor, as quoted by G. O. Ferguson, Jr., in *The Psychology of the Negro: An Experimental Study* (New York: The Science Press, 1916) p. 407.

13. A. de Gobineau, *The Inequality of Human Races* (New York: Putnam, 1915) pp. 205–211.

14. Ibid., p. 211.

15. George A. Miller, *Psychology* (New York: Harper and Row, 1962) p. 129.

16. Galton divided races into sixteen defined grades of ability, eight above the median and eight below. The darker peoples of the globe occupied the lower eight grades.

17. F. Galton, "Annals of Eugenics," *Galton Laboratory for National Eugenics*, 1:1 (October 1925), p. 3.

18. D. P. Schultz, *A History of Modern Psychology* (New York: Academic Press, 1969) p. 31.

19. M. Bache, "Reaction Time with Reference to Race," *Psychological Review*, 2 (1895), pp. 475–586.

20. R. S. Woodworth, in *History of Psychology in Autobiography*, ed. Carl Murchison (Worcester, Mass.: Clark University Press, 1932) vol. 2, p. 373.

21. H. Miller, "Some Psychological Considerations on the Race Problem," in *The Health and Physique of the Negro American*, ed. W. E. Burghardt Du Bois (Atlanta: Atlanta University Press, 1906) pp. 54–59.

22. M. J. Mayo, *The Mental Capacity of the American Negro,* Archives of Psychology: 28 (New York: The Science Press, 1913) p. 17.

23. Mayo, ibid., p. 17.

24. Ferguson, *op. cit.,* p. 125.

25. Ferguson, Ibid., p. 125.

26. A. L. Crane, "Race Differences in Inhibition," *Archives of Psychology,* 63 (New York: The Science Press, 1923) p. 15.

28. Ibid.

29. Ibid.

30. Ibid.

31. Ibid.

3
Psychometric scientism

WATER IS H_2O, HYDROGEN TWO PARTS, OXYGEN ONE,
BUT THERE IS ALSO A THIRD THING THAT MAKES IT
WATER, AND NOBODY KNOWS WHAT IT IS.

D. H. Lawrence

Nativism, elitism, social class bias, and racism were as essential to
the development of psychometric thought in America as the requirement of free enterprise was to capitalism. The psychological
test of mental ability, with its commonplace term, the IQ, was the
tour de force that replaced anthropometric attempts to establish
racial stratifications. Armed with messianic self-concepts, many
psychologists became early twentieth century helmsmen for
American racism. By presenting an imposing array of statistics
declaring that lower-median IQ scores truly reflected most non-
white peoples' abilities, many psychologists inadvertently justified
racial prejudice and discrimination as an intellectual necessity.
Even at an embryonic stage, mental measurement was regarded
as an empirical proposition of enormous accuracy. A brief look at

some theoretical antecedents of psychological testing will help to show how this condition of faith developed.

Theoretical Antecedents

Concepts of inherited individual differences, and the requirement that these differences be measured statistically, were firmly established in Western thought before the 1900s. Three events strongly contributed to these views: a report that astronomers differed in reaction time suggested that differences in human behavior could be evaluated quantitatively;[1] Sir Francis Galton's subjective studies of familial genius and individual achievement set the stage for blood-lineage biases; and Wilhelm Wundt's laboratory procedures helped lead the discipline of psychology to establish taxonomic-like investigations.

Though the term *mental test* was employed as early as 1890 by Cattell, it was the later description of mental processes and classifications by French psychologists Alfred Binet and Victor Henri that served as a framework for theorizing the possibilities of mental measurement. So impressive were Binet's descriptions (idiot, imbecile, moron, etc.) that he was soon being described as the leading innovator in psychometrics. Consequently, in 1904, when French government officials formed a commission of medical men, educators, scientists, and public officials to study the problem of teaching retarded children in the Paris public schools, Binet was selected as a participant. Teaming with Theophile Simon, a medical doctor, Binet constructed a test of intelligence which, in a few years, was to play a major role in the attempt to identify racial differences in America. The end result was a psychomedical model of measurement which was viewed as *scientific* from its very beginning—in spite of Binet's own warning of its limitations. (He had pointed out that while his tests could safely be used to arrive at individual differences, the individuals tested must have had the same, or approximately the same, environmental and educational opportunities.) Binet's test, unlike the later revisions, employed simple, everyday problems unrelated to formal classroom instruction. (Examples of these test problems are given in Table 7.)

At about the same time, across the English channel, psychologist Charles Spearman (1904) introduced a two-factor theory of intelligence leading to the belief that every mental test measured two components: a *general factor* and a *specific factor*.[2] The general, or g factor, expressed the belief that abstract reasoning was

Table 7 Sample of Items Used by Binet in the 1908 and 1911 Versions of the Binet-Simon Tests

AGE 1 YEAR
Visual coördination of the head and eyes
  in following an object.

AGE 3 YEARS
Points to nose, eyes and mouth.
Repeats two digits.
Names objects in a picture.

AGE 4 YEARS
Names a key, knife and penny.
Repeats three digits.
Compares two lines.

AGE 5 YEARS
Copies a square.
Repeats a sentence of ten syllables.
Unites the halves of a divided rectangle.

AGE 6 YEARS
Defines familiar words in terms of use.
Copies a diamond.
Counts 13 pennies.

AGE 7 YEARS
Points to right and left ears.
Executes three commands given together.
Names four colors.

AGE 8 YEARS
Compares two objects from memory.
Counts backwards from twenty.
Notices missing parts from pictures.

AGE 9 YEARS
Gives change from twenty sous.
Defines familiar words in other terms than
  use.
Names the months of the year in order.

AGE 10 YEARS
Copies two drawings from memory.
Can tell what is wrong with absurd state-
  ments (The body of a girl was found cut in
  18 pieces; they think she killed herself.
  What is wrong with that?).
Arranges five blocks in order of weight.

AGE 12 YEARS
Names 60 words in three minutes.
Defines three abstract words.
Can rearrange a disarranged sentence.

AGE 15 YEARS
Repeats seven digits.
Repeats a sentence of 26 syllables.
Finds three rhymes for a given word in one
  minute.

SOURCE: James Deese, *General Psychology.* © 1967 by Allyn and Bacon, Inc. Reprinted by permission.

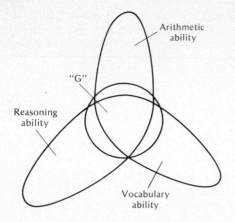

Figure 3.1 Illustrates the Spearman general factor theory: Tests of ability correlate because they, in part, measure an underlying general ability. In addition, however, each test has an uncorrelated part that is an ability unique to that test. The general ability is labeled "G" in the diagram. (*Source:* From James Deese, *General Psychology.* Copyright © 1967 by Allyn and Bacon, Inc., Boston. Reprinted by permission.)

positively correlated with verbal knowledge because a single ability ran through both performances (Figure 3.1). This speculation strongly influenced the conceptualization by other psychologists of the nature of intelligence.

It is important to note that Binet's definition of intelligence included "the tendency to take and maintain a definite direction; the capacity to make adaptations for the purpose of attaining a desired end; and the power of auto-criticism."[3] Spearman's concept suggested that Binet's notion of individual learning styles and conditions of affective behavior were not pertinent to the definition; Spearman, therefore, focused on a narrower aspect of intelligence. As his dichotomous view of intelligence was in accord with existing middle-class Anglo-Saxon values, it was quickly accepted by those who shared backgrounds emphasizing abstraction and verbalization criteria.

Acceptance of the g factor theory encouraged the creation and utilization of verbal- and quantitative-type test items as appropriate measures of "pure intellectual capacity" while deemphasizing the importance of measuring other intellectual qualities.[4] This reasoning led to unrealistic psychometric evaluation of children whose backgrounds, cultures, and life styles emphasized other values. Arithmetic and vocabulary problems, couched in varying degrees of difficulty and demanding a firm knowledge of the English language, became the eventual yardstick for measuring the mental abilities of children from America's oppressed minorities and low-status immigrants.

Stanford-Binet Revisions

The Americanization of the Binet-Simon scales occurred at approximately the same time that the g factor became entrenched in mental measurement theory. Before the Stanford University revision of the scales gained its overwhelming popularity, the Binet-Simon scales had undergone many not so successful translations and revisions: Goddard (1911) and Kuhlmann (1911) in America, Ferrari (1908) and Treves and Soffiotti (1909) in Italy, Descoeudres (1911) in Switzerland, Bobertag (1912) in Germany, and Johnson (1922) in England. These and the Stanford revisions were all influenced by an interesting, unique concept which enabled test results to be interpreted and calculated as a single score, the intelligence quotient (IQ):[5]

$$IQ = \frac{\text{Mental Age}}{\text{Chronological Age}} \times 100$$

This formula assumed that the ratio between mental age and chronological age would remain constant throughout the various stages of human development; a debatable assumption, it has had an enormous impact on psychometric and educational theory for many years.

Lewis Terman

When Lewis Terman of Stanford University revised the Binet scales in 1916, he directed their use in a manner of which the professor from the Sorbonne had never dreamed. Whatever benefits might have been achieved by the revision were overshadowed by Terman's bias and his narrow-minded declarations to future psychologists: "(Mental retardation) represents the level of intelligence which is very, very common among Spanish-Indians and Mexican families of the Southwest and also among negroes. Their dullness seems to be racial."[6] Terman further predicted that when future IQ testing of these groups was done, "there will be discovered enormously significant racial differences which cannot be wiped out by any scheme of mental culture."[7]

It is amazing how the Stanford psychologist, later president of the American Psychological Association (APA), reached these incredible conclusions from a scale that was standardized on a sample of approximately 1,000 children and 400 adults—none of them black or brown people. Nevertheless, in the same breath, he called for special education classes and prescribed their content and pedagogy: "Children of this group should be segregated in special classes and be given instruction which is concrete and practical. They cannot master abstractions."[8] Finally, speaking of these same minorities, Terman's racism reached dangerous proportions: "There is no possibility at present of convincing society that they should not be allowed to reproduce, although from a eugenic point of view they constitute a grave problem because of their unusually prolific breeding."[9] In line with this view, Terman felt that every retarded youngster was a potential criminal.

It was no accident, even beyond Gaussian predictions, that twenty-six percent of Terman's population would have IQs designated *below average* (or often referred to as *abnormal*).[10] Furthermore, at a time when massive numbers of disfranchised immigrants, laborers, and racial minorities occupied the working-class strata of America's economy, the Terman revision asked for explanations of middle-class proverbs ("He who would eat the kernel must crack the nut" and "One swallow does not make a summer"). It required a child to remember and repeat sentences based on his ability to handle the English language ("The red-headed woodpeckers made a terrible fuss as they tried to drive the young away from the nest" and "The early settlers had little idea of the great changes that were to take place in this country").[11]

It is not too difficult to visualize the barrio or ghetto child struggling not only with pronunciation but repeating words which meant little or were seldom heard in his culture. The ultimate disregard for cultural differences appeared in the task requiring the child to utilize Anglo-Saxon criteria for discriminating between "prettiness" and "ugliness." Not only was this an insensitive exercise, it was damaging to a developing self-image and to a standard of beauty that is subjective for each culture.

Discussions of social class boundaries were interwoven throughout most theoretical psychology papers of this era. Terman et al. (1917) lent early credence to this viewpoint when they assigned the categories *very inferior* (IQ below 80), *inferior* (IQ 80–90), *average* (IQ 90–109), *superior* (IQ 110–119), and *very superior* (IQ 120 and above) to socioeconomic status categories. Arguing that IQ scores were primarily due to a matter of innate endowment, Terman assigned the following occupational descriptions to his IQ calculations:

> Preliminary investigations indicate that an IQ below 70 rarely permits anything better than unskilled labor; that the range from 70 to 80 is preeminently that of semi-skilled labor, from 80 to 100 that of the skilled or ordinary clerical labor, from 100 to 110 or 115 that of the semi-professional pursuits; and that above all these are grades of intelligence which permit one to enter the professions or the larger fields of business. Intelligence tests can tell us whether a child's native brightness corresponds more nearly to the median of (1) the professional classes, (2) those in the semi-professional pursuits, (3) ordinary skilled workers, (4) semi-skilled workers, or (5) unskilled laborers. This information will be of great value in planning the education of a particular child and also in planning the differentiated curriculum here recommended.[12]

The sociopolitical aspect of these classifications clearly indicates the potential power and control inherent in these concepts in mental testing.

With the exception of the gross mental deficiencies discussed by Binet, it was the American psychologists who extended the range of classification from idiocy to a vague notion of genius—with various classifications along the way. It was also the American psychologists, led by Lewis Terman, who chorused the blood lineage theme to explain differing scores along the continuum. And it was educational psychologist Edward Thorndike who announced that intelligence was "roughly" 80 percent genetic, 17 percent based on educational opportunities, and 3 percent accidental.[13] Thorndike's speculations placed an unfair emphasis on the role of heredity; he undoubtedly set the intellectual biases for present-day prognosticators of black-white mental abilities.

Throughout this period of intelligence testing, few attempts were made to censure the tests or even to voice skepticism; Terman's views soared as words of great wisdom for aspiring neophyte psychologists. As the testing mystique grew, the cloak of secrecy increased. Only "the informed" knew about the IQ formula and its calculation. Individuals submitted to IQ testing but the results were kept under lock and key, protected from unsophisticated eyes. The mental testers, with the sanction of school officials, were given free rein to test any school-age child. Parental consent was unthought of, much less considered a normal condition. There was no code of ethics or standards to check the profession; it was in fact a system in complete control of its subjects.

The 1916 Stanford-Binet scales maintained their dominance in the testing world for twenty years—until the 1937 revision. This revision retained the majority of the old test items but was extended downward to the two-year-old level and upward to the twenty-two-year-old level. As had the original revision, this version also omitted the use of black children in preparing its normatization data.

Black-White Mental Testing

The earliest effort by American researchers to investigate black-white differences using intelligence tests was made in 1897 when G. R. Stetson tested 500 black and 500 white public school children in Washington, D. C. The test utilized by Stetson consisted of four stanzas of poetry which the experimenter read aloud and the children were required to repeat.[14] It is interesting to observe that in this exercise, of which little publicity was made, the black children excelled the white children; consequently, it was determined that the memory technique was not a valid measure of intelligence.

The first reported study utilizing the Binet scales to determine whether racial differences existed was made in Columbia, South Carolina, in 1912. In this study, Josiah Morse of the University of South Carolina directed his graduate student, Alice C. Strong, to measure, with the Goddard revision of the Binet scale, the intelligence of 225 white children and 125 black children. Strong went so far as to divide the black children into groupings based on the degree of their skin pigmentations: dark, medium, and light-colored. Her purpose for this grouping was "to determine the effect of white blood on intelligence."[15] (This was an effort in support of the *mulatto hypothesis,* which held that the degree of intelligence increased with the proportion of white blood in black children [see page 62].) Her findings concluded that "colored children are mentally younger than the White" and that lighter-complexioned black children obtained higher mental scores. Morse later reported that while the Strong study showed that

> the colored children did excel in rote memory . . . (they) are inferior in esthetic judgement, observation, reasoning, motor control, logical memory, use of words, resistance to suggestion and in orientation or adjustment to the institutions and complexities of civilized society.[16]

Despite this egregious indictment, Morse at least recognized one flaw in the testing instrument when he observed that "the picture tests gave the colored children considerable trouble, probably due to difference in racial esthetics."[17] Later, in a stroke of rare intellectual insight for 1913, Morse noted:

> . . . if Binet and Simon had originally tested southern negro children they would have worked out from the results a scale which would have been different from their present one in several respects, and which when applied to southern white children would be found to be, for the most part, a year or more too young. . . . Perhaps some day each branch of the human family will have a Binet scale of its own.[18]

In 1914, B. A. Phillips compared the test scores of 137 white and 86 black children and then went beyond the mere recording of scores by raising the question of providing separate educational training for blacks:

> If the Binet tests are at all a gauge of mentality it must follow that there is a difference in mentality between the colored and the white children, and this raises the question: Should the two groups be instructed under the same curriculum?[19]

This analysis was one of the earliest psychological appraisals of intelligence test scores which suggested separate educational programs for black and white children. Prior to this, evidence supporting the existence of segregated educational programs consisted of philosophical opinions. For example G. Stanley Hall, the founding father of the American Psychological Association, maintained that:

> No two races in history, taken as a whole, differ so much in their traits, both physical and psychic, as the Caucasian and the African. The color of the skin and the crookedness of the hair are only the outward signs of the many far deeper differences, including cranial and thoracic capacity, proportions of body, nervous system, glands, and secretions, vita sexualis, food, temperament, disposition, character, longevity, instincts, customs, emotional traits, and diseases. All these differences as they are coming to be better understood, are seen to be so great as to qualify if not imperil every inference from one race to another, whether theoretical or practical, so that what is true and good for one is often false and bad for the other.[20]

With the acceptance of psychology (with its tests of mental ability) as a science, unquestioning credence was given to reports like those of Phillips. Ferguson (1916) echoed a similar contention that blacks, as a result of recorded IQ test differences, should be trained as manual laborers:

> Without great ability in the processes of abstract thought, the negro is yet very capable in the sensory and motor powers which are involved in manual work. And economy would indicate that training should be concentrated upon these capacities which promise the best return for the educative effort expended.[21]

As racist research efforts continued, statistical measures of central tendency evolved into mental percentage comparisons between blacks and whites. When W. H. Pyle (1915) tested 408 black children in the Missouri public schools and compared them to white children in the same area, he concluded: "In general the marks indicating mental ability of the Negro are about two-thirds of the whites."[22] The two-thirds statistic was historically interesting in that it also supported a political contention which had previously regarded the black as a "fractionated" man.[23]

Children to Adults and Individual to Mass Testing

The advent of World War I increased and shifted testing emphases in two directions, from children to adults and from individual to group tests. During the period 1917–1919, over one and one-half million soldiers were administered group tests developed by a special committee appointed by the American Psychological Association (APA). It was through this committee, headed by APA President Robert M. Yerkes, that group IQ tests were nurtured. The APA and the National Research Council (NRC) set the stage for mass testing and the Committee for Classification of Personnel in the Army (CCPA) carried out the movement. The Army Alpha and Army Beta tests, created by Army psychologist Arthur Otis, were the most important products of this committee and the forerunners of educational group tests.[24]

Table 8 Sample Items from the Army Alpha Test, 1917

MATHEMATICS
"If it takes six men three days to dig a 180-foot drain, how many will dig it in half a day?"

SYNONYM—ANTONYM
Fallacy—Verity (Same/Opposite?)
Innuendo—Insinuation (Same/Opposite?)

ANALOGIES
Lion : animal as rose : smell *or* leaf : plant
Tolerate : pain as welcome : pleasure *or* unwelcome : friend

GENERAL INFORMATION
The *dictaphone* is a kind of *typewriter, multigraph, phonograph, adding machine?*
Mauve is the name of a *drink, color, fabric, food?*
"Why is wheat better for food than corn?" Because ( ) it is more nutritious; ( ) it is more expensive; ( ) it can be ground finer.

SOURCE: U.S. Government Printing Office, Washington, D.C., 1918.

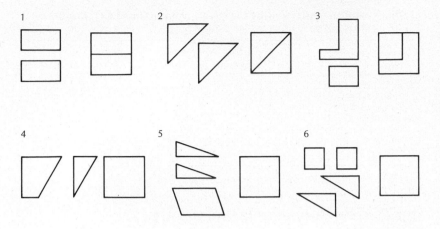

Figure 3.2 A set of sample items from the Army Beta Test: Individuals being examined are instructed to mark the square at the right to show how the figures at the left will fit into it. (*Source:* Ladd Wheeler, Robert Goodale, and James Deese, *General Psychology*. Copyright © 1975 by Allyn and Bacon, Inc., Boston. Reprinted by permission.)

The Army Alpha, which made little attempt to measure abilities independent of prior education, was quickly regarded as a bona fide measure of innate mental ability; it contained typical arithmetic, analogy, and general information items (Table 8).

The Army Beta, a non-verbal parallel to the Alpha, contained mazes, picture completions, and geometric constructions created especially to measure the mental abilities of illiterate and non-English-speaking recruits (Figure 3.2).

Between 1919 and 1926, the military human assessment turf was parceled among psychologists for research testing data: R. M. Yerkes had Camps Dix, Sevier, and Dodge; M. R. Trabue had Camp Grant; and G. O. Ferguson gleaned data from Camp Lee.[25] Immediately after the war, released Army data illustrated the magnitude in which psychologists had explored black and white IQ test score differences in soldiers. These data were discussed and displayed in hundreds of journal articles and textbooks with outspoken discussions supporting racial and regional IQ differences. The most frequently quoted data came from the comparisons between black and white, northern and southern Army recruits (Table 9).

The membership rolls of the APA increased nearly threefold during the 1920s, a large percentage of these members being employed by educational institutions. As the number of psychologists grew, added to from the training ranks, so interest in the area of mental testing expanded.

Table 9 Median Alpha Scores for Given Amounts of Education (1916–1918)

Group	0 to 4 Grades	5 to 8 Grades	High School	College
White soldiers				
(Native-Born)	22.0	51.1	92.1	117.8
(Foreign-Born)	21.4	47.2	72.4	91.9
Negro Soldiers				
(Northern)	17.0	37.2	71.2	90.5
(Southern)	7.2	16.3	45.7	63.8
White Officers	112.5	107.0	131.0	143.2

SOURCE: U.S. Government Printing Office, Washington, D.C., 1930.

Postwar Psychological Measurements

World War I practices led to the creation of group testing to pre-dict and measure potentialities in school children. Group IQ tests were constructed for each educational level: elementary, high school, and college. Leading examples of this era included the Otis IQ test, National Intelligence Test, Kuhlmann-Anderson IQ test, Peterson Rational Learning Test, Pitner-Patterson Series, and the Goodenough Draw-A-Man Test. The general public accepted the IQ concept and expressed unwavering faith in the validity of the new tests. Schoolteachers, social workers, guidance coun-selors, and personnel workers became official examiners and inter-preters of the new devices; the group tests were not only readily available but were easily scored and interpreted. Very little de-bate arose concerning the rationale of the test questions, which allowed the items to be designed without contest. Examiner's manuals became test appendages with an impressive entangle-ment of figures and tables that increased acceptance of the "scientific quality" of the tests.

In addition to grade-level stratifications, every possible human variation was examined and compared—usually after the tests were constructed. In short order, specialists (as well as publishers) began to appear claiming expertise in the measurement of human differences. The native American, along with the immigrant white ethnic groups, Asian-Americans, and blacks, were constant ob-jects of mental testing efforts.

The United States Indian Schools

Like black children, native American youngsters were easily iden-tifiable and conveniently segregated. But, unlike the segregated black schools in urban and rural America, reservation schools grouped Indian children along tribal lines, which facilitated inter-group comparisons by researchers. The added variable of lan-guage difference offered still another dimension for educational psychologists in their discussions and debates of mental capaci-ties; opinions expressing the need for the native American to absorb the white man's culture in order to improve his "innate inferiority" (as measured by the tests) were frequently discussed.

Some of the principal examples of early testing efforts of na-tive American children occurred in the mid-1920s. Jamieson and Standiford (1928) administered the National Intelligence, the Pit-ner Non-Language, and the Pitner-Patterson Performance Tests to a large sample of Ontario Indians and concluded that the ob-served disparity between verbal and written performance test scores was correlated to the degree of "their contact with white culture."[26] In support of this hypothesis, Hunter (1922) had re-ported earlier:

> there is a positive correlation between increasing degree of white blood in the American Indian and score on the Otis Intelligence test which would seem to indicate a racial difference probably of intelligence although possibly of temperament.[27]

While a study by Fitzgerald and Ludeman (1926) flatly reported that the Indian child was an inferior being,[28] Hunter, this time teaming with Sommermier (1922), tested 711 native Americans from different tribes who were students at the Haskell Indian In-stitute (Lawrence, Kansas) and concluded that a correlation of .41 existed between IQ score and degree of white blood.[29] Finally, Garth et al. (1927), using the popular National Intelligence Test, examined nearly 700 native Americans in South Dakota, New Mexico, Oklahoma, and Colorado and concluded that significant correlations existed between the degree of white ancestry and IQ test scores.[30]

These studies supported the popular belief that white blood increased the Indian's intellectual capability until Klineberg (1928), after testing 100 Yakima Indians in Washington, reported a lack of any conclusive relationship between white ancestry and IQ scores.[31] Klineberg's subsequent research efforts reported similar findings, and it was not long before he was labeled an egalitarian in the human affairs arena. Within a few years he began to ques-tion cultural biases found in IQ tests. For example, in 1935 he ob-served that Dakota Indian children considered it to be in bad taste to answer a question in the presence of others who did not know the answer.[32] This observation was soon extended to events in United States reservation school rooms where individual com-petition was expected to prevail. Porteus (1931) had expressed similar notions while testing native Australians: ". . . the aborigine is used to concerted thinking. Not only is every problem in tribal life debated and settled by the council of elders, but it is always discussed until a unanimous decision is reached."[33] Nevertheless, in spite of Klineberg's and Porteus's findings, there was little visible effort to take cultural factors into consideration in IQ testing.

Mexican Americans and IQ Testing

Mexican-American children, too, were victimized and frequently labeled "racially inferior" as a result of IQ tests that expected all children to have had the same cultural experiences. Bilingualism was thought to induce a state of "mental confusion" in these children, and this theory led to the practice of literal translation of the standardized tests from English into Spanish. However, the assumption that Anglo-cultural references were omnipotent and needed only language translation was a major fallacy; as little consideration for the Mexican-American culture was made during the construction of the tests.

Among those tests translated, the International Group Mental Test (IGMT) gained the most recognition for its use with Spanish-speaking subjects. Beatrice Blackwood (1927) administered the IGMT to 413 Indian and 200 "Spanish-American" children in New Mexico and Arizona in typical fashion for this time.[34] Her purpose was to offer suggestions for the refinement of a "test suitable for primitive conditions" and to determine if any differences existed between the two populations. While she reported no new testing refinement, she concluded that significant IQ differences existed between the Mexican-American and the Indian children.

Among the few voices sounded against the acceptance of reports such as Blackwood's was that of George Sanchez, then (1932) Director of the Division of Information and Statistics, New Mexico State Department of Education. He criticized the translated tests because they were "used as actual measures rather than as experimental tools . . . (and) may be still further questioned as to their value in revealing the mental confusion resulting from a 'dual language handicap'."[35] Sanchez also stressed the importance of the *linguistic* variable, the neglected third factor in the heredity and environment debates of the 1920s. His classic article, "Group Differences and Spanish-Speaking Children—A Critical Review," carefully evaluated the large-scale IQ testing of Mexican-American children. (Table 10 lists the studies on which Sanchez focused his critique.) In spite of Sanchez's many criti-

Table 10 Studies of Test Results of Spanish-Speaking Children

Student	Date	Measure	Cases[a]	Place
Davenport	1931	Goodenough	420 Ss sibs 126 Es sibs	Texas Texas
Delmet	1930	Det. Kdgtn. Pint. Cun. Pres. Prim. Haggerty In. Otis Grp. Stfd. Ach.	341 Ss	Calif.
Fickinger	1930	Pint. Cun. (Eng. & trs.)	95 Ss	N. Mexico
Garretson	1928	N. I. T. Pantomime Pint. Cun.	117 Ss 197 Es	Arizona Arizona
Garth	1923	N. I. T.	307 Ss 634 Ind.	Texas Okla. & N. Mexico
Garth	1928	N. I. T.	1006 Ss	Texas, N. Mexico & Colo.
Goodenough	1928	Goodenough	367 Ss 500 Es 1590 others	Calif. La., & Tenn.
Haught	1929	Pint. Cun. N. I. T. German grp.	All Ss in 4(?) scho. systems	N. Mexico
Hughes	1928	Goodenough	440 Ss 396 Es	Texas Texas
Knight	1931	Eye-movement (Read.)	21 Ss Controls Es	Texas Texas
Koch & Simmons	1928	Pant. & 1 of N. I. T., Det. 1st Gr., or Pint. Cun.	1492 Ss 1211 Es 613 Negro	Texas Texas Texas
Paschal & Sullivan	1925	Perf. Tests Anthro. Meas.	415 Ss	Arizona
Sanchez	1931	Stfd. Ach. Haggerty In.	45 Ss	N. Mexico
Sheldon	1924	Stfd. Binet	100 Ss 100 Es	N. Mexico N. Mexico
Sininger	1930	Mon. S. Read.	3336 Ss 6563 Es	N. Mexico N. Mexico
Stoltz	1931	Meier-Seashore McAdory	82 Ss 103 Es	Texas Texas
Tireman	1929	Mon. S. Read.	3366 Ss 6119 Es	N. Mexico N. Mexico
Wright & Manuel	1929	Stfd. Read. (Eng. & Trs.)	128 Ss 450 Es	Texas Texas
Young	1922	Army Alpha Army Beta	51 Ss 402 Es 325 others	Calif. Calif. Calif.

SOURCE: George I. Sanchez, "Group Differences and Spanish-Speaking Children," *Journal of Applied Psychology*, 16 (1932), pp. 552–553. Copyright 1932 by the American Psychological Association. Reprinted by permission.

[a] Ss: Spanish-speaking; Es: English-speaking.

George I. Sanchez *(Jorge Isidoro Sanchez y Sanchez),* *1906–1971.* Dr. Sanchez was an early critic of psychological testing that claimed Mexican-American mental inferiority. He was a University of Texas professor and author of numerous monographs and research articles.

cisms (1932 and 1934), the practice of administering the tests continued.

In spite of the decline of anthropometry in American research, physical measurement was often used in conjunction with the IQ testing of Mexican-American children. A case in point were the investigations of nine- and twelve-year-old children in the public schools of Tucson, Arizona. Paschal and Sullivan (1925), after recording an enormous amount of physical data and mental test scores, reported seventeen conclusions, including this one: "Tucson Mexicans who are partially of Indian origin have (a) a lower mental score, (b) a lower social or economic status, (c) a lower school standing in grade, than those Tucson Mexicans who are wholly of white origin."[36] Studies such as this led many investigators to agree that a definite relationship existed between the proportion of Indian blood in Mexican Americans and their mental test scores. This view in turn supported popular assumptions concerning the importance of "white blood" in blacks in relation to their IQ test score performances.

The Mulatto Hypotheses

Between 1916 and 1930, the black child was continuously subjected to massive assessment studies (Table 11). Dialectal and cultural differences received little or no consideration; mental test

62

Table 11 Geographical Location of Investigations of Intelligence of Negroes with Standard Tests, 1916–1930

Place	Investigator
Arkansas	Jordan
California	Clark; Goodenough
Florida	McGraw
Indiana	Lenoir; Pressey and Teter
Jamaica, British West Indies	Davenport
Louisiana	Arlitt; Goodenough; Sunne
Mississippi	Boots
New York City	Klineberg; Murdock
North Carolina	Leggett
Oberlin, Ohio	Wells
Oklahoma	Lacy
South Carolina	Derrick; Strong
South Africa	Loades and Rich
Tennessee	Goodenough; Leggett; Peterson
Texas	Davis; Garth and Whately
Virginia	Ferguson
West Virginia	Klineberg; State Dept. of Education
Wisconsin	Martell

SOURCE: J. St. Clair Price, "Negro-White Differences in General Intelligence,"*Journal of Negro Education,* July 1934, p. 438. Reprinted by permission of the publisher.

scores of black and white English-speaking populations were frequently matched and correlated with little regard for those differences, leaving questionable conclusions to be drawn. One outgrowth of these and similar comparisons led to specific issues surrounding the mulatto hypotheses.

The mulatto hypotheses were formulated from two perspectives: one held that persons of racially mixed ancestry were *inferior* to those of "pure" (unmixed) backgrounds; the other view held that racially mixed persons were *superior* to those of "pure" backgrounds. For both views, scientific data were recorded. One bizarre study claimed that black-white crosses in Jamaica left the individuals with "long legs of the Negro and the short arms of the white, thus putting them at a disadvantage in picking up objects from the ground."[37] This view was studied under a theory of *disharmonic* results from racial-mixturing.

Significant numbers of psychological studies during the 1920s and 1930s purported to show a relationship between white ancestry and IQ test scores of black children. Klineberg (1931), Eells (1933), and Herskovits (1935) were among the few white scholars refuting these studies by performing and reporting their own research efforts. Herskovits reported the most extensive review on this issue and concluded that ". . . no significant correlations have been made between the amount of Negro blood represented in individuals—whether estimated on the basis of inspection, by the use of genealogies, or by anthropometric measurements—and standing in tests. . . ."[38] Yet, in spite of these findings, the mulatto hypotheses continued to maintain widespread support among many researchers.

In order to determine the acceptance level of the mulatto hypotheses among white behavioral scientists, a Howard University professor, C. H. Thompson, queried 169 leading white scholars during the school year 1929–1930.[39] One hundred psychologists were chosen from the membership lists of the Ninth International Congress of Psychology, while educators, sociologists, and cultural anthropologists were selected from random lists.[40] With a 76 percent response rate to the question "Does experimental evidence support or refute the 'mulatto hypothesis'?" 70 percent of the respondents felt that the evidence was inconclusive. However, the group with the largest percentage supporting the hypothesis were the psychologists. Further analysis of Thompson's data revealed that nearly two-thirds of the total group felt that investigations concerning the "inferiority or equality of inherent black mental ability" were also inconclusive. But, as before, one-fourth of the queried psychologists felt that substantial evidence existed to prove the mental inferiority of blacks. Interestingly, more than one-third of the sociologists and anthropologists felt that the evidence supported the existence of mental *equality* between blacks and whites (Table 12).

Table 12 Conclusions from Investigations of the Relative Inherent Mental Ability of the Negro (1929–1930)

1. Do investigations show the inherent mental ability of the Negro to be inferior or equal to that of the White?

GROUP	DATA INCONCLUSIVE	NEGRO INFERIOR	NEGRO EQUAL
Psychologists	64%	25%	11%
Educationists	61	14	15
Sociologists and Anthropologists	57	5	38
Total	62%	19%	19%

2. Does experimental evidence support or refute the "mulatto hypothesis"?

GROUP	INCONCLUSIVE	SUPPORTS	REFUTES
Psychologists	68%	23%	9%
Educationists	65	10	25
Sociologists and Anthropologists	76	—	24
Total	70%	15%	15%

SOURCE: Charles H. Thompson, "The Conclusions of Scientists Relative to Racial Differences," *Journal of Negro Education*, July 1934, p. 499, 507. Reprinted by permission of the publisher.

Horace Mann Bond *(1904–
1972)*. Dr. Bond, author of
numerous books and research
articles, became the first black
president of Lincoln University
(Pennsylvania) and of Fort
Valley State College (Georgia).
He was an early critic of psychometric studies that claimed
mental inferiority of black
children.

Reactions of Black Scholars
and Communities

With black psychologists practically nonexistent during the 1920s
and 1930s, it fell to black educators to protest the mulatto hypotheses and the psychological testing movement. Among the
most vocal critics was Horace Mann Bond, an outstanding twenty-
year-old professor at Langston University (Oklahoma). Much of
Bond's early criticisms were couched in the form of instruction
and warnings to black people to become aware of the conclusions reached by white psychological examiners.[41] He specifically
called for active participation against what he called: ". . . insidi-
ous propaganda . . . which seeks to demonstrate that the Negro
is intellectually and physically incapable of assuming the digni-
ties, rights and duties which devolve upon him as a member of
modern society."[42] Bond criticized the practice of generalizing
from conclusions based on comparisons of unequal social groups:
"To compare the crowded millions of New York's East Side with
the children of some professorial family on Morningside Heights
indeed involves a great contradiction. . . ."[43] He felt these interpretations were especially dangerous to the "newly born race
consciousness" of black people, and he called for immediate actions against these inequities:

The time has passed for opposing these false ideas with silence; every university student of Negro blood ought to comprise himself into an agent whose sole purpose is the contravention of such half-truths . . . There is no longer any justifications for the silence of the educated Negro, when confronted with these assertions; and only through his activity and investigation will the truth be disclosed and the ghosts of racial inferiority, mental or physical, set at rest, forever.[44]

Herbert Miller, addressing the Sixteenth Annual Conference of the National Association for the Advancement of Colored People (NAACP) in 1925, spoke out against "aspects of intelligence tests" and described the alleged psychometric evidence supporting the inherent inferiority of blacks as a popular form of "pseudoscience."[45] The speaker found humor in the use of statistics to measure mental differences with the same accuracies and expectations found in the physical sciences. He commented that, while it is true that "figures do not lie," it was also true that "there are lies, damned lies, and statistics." Miller acknowledged that it would be difficult to comprehend the mass of social phenomena without the use of numbers, but he said:

. . . in the vast variety of human concerns there are possibilities of counting many unimportant things and of mixing the important with the unimportant, and then drawing misleading conclusions. Thus racial groupings for intelligence tests will give very different results in different cultural areas. . . .[46]

In a classic 1927 article, the prolific Horace Mann Bond called the testing of black children a major indoor sport among white psychologists and outlined rules for the game: "First one must have a *white* examiner; a group of *Negro* children; a test standardized for *white* children tested by white examiners; and just a few pre-conceived notions regarding the nature of "intelligence."[47] Bond noted that when examining white children the examiner must be careful to establish "rapport" with his subject and that an "esprit cordiale" must exist between himself and the person being tested. "If this was not done, so long as white children are being tested, the results of the game may not be valid," Bond explained. On the other hand, this was not true, as he noted, when testing black children. Black children were often criticized for being withdrawn during the testing situation; their docility was assumed to be an inherited trait and of no significance in determining the final test score.

As a result of these feelings, Bond decided to "play the game" of psychometry—with some alterations. He selected black children from professional homes and middle-class homes, rather than from the laboring-class homes which were the favorite source of subjects for white psychologists. Using the Stanford-Binet Test, he made special efforts to gain "fullest rapport" during the testing, and he "leaned over backwards" in order to maintain "scientific accuracy." The results were so striking that they even surprised Bond: 63 percent made scores above 106; 47 percent equalled or exceeded IQs of 122; 26 percent made scores over 130. Bond concluded that these exceptional children "were not out of the ordinary . . . the same sort of a group could be selected in any Negro community" provided the same sociocultural background of the subjects existed. Bond's study received no published reaction from white psychologists, but his article did serve notice of the importance of the race of the examiner relative to that of the subject, of the rapport between examiner and subject, and social-class variables.

Black Graduate Students Respond

During the 1930s, a few black students of psychology began to filter through the northern university training centers. These students became a small legion of protestors, frequently directing their theses, dissertations, and other academic energies toward refuting beliefs of black mental inferiority. Among these students were Herman G. Canady, masters degree candidate at Northwestern University; Howard H. Long, doctoral candidate at Harvard University; Albert S. Beckham, doctoral candidate at New York University; and Martin D. Jenkins, doctoral candidate at Northwestern University.

Herman G. Canady's master's thesis (1928) provided empirical evidence supporting the importance of the effects of rapport on the IQ—data later regarded as classic in psychological testing. His study in "racial psychology" presented statistical evidence across two dimensions: (1) effects of rapport and (2) race of the examiner. Canady's initial concern regarding these questions was stimulated by an anonymous article of 1916, "Some Suggestions Relative to the Study on the Mental Attitude of the Negro," which questioned the appropriateness of the Binet test for black children, the unconscious mental biases of the examiners, the tendency of black children not to "let a white person know anything about him," and the importance of rapport: ". . . it is not too much to say that the mere presence in the room of a member of the dominant race creates an atmosphere in which it is impossible to get a normal response."[48] Inspired by this article, Canady used the Stanford-Binet test on 48 black and 25 white children from the elementary schools of Evanston, Illinois. Employing black and white examiners, he set about testing the assumption ". . . if it is true that a white examiner cannot gain the full cooperation of Negro children because of racial barriers, it might also be true that a Negro examiner would encounter the same difficulty in testing white children."[49] His results showed that the testing environment was in jeopardy under both reversed-examiner conditions, indicating the influence that rapport played on the testing situation.

Howard H. Long's dissertation (1933) at Harvard explored the relationship between IQ test scores of poor and middle-class black children. Long's study underscored the inappropriateness of utilizing white socioeconomic classification schemes (SES) for describing all black populations. Most important was his research data that illustrated the wide range of intellectual ability found in black children.[50]

Albert S. Beckham's dissertation (1933) compared IQ test results of black children from the public schools of Washington, D.C., Baltimore, and New York City.[51] He produced evidence showing that median IQ scores of black children from these major cities fell well into the range of average intelligence. Beckham's investigation countered evidence by white psychologists which had shown that the black child was at least ten points below the white child in IQ score level.

Martin D. Jenkins's dissertation (1935) was an important sociopsychological study of black children with superior intelligence. He showed that the proportion of gifted black children was about the same as that for gifted white children, provided that equal educational opportunities were provided.[52] Jenkins, later president of Morgan State College, reported finding a black girl with a Stanford-Binet IQ score of 200.[53] This research was significant because it provided authenticated data that counteracted popular beliefs of black inferiority and underlined, again, the importance of testing rapport.

Intelligence Testing and the Courts

The Stanford-Binet test was contested in several early court cases in which institutionalization of a patient was the issue. A precedent was established in 1916 when New York State Supreme Court Justice Goff "refused to accept the Binet test as sufficient ground for committing a delinquent girl to an institution for feebleminded."[54]

While the Binet test encountered early legal difficulties, it gained popularity and met little resistance among educators, who used its results for the assessment of school children. It was not until the mid-1960s that intelligence tests scores, used to decide which students should be taken out of regular classrooms and placed in special situations, were legally contested (see Chapter 8 for further discussion).

Wechsler-Bellevue Scale

Fortunately, just when clinical psychology was emerging as an accepted profession, the Wechsler-Bellevue Scale (1939) was developed chiefly for the measurement of adult intelligence. Within a short time, the Wechsler-Bellevue and its later revisions became leading psychological tests of intelligence and a standard instrument in public mental hospitals, child-guidance clinics and veterans' hospitals. The tests not only combined Binet and performance-type items for ability assessment, but the pattern of scores was also used as a guide for other clinical purposes. Wechsler also rejected the mental age concept of former tests in favor of point scales which allowed test scores to be contrasted with "normed" scores with age as the only criterion.

Wechsler defined intelligence as the "aggregate or global capacity of the individual to act purposefully, to think rationally and to deal effectively with his environment."[55] He did not use blacks in his normed test data; rather, the test was standardized on 670 white children and 1081 white adults. In justifying the population he used, Wechsler frankly discussed the issue of racial norms and his solution: "Thus, we have eliminated the 'colored' vs. 'white' factor by admitting at the outset that our norms cannot be used for the colored population of the United States."[56] Apparently psychologists and educators paid little heed to this statement; for many years the tests were used indiscriminately in the mental measurement and other clinical diagnoses of minority-group populations.

Personality Testing of Minority Groups

Widespread personality stereotyping had categorized the black American as easygoing and happy, the Mexican-American as hot-blooded and excitable, and the native American as stolid and a savage. All American minority groups were generally classified as lazy. Psychologists attempted to measure these and other personality attributes by using *temperament* and *personality* tests of the late 1920s. The leading tests at this time included the Pressey X-O tests, the Downey-Will Temperament test, the Carnegie test, the Woodworth-Matthews questionnaire, the Thurstone Personality schedule and the Allport Ascendence-Submission test.

As early as 1922, psychologist June Downey felt that "in racial psychology important results may be expected to follow temperamental testing."[57] She believed the results of mass temperamental testing would determine whether different personality characteristics could be attributed to racial groups. In subsequent years, much effort was expended in an attempt to detect and measure these characteristics. Sunne (1925) compared personality test results of black and white teenagers and reported that

> negroes were slower in movement than the whites, that they have a slightly greater inertia, greater motor impulsion and the same interest in detail, volitional perseveration, and co-ordination of impulses, and less motor inhibition.[58]

In 1927, Garth studied "170 full blood Indians" from the United States Indian Schools at Santa Fe and Albuquerque, New Mexico, and Rapid City, South Dakota, and compared will-temperament test scores with scores made by blacks in a previous study. He concluded that the native Americans were less speedy in decision-making and exhibited more motor inhibition than the blacks.[59]

McFadden and Dashiell (1923) administered the Downey Will-Temperament test to an equal number of black and white high school and college students and concluded that only minor differences existed between the groups.[60] Hurlock (1930) reported no significant difference of personality traits when the Downey test was administered to 110 white and 101 black seventh- and eighth-grade students.[61] In the same study, she analyzed most of the previous major attempts to measure black-white personality differences and questioned the practicality of attempting to measure these differences. In support of the Hurlock study, Cooper, a white professor in a black college, administered (1930) the Allport Ascendance-Submission Reaction Study to large numbers of black college students and found no racial differences, concluding that "this test disproves the traditional view that the Negro is innately more submissive than the white man."[62]

As test data disagreements began to plague the area of personality assessment, doubts of test validity and reliability arose. No two tests seemed to measure the same thing. Moore and Steele (1934) reported that they found little correlation between the results of any two tests.[63] With the added possibility of individuals "faking" answers, it was apparent that paper-and-pencil personality tests were in jeopardy from several perspectives.

In the early 1930s a new technique of personality assessment appeared, the Rorschach ink blot technique, later to be classified as a *projective technique*. The first published research in the United States involving this test appeared in 1930; within eight years nearly 150 articles had been published on its clinical applications. But standardization was an immediate problem, and relatively few studies were made evaluating the test's reliability or validity.

With the Rorschach's dependence upon psychoanalytic theory for interpretation, there was some question of its validity for individuals who had been systematically excluded from equal participation in the majority culture; nevertheless, most psychologists viewed the test as a promising instrument because of its relative independence of language and other culturally restricted content. In reality, the test was far from being "culturally free," for the Freudian-based philosophical underpinnings were biased, and the psychologists who administered and interpreted the test were not culturally free.

It was not long before the Rorschach technique was joined by other projective devices. For instance, rather than rely on ambiguous stimuli to elicit examinee responses, as on the Rorschach, the Thematic Apperception Test (TAT) consisted of thirty pictures of people in a variety of situations.[64] The process of identifying the hero (called *needs*) and the environmental forces (called *press*) in the stories created by minority examinees called for abilities more often found lacking in the background of white clinicians.

Race Studies and Anti-Semitism

As European anti-Semitism simmered in the pre-World War II period, several American professional organizations began to issue disclaimers for "misterpretation" of their racial-difference data. In several instances, claims of Jewish "racial" inferiority had been gleaned from psychological studies of the 1920s and 1930s; frequent references to these studies by the Nazis became a source of embarrassment and shame. Consequently, the Council of the Society for the Psychological Study of Social Issues (SPSSI) published an "official protest against the non-scientific interpretations of American findings."[65] This statement declared in part: "In experiments which psychologists have made upon different peoples, no characteristic, inherent psychological differences which fundamentally distinguish so-called 'races' have been disclosed." The statement, directed at the Nazi call for the maintenance of an "Aryan-pure race" and the categorization of a "Jewish race," concluded, ". . . there is no indication that members of any group are rendered incapable by their biological heredity of completely acquiring the culture of the community in which they live."[66] The statement included no specific reference to American minorities.

The German "race-betterment" movement and the concept that a "super race" could be bred was also a derivative of an interesting entanglement between psychology and the "science" of eugenics.

Notes

1. For an account of this incident, see J. M. Reisman, *The Development of Clinical Psychology* (New York: Appleton, 1966) pp. 26–27.
2. C. Spearman, "General Intelligence Objectively Determined and Measured," *American Journal of Psychology*, 15 (1904), pp. 193–201.
3. L. J. Cronbach, *Essentials of Psychological Testing* (New York: Harper and Row, 1949) p. 200.
4. The contemporary concept of fluid or analytic ability, as expressed in Raven's *Progressive Matrices Test*, is an extension of the g factor.
5. W. Stern, *Uber Psychologie der Individuellen Differenzen* (Leipzig, 1900) p. 146.
6. L. M. Terman, *The Measurement of Intelligence* (Boston: Houghton Mifflin, 1916) p. 92.
7. Ibid., p. 92.
8. Ibid., p. 92.
9. Ibid., p. 93.
10. Sharing the same broad academic discipline with clinical psychologists, educational psychologists interchangeably used jargon from the clinical setting. In this way, many educational psychologists regarded themselves as clinicians with access to medical diagnoses. The frequent use of Freudian jargon and psychiatric terminology by psychometrists was common. These tandem boundaries led educational psychologists to speculate frequently in areas of psychiatry and genetics with less than adequate backgrounds in these disciplines. With a partisan cohort, they were rarely challenged on the appropriateness and accuracy of their conclusions. Recently, educationalists speculating in genetics have experienced far more criticism and are unable to receive wholehearted endorsement of their pronouncements.
11. L. Terman and M. A. Merrill, *Measuring Intelligence* (Boston: Houghton Mifflin, 1937) pp. 122–123.
12. L. Terman, *Intelligence Tests and School Reorganization* (New York: World, 1923) pp. 27–28.
13. E. L. Thorndike, *Human Nature and the Social Order* (New York: Macmillan, 1940) p. 320. After fifty years, educators are still attempting to estimate the percent of variance that genes and environment may affect IQ test scores.
14. G. R. Stetson, "Some Memory Tests of Whites and Blacks," *Psychological Review*, 4 (1897), 285–289.

15. A. C. Strong, "Three Hundred Fifty White and Colored Children Measured by the Binet-Simon Measuring Scale of Intelligence," *Pedagogical Seminary,* 20 (1913), pp. 485–515.

16. J. Morse, "A Comparison of White and Colored Children Measured by the Binet Scale of Intelligence," *The Popular Science Monthly,* 84:1 (January 1914), pp. 75–79.

17. Ibid., p. 77.

18. Ibid., p. 79.

19. B. A. Phillips, "The Binet Test Applied to Colored Children," *Psychological Clinic,* 8 (1914), pp. 190–196.

20. G. S. Hall, "The Negro in Africa and America," *Pedagogical Seminary,* (1905) p. 358.

21. G. O. Ferguson, Jr., *The Psychology of the Negro: An Experimental Study* (New York: The Science Press, 1916) p. 125.

22. W. H. Pyle, "The Mind of the Negro Child," *School and Society,* I (1915), p. 358.

23. Article 1, Section 3, of the Constitution of the United States in discussing tax apportionment declared that free persons, including indentured servants, would be counted as a whole and that the vast majority of blacks would be considered as *three-fifths* of a person.

24. Dr. Otis parlayed this advantage into the first successful commercial test publication in America through an arrangement with a textbook publisher. Several profit-making test producers were born during this era and at least one "test publisher's board of directors read like a Who's Who in psychology." See Milton Holmen and Richard Docter, *Educational and Psychological Testing* (New York: Sage Foundation, 1972) for an excellent discussion.

25. After World War I, researchers maintained this educational-military relationship and continued such studies. Among early participants were Klineberg, Garrett, and Montague. This arrangement led to increasing numbers of educational psychologists working on military concerns and was the backdrop leading to the establishment of Division 19, Military Psychology, of the American Psychological Association (APA).

26. E. Jamieson and P. Standiford, "The Mental Capacity of Southern Ontario Indians," *Journal of Educational Psychology,* 19 (1928), pp. 536–551.

27. W. S. Hunter, "Indian Blood and Otis Intelligence Test," *Journal of Comparative Psychology,* 2 (1922).

28. J. A. Fitzgerald and W. W. Ludeman, "Intelligence of Indian Children," *Journal of Comparative Psychology,* 6 (1926).

29. W. S. Hunter and E. Sommermier, "The Relation of Degree of Indian Blood to Score on the Otis Intelligence Test," *Journal of Comparative Psychology,* 2 (1922), pp. 257–277.

30. T. R. Garth, "The Will-Temperament of Indians," *Journal of Applied Psychology,* 11 (1927), pp. 512–518.

31. O. Klineberg, "An Experimental Study of Speed and Other Factors in 'Racial' Differences," *Archives of Psychology,* 93 (1928), p. 111.

32. O. Klineberg, *Race Differences* (New York: Harper and Row, 1935) p. 367

33. S. D. Porteus, *The Psychology of a Primitive People* (New York: Longmans, 1931) p. 438.

34. B. Blackwood, "A Study of Mental Testing in Relation to Anthropology," *Mental Measurement Monographs,* 4 (December 1927), p. 113.

35. G. I. Sanchez, "Group Differences and Spanish-Speaking Children—A Critical Review," *Journal of Applied Psychology,* 16 (1932), pp. 549–558.

36. F. C. Paschal and L. R. Sullivan, "Racial Factors in the Mental and Physical

Development of Mexican Children," *Comparative Psychology Monographs,* 3 (October 1925), pp. 46–75.

37. C. B. Davenport and M. Steggerda, "Race Crossing in Jamaica," *Publication,* Carnegie Institution of Washington, D.C., 395 (1929), pp. 469–471.

38. M. J. Herskovits, "A Critical Discussion of the 'Mulatto Hypotheses'," *Journal of Negro Education,* 3 (July 1934), p. 401.

39. C. H. Thompson, "The Conclusion of Scientists Relative to Racial Differences," *The Journal of Negro Education,* 3 (July 1934), pp. 494–512.

40. For a complete listing, see Appendix.

41. Traditional psychologists rarely considered any form of scholarship, let alone criticism from black scholars. This academic racism led black scholars to publish their own journals and to establish other media of communication. A leading periodical of this era was *The Crisis,* edited by W. E. B. Du Bois at Fisk University.

42. H. M. Bond, "Intelligence Tests and Propaganda," *The Crisis,* 28:2 (June 1924), p. 61.

43. Ibid., p. 64.

44. Ibid., p. 64.

45. H. Miller, "Science, Pseudo-Science and the Race Question," *The Crisis,* 30:6 (October 1925), pp. 287–290.

46. Ibid., p. 289.

47. H. M. Bond, "Some Exceptional Negro Children," *The Crisis,* 34 (October 1927), pp. 257–280.

48. Anon., "Some Suggestions Relative to a Study of the Mental Attitude of the Negro," *Pedagogical Seminary,* 23 (1916), pp. 199–203.

49. H. G. Canady, "The Effect of 'Rapport' on the IQ: A New Approach to the Problem of Racial Psychology," *Journal of Negro Education,* 5 (1936), pp. 209–219.

50. H. H. Long, "Analyses of Test Results From Third Grade Children Selected on the Basis of Socio-Economic Status," Unpublished Doctor's Dissertation, Harvard University, 1933.

51. A. S. Beckham, "A Study of the Intelligence of Colored Adolescents of Different Socio-Economic Status in Typical Metropolitan Areas," *Journal of Social Psychology,* 4 (1933), pp. 70–91.

52. M. D. Jenkins, "A Socio-Psychological Study of Negro Children of Superior Intelligence," *Journal of Negro Education,* 5 (1936), pp. 175–190.

53. P. Witty and M. Jenkins, "The Case of 'B'—A Gifted Negro Girl," *Journal of Social Psychology,* 6 (1935), pp. 117–124.

54. "The Binet Test in Court," *Eugenical News* (August 1916), p. 55.

55. D. Wechsler, *The Measurement of Adult Intelligence* (Baltimore: Williams and Wilkins, 1939), p. 3.

56. Ibid., p. 109.

57. J. E. Downey, *The Will-Temperament and Its Testing* (Yonkers, New York: World, 1924).

58. D. Sunne, "Personality Tests—White and Negro Adolescents," *Journal of Applied Psychology,* 9 (1925), pp. 256–280.

59. T. R. Garth, "The Will-Temperament of Indians," *Journal of Applied Psychology,* 11 (1927), pp. 512–518.

60. J. H. McFadden and J. F. Dashiell, "Racial Differences as Measured by the Downey Will-Temperament Test," *Journal of Applied Psychology,* 7 (1923), pp. 30–53.

61. E. B. Hurlock, "The Will-Temperament of White and Negro Children," *Pedagogical Seminary,* 38 (1930), pp. 91–99.

62. P. Cooper, "Notes on Psychological Race Differences," *Social Forces,* 8 (1929), p. 426.

63. H. Moore and I. Steele, "Personality Tests," *Journal of Abnormal and Social Psychology,* 29 (1934–1935), pp. 45–52.

64. C. D. Morgan and H. A. Murray, "A Method for Investigating Fantasies: The Thematic Apperception Test," *Archives of Neurological Psychiatry,* 34 (1935), pp. 289–306.

65. M. Van de Water, "Racial Psychology," *Science-Supplement,* 30 (September 1938), pp. 7–8.

66. See Appendix for the full text of the protest.

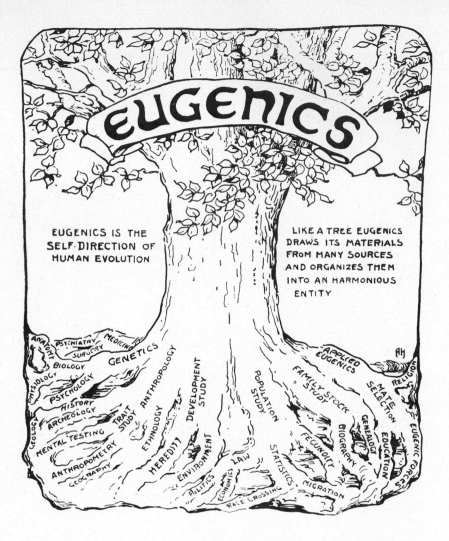

Third International Eugenics Congress

New York City, August 21–23, 1932.

Introductory Wall Panel at Entrance to the Exhibit.

EUGENICS TREE. From the introductory wall panel at the entrance to the exhibit of the Third International Eugenics Congress, New York City, August 21–23, 1932. (*Source: Eugenical News*, 1932, p. 138.)

4
Psychology and eugenics

FOR A GOOD TREE BRINGETH NOT FORTH CORRUPT FRUIT;
NEITHER DOTH A CORRUPT TREE BRING FORTH GOOD FRUIT.
FOR EVERY TREE IS KNOWN BY HIS OWN FRUIT.
FOR OF THORNS MEN DO NOT GATHER FIGS,
NOR OF A BRAMBLE BUSH GATHER THEY GRAPES.

—Luke 6:43–44

Views supporting the importance of heredity, birth control, and sterilization can be found in the earliest writings of western philosophy and religion. In the *Republic,* Plato (427–347 B.C.) suggested that in order to improve the human species, "the best men must cohabit with the best women in as many cases as possible and the worst in the fewest, and that the offspring of the one must be reared and that of the other not, if the flock is to be as perfect as possible."[1]

Mention of the significance of heredity can be found in biblical verse. In the New Testament, reference to heredity was made when Jesus delivered the immortal Sermon on the Mount and warned of false prophets who appear in sheep's clothing:

> Even so every good tree bringeth forth good fruit; but a corrupt tree
> bringeth forth evil fruit.
> A good tree cannot bring forth evil fruit, neither can a corrupt tree
> bring forth good fruit. —*Matthew 7:17–18*

A recommendation for birth control appeared in the early writings of economic theory in the eighteenth century, when Thomas Malthus held that if the world's population were allowed to reproduce at a constant rate, many people would face the prospect of malnutrition or starvation. The Malthusian Doctrine suggested the necessity for controlling human growth in relation to world economic growth.[2]

In the nineteenth century, Charles Darwin's *On the Origin of Species by Means of Natural Selection* (1859) examined the struggle for existence and the effects of environment on one's chances for survival. Darwinian concepts of *natural selection* and *survival of the fittest* became shibboleths for generations of advocates of birth control measures and other "race betterment" philosophies.

In 1883, Darwin's cousin, Francis Galton, coined the term *eugenics* and defined it as "the study of the agencies under social control that may improve or impair the racial qualities of future generations either physically or mentally."[3] In *Hereditary Genius: Its Laws and Consequences* (1869), Galton expressed a platonic belief that "it would be quite practical to produce a highly gifted race of men by judicious marriages during several consecutive generations." As a mechanism to popularize and expand this notion, Galton established the Eugenics Society of Great Britain in 1908 and the following year published the *Eugenics Review,* a monthly journal that served as the chief medium of communication for eugenicists throughout the world.

Similar efforts aimed at race betterment were initiated in other countries settled by peoples of western European descent. In the United States, the movement grew with the establishment of the American Eugenic Society in 1905. Henry H. Laughlin, one of its founders,[4] proudly declared that "the English-speaking people seem to take the lead in the study of human breeding, just as they have in the production of superior domestic animals . . . the English are, in truth, the world's most skillful breeders."[5] Figure 4.1 illustrates the "idealized man" as perceived by eugenicists at the turn of the century.

Charles B. Davenport, another leading figure in the American eugenics movement, offered a parallel and a prediction: "Man is an organism—an animal: and the laws of improvement of corn and race horses hold true of him also. Unless people accept this

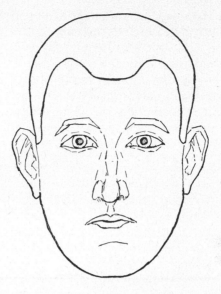

Figure 4.1 The idealized man of colonial ancestry, drawn to scale from Ales Hrdlicka's studies. The outline of the face is almost oblong; the head is high and "well-developed," which was supposed to denote "superior intelligence." Eugenicists strived to maintain this type in the American population. (*Source:* Paul Popenoe and D. Johnson, *Applied Eugenics,* 1920, p. 425. Reprinted by permission of the author.)

simple truth and let it influence marriage selection, human progress will cease."[6]

Carnegie Station for Experimental Evolution

In Washington, D.C., steel magnate Andrew Carnegie established the Carnegie Institution for Experimental Evolution in 1904 and placed Davenport in charge. This was the first formal eugenics organization in North America. Under the auspices of the institution, the Carnegie Station for Experimental Evolution was established at Cold Spring Harbor, New York. Davenport was also placed in charge of this operation.

Eugenicists, following the "rediscovery" of Mendel's laws of heredity in 1900, placed extreme faith in the concept that "like produces like." This theory was interpreted to mean that superior reproduces superior, inferior reproduces inferior, and the criminal reproduces the criminal. The purpose of the Carnegie Station, then, was to expand the study of hereditary traits in plants and lower animals to include humans. In 1910, with funds donated from the E. H. Harriman family, the Eugenics Record Office was established as an adjunct to the Eugenics Section of the American Breeders Association.[7] The establishment of the Record Office provided eugenicists with the facility and funds needed to document and maintain files on human traits. One of the largest centers of its kind in the world, the Eugenics Record Office proclaimed ten ambitious purposes:

1. To serve eugenical interests in the capacity of repository and clearinghouse.
2. To build up an analytical index of the traits of American families.
3. To study the forces controlling and the hereditary consequences of marriages-matings, differential fecundity, survival and migration.
4. To investigate the manner of inheritance of specific human traits.
5. To advise concerning the eugenical fitness of proposed marriages.
6. To train field workers to gather data of eugenical import.
7. To maintain a limited field force actually engaged in gathering data for eugenic studies.
8. To co-operate with other institutions and with persons concerned with eugenical study.
9. To encourage new centers of eugenics research and education.
10. To publish the results of researchers and to aid in the dissemination of eugenical traits.[8]

A unique aspect of the Eugenics Record Office programs was the system of record keeping for family histories. It employed a catalog-analysis of human traits based on an elaborate, expansible decimal system:

    0—General traits
    08—General diseases
    09—Occupations
     1—Integumentary system
     2—Skeletal system
    25—Muscular system
     3—Nervous system
    35—Criminality
     4—Mental traits
    43—Movements

5—Sense organs
6—Nutritive system
7—Respiratory system
8—Circulatory system
85—Lymphatic system
9—Excretory system
94—Reproductive system[9]

Each trait was assigned a numerical rating, for example:

> The number "4598" represents ability at chess playing, the "4" standing for mental traits, "45" for special mental ability, "459" for special ability in athletic or other games, "4598" for special ability in chess playing.[10]

The Trait Book, published by the Record Office, was designed to standardize record keeping for the growing number of eugenic field workers. (Catalog-analysis information for Section 4, "Mental Traits" was coordinated by the well-known psychologists E. L. Thorndike and R. M. Yerkes.)

An important program within the Record Office was a two-month training course for prospective field workers, taught by C. B. Davenport and H. H. Laughlin, and designed to provide laboratory and clinical studies in human heredity and instruction in making firsthand pedigree studies (Figure 4.2 shows one of the training charts used). Between 1910 and 1918, nearly two hundred people were trained in these courses. The graduates scattered across the United States and the Caribbean Islands, performing and reporting their field-work findings to the Record Office. Some returned to colleges and universities to spread to their students the techniques and philosophy of eugenic investigation.

Psychology courses often became vehicles for eugenic propaganda. One graduate of the Record Office training program, a professor of psychology, wrote, "I hope to serve the cause by infiltrating eugenics into the minds of teachers. It may interest you to know that each student who takes psychology here works up his family history and plots his family tree."[11] Harvard, Columbia, Brown, Cornell, Wisconsin, and Northwestern were among the leading academic institutions teaching eugenics in psychology courses. But psychology served the eugenicists' cause in a far more important way than merely being an outlet for its propaganda. Psychology made its chief contribution by providing much of the philosophical discussion purporting to validate the existence of "fine-lined" individual differences. While psychology's measuring devices conveniently labelled these mental variations, its developmental theories helped guide the eugenicists from theoretical positions to applied programs.

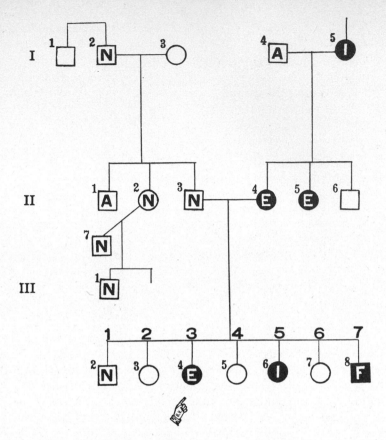

Figure 4.2 Example of a simple pedigree chart and (opposite) key. (*Source:* C. B. Davenport, *The Family-History Book,* Eugenics Record Office Bulletin No. 7, September 1912, pp. 96, 100.)

Recapitulation Theory

A theory which stressed the relationship between an individual's racial background and his developmental stages played an influential role in shaping the foundation of several psychological concepts and, eventually, eugenic views. This idea, the *recapitulation theory,* held that an individual organism, in the process of growth and development, passes through a series of stages representing those in the evolutionary development of the species.[12] G. Stanley Hall, for example, believed "that in its play activity the child exhibits a series of phases corresponding to cultural phases of human society, a hunting period, a building period, and so on."[13] Hall's attempt to mold individual development (ontogeny) with racial characteristics (phylogeny) was supported by many leading behavioral scientists of this time. (John Mark Baldwin's *Mental Development in the Child and the Race,* for example, was a frequently quoted source.)

KEY TO HEREDITY CHART.

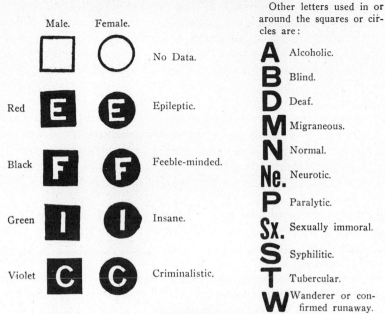

Male.   Female.

Other letters used in or around the squares or circles are:

No Data.

A   Alcoholic.

B   Blind.

D   Deaf.

Red   Epileptic.

M   Migraneous.

N   Normal.

Black   Feeble-minded.

Ne.   Neurotic.

P   Paralytic.

Green   Insane.

Sx.   Sexually immoral.

S   Syphilitic.

Violet   Criminalistic.

T   Tubercular.

W   Wanderer or confirmed runaway.

FIGURES.

Above the line—Order in the line of birth.
Above the square or circle—Individual reference number.
Below the square or circle—Age at time of death or date of birth or death.
In squares or circles—Number of individuals of that sex.

SMALL LETTERS.

b—Born.   † or (d)—Died or dead.
† (d) inf.—Died in infancy.   m—Married.

LINES.

Solid—Connects married individuals and fraternities.
Dotted—Not married or illegitimate.
For   { Green—Paternal side } of individual under study.
display { Red—Maternal side }
charts. { Violet—Connects related charts or individuals on more than one chart.

SYMBOLS.

   --   Shows patient at institution reporting.

Miscarriage or stillbirth.

Institutional care (place under symbol).

Since it was generally believed that the human race was sub-divided into primitive groups and advanced groups, with stratifications in between, early psychologists were of the opinion they could evaluate the level of group attainment by observing individual developmental stages. Supporting and concurrent views held by sociologists reinforced the recapitulation theory with characterizations of various societies based on their developmental stages. Anthropologists, too, described human adjustments to varying environments in terms of the recapitulation theory. Even though these evaluations were made from highly subjective and cultural positions, they did not lessen the acceptance of the theory and its ensuing foothold on the behavioral sciences. The recapitulation theory was attractive and it caught the fancy of many early scientists.

From this theory also evolved the belief that group psychological variables dealing with human competency and desirability could be measured and evaluated by observation. Thus, as the Mendelian concept of genetic transmission of individual traits grew in acceptance, so did the beliefs that group superiority and inferiority stem from hereditary causes. Mendelizing of human traits came of age during this era, and many attempts to search for single causative genes reached preposterous stages. Frequently, social scientists tried to link human conditions of poverty and "unacceptable" social behavior to Mendelian dominance. All these attempts to explain human variability were eagerly embraced by those who considered the control of human behavior a desirable goal. And the desire to predict and control human conditions led to the acceptance of two action-oriented programs during the early part of the twentieth century.

Applied Eugenics and Euthenics

The assertion that individuals and groups of people were either "desirable" or "not desirable" led to two applied lines of approach to the concept of increasing the quality of human beings. These were *eugenics* and *euthenics*. Eugenic programs were concerned with the control of individual heredity while euthenic programs sought control of the environment.

Eugenic programs were by far the more popular and more expansive attempts at race-betterment. Euthenic advocates were small in number and correspondingly less vocal in their influence, while the eugenicists, large in number, were very vocal. Both were quick to point to the results of warfare, in which the strongest and most healthy young men were eliminated, and, consequently, both groups advocated peace programs and armed forces composed of volunteers rather than conscripts.

Eugenicists were usually middle-class professionals, including a large number of college and university teachers, researchers, and administrators. The movement against the "socially unfit" made many connections and allies with those against the "racially unfit." Psychologists unwittingly contributed to both views by calling attention to individual differences found through army testing in World War I and by the announcement of "discovered" racial differences in IQ scores. When eugenicists took the lead and proposed a number of programs to carry out their mandate of race-betterment, it was to be expected that psychologists would be in the vanguard.

Findings of the Research Committee

Fearful that natural selection would not operate to accomplish the "survival of the fittest," the Research Committee of the Eugenics Section of the American Breeders Association unanimously adopted a resolution establishing a group of scholars to "study the best practical means, so far as the innate traits are a factor, of purging the blood of the American people of the handicapping and deteriorating influences of . . . anti-social classes."[14] Leading representatives from the fields of psychology, sociology, and anthropology, as well as from medicine and law, were called to membership in this comittee. Psychology's role was to provide analyses of the "standards and tests for determining the types of mental degenerates and defectives proposed for sterilization."[15] Additionally, psychologists were charged with the analyses of the effects of sterilization on the "mental processes, industry, habits of life, and sex instincts." Sociologists were to be concerned, among other things, with methods of reaching "defectives and potential parents of defectives not in institutions." For discussion purposes, this committee utilized an interesting classification of social misfits: (1) the feeble-minded, (2) the pauper, (3) the inebriate, (4) the criminalistic, (5) the epileptic, and (6) the insane.

One outgrowth of the committee's report was the suggestion of a number of remedies for "purging the blood of the race" in which defective strains were found. These suggestions included: segregation, birth control, rewards for parenthood, restrictive marriage laws, eutelegenesis (artificial insemination), and sterilization.

Segregation called for the separation of men and women confined to institutions, such as mental hospitals, prisons, and other "homes," in order to prevent the inmates, characterized as socially undesirable, from reproducing.

Birth control procedures were encouraged to reverse the alleged trend of larger families to be produced by "lower economic status" and "lower IQ" groups; free clinics and supplies were to be provided to specially selected groups.

Rewards for parenthood meant the offering of bonuses to parents of "superior ability" as an inducement; financial assistance resembling scholarships would encourage select groups to have as many children as they wanted.

Restrictive marriage laws and customs were designed to prevent consanguineous matings which would increase the number of persons homozygous for recessive genes (those designated as negative); legal restrictions and taboos were created to decrease "socially inadequate and unfit" reproductions. (Restrictions prohibiting marriage between whites and blacks drew support from this philosophy. See Appendix for a compendium of miscegenation laws in the United States.)

Eutelegenesis. Since the "pure sire method" was considered the most advanced technique for animal breeding, eugenicists suggested the extensive use of selected sires for artificially inseminating prospective human mothers. This process was called eutelegenesis.

Sterilization was the leading remedy of those suggested; its appeal, both abroad and in the United States, is a matter of record, noticeably among a number of state judicial and legal organizations advocating race-betterment philosophies.

Sterilization Laws

"Whereas, heredity plays a most important part in the transmission of crime, idiocy, and imbecility . . ."—thus began the text of the first state law permitting mental institutions to perform sterilization operations upon inmates. This Indiana law of 1907 stimulated concerted efforts by other state governments to enact and enforce similar sterilization procedures. The State of Washington (1909) followed Indiana with similar legislation as a part of its criminal code, making it clear that sterilization would also be a form of punishment for those guilty of "carnal abuse of a female person" or those classed as "habitual criminals." California (1909) enacted laws to permit "asexualization of inmates" at state hospitals, the Sonoma State Home, and state prisons.

By 1930, twenty-four states had sanctioned sterilization as an eugenic measure, and over ten thousand individuals were sterilized under the provisions of these laws (Table 13). (*Vasectomy,* the excision of the vas deferens, and *salpingotomy,* the cutting of the oviducts, were the primary surgical procedures.) California, using the Stanford-Binet Intelligence Test as the primary psychometric measure of mental deficiency, led the Nation with 6787 court-ordered sterilizations. By 1935, sterilization laws had been passed in several European countries: Switzerland, Denmark, Germany, Sweden, and Norway. By 1945, more than two-thirds of the United States had passed some form of sterilization law and nearly forty-four thousand such operations had been performed.

The constitutionality of the sterilization laws was debated from the beginning. These laws were often confusing because the distinction between sterilization for eugenic purposes and sterili-

Table 13 States Having Sterilization Laws and Number of People Sterilized by January 1, 1930

State	Number of persons sterilized		
	MALES	FEMALES	TOTAL
Alabama	32	12	44
Arizona	0	0	0
California	3,636	3,151	6,787
Connecticut	7	193	200
Delaware	171	107	278
Idaho	0	0	0
Iowa	43	14	57
Indiana	120	3	123
Kansas	414	243	657
Maine	4	8	12
Michigan	62	326	388
Mississippi	0	0	0
Montana	27	33	60
Nebraska	109	199	308
New Hampshire	4	57	61
North Carolina	2	1	3
North Dakota	22	17	39
Oregon	257	393	650
South Dakota	19	42	61
Utah	43	36	79
Virginia	94	274	368
Washington	1	8	9
West Virginia	0	0	0
Wisconsin	35	270	305
Total (24 states)	5,134	5,743	10,877

SOURCE: *Progressive Labor,* vol. 9, Number 1, April 1973, p. 95. Reprinted by permission.

zation for punitive reasons was vague; the laws presented a con-
glomeration of racial and eugenic phraseologies that were open
to subjective interpretations; and many of the statutes considered
sterilization a sanitary measure to be determined by authorities
and not requiring due process of law. Consequently, court cases
were debated at all levels of jurisdiction. For example, in 1912 a
suit was filed in New Jersey challenging the right of state institutions to sterilize mentally deficient patients. The court later ruled
in favor of state institutions performing such operations. In *Buck*
v. *Bell* (1927), argued from a Virginia statute which permitted the
sterilization of an institutionalized, feeble-minded white woman,
the United States Supreme Court ruled that sterilization was not a
violation of due process and equal protection of the laws of the
Fourteenth Amendment.[16] The *Buck* v. *Bell* decision became a
major precedent for future litigation, encouraging advocates of
enforced sterilization procedures.

Heredity and Environment: White Rats and Mazes

In the year of the *Buck* v. *Bell* decision, the first extensive psychological experiment in behavior genetics was begun at the University of California at Berkeley. Robert Choate Tryon, then an associate professor of psychology, designed an elaborate selective
breeding experiment to produce a line of maze-bright and a line
of maze-dull rats.[17] Just the year before, the first study of sibling
resemblance in laboratory rats had been conducted by Stanford
University psychology student Mildred Burlingame.[18] While Burlingame's study was based on a short-term series of maze-running
tasks by albino rats, Tryon began with a "parental" generation of
male and female albino rats and conducted his experiment over
decades of time.

The primary aims of Tryon's experiment were to

> establish under environmental control a maze-bright and a maze-
> dull strain of rats, to determine the nature of the genetic deter-
> miners at work, to discover the constancy of this psychological dif-
> ference throughout a large range of the rats' life span, and to find
> important biological and psychological correlates of the difference
> in this maze ability.[19]

Tryon's automatic mechanical device, which delivered the animals into the maze, claimed to control the intervening variable of
environmental conditions. In order to offset calculation errors,
electric recorders were used. In 1940, Tryon reported findings

concluding that "proof of the inheritance of individual difference in maze ability" was found.

As a result of this evidence, many leading researchers and large numbers of laymen quickly inferred that maze running by white rats was directly related to general intelligence in human beings, and that these abilities were Mendelian dominant. Moreover, it was felt that Tryon's study produced evidence substantiating inherited intellectual differences in human beings across racial lines. But in 1949, L. V. Searle reported contradictory findings after testing Tryon's strains of rats on learning tests other than maze-running ability (discrimination of distance, angles, and brightness). He illustrated that the so-called bright rats were not bright on everything and that the dull rats were not dull on everything.[20] This evidence should have undercut the parallel drawn between maze running in rats and general intelligence in human beings—but this was the age of the eugenicists.

Searle's study was not quoted by the eugenic media; instead, eugenicists extolled the importance of heredity in every quarter. Leading articles in the *Eugenical News* were devoted to describing the parental backgrounds of prominent white Americans. Each history stressed the importance of "good heredity" in successful men; such descriptions as "He was a fighter like his father," "He showed his Scottish blood," and a "heritage from the gentry that formed the first good families" were typical.

Davenport, discussing the "royalty" sent from England to colonial Virginia, wrote:

> Soon better blood crowded into Virginia to redeem the colony. Upon the execution of Charles I, a host of royalist refugees sought an asylum here and the immigration of this class continued even after the Restoration. By this means was enriched a germ plasm which easily developed such traits as good manners, high culture, and the ability to lead in all social affairs—the traits combined in a remarkable degree in the first families of Virginia.[21]

Even discussions of black people were characterized by the same misguided and misunderstood notions of heredity:

> . . . only the bad ones were "sold South." Thus the tendency was to keep well behaved negroes in Virginia and to supply the other states with the unruly ones. Naturally then, the Virginia negro of today, being descended from "selected stock" . . . may be expected to average some what higher in human virtues than the offspring of slaves of the black belt.[22]

Not only were attempts made to identify and describe the backgrounds of "desirable" individuals, but similar efforts were made to identify and describe families with a predominance of intellectual defect, pauperism, and crime. In an effort to document and thus verify the popular adage, "like father, like son," the family history method of investigation grew to become a leading technique in research efforts.

"Degenerate" Families

The earliest "degenerate" family pedigree was published by Richard L. Dugdale in 1875 and followed up by Arthur H. Estabrook in 1915 under the auspices of the Eugenics Record Office. This family, called the Jukes, became a eugenic cause celebre for those who argued in support of theories of the inheritance of mental and social defects—in spite of Dugdale's warning of "environmental considerations."[23] The family was alleged to have produced many offspring classified as "immoral," "harlots," "lechers," "paupers," "drunkards," "fornicators," "murderers," "rapists," and "thieves." The Industrial Revolution scattered the Juke families from Connecticut to Minnesota in search of new employment opportunities. It was at this point that Estabrook, with the financial assistance of a Carnegie grant, traced the families noting their social and mental conditions. The original investigation by Dugdale was from a sociological stance, whereas Estabrook's followup emphasized only the genetic aspect of inbreeding.

In 1897, eight-year-old Deborah Kallikak (a fictitious name created by Henry Goddard from the Greek *kalos*, "good," and *kakos*, "bad") was committed to the Vineland (New Jersey) Training School for Backward and Feebleminded Children. Shortly after her commitment, Goddard, who had established a research department at Vineland, began a number of family history research ventures. With a team of researchers, an extensive investigation was launched into Deborah Kallikak's family history. The results of this study were documented as proof-positive supporting the bad seed concept because the family was purported to consist of two branches, one "normal" and the other "degenerate."[24] The investigation claimed to produce documentary evidence that Martin Kallikak, a Revolutionary War soldier, fathered both good and bad progeny as a result of his involvement with a feebleminded tavern girl and his later marriage to a "good" Quaker girl (Figure 4.3). Goddard reported finding 480 descendents, of which 143 were feebleminded, 33 were sexually immoral, 24 were alcoholics, and many others were brothel keepers and criminals.

A number of family histories were published during this period

He dallied with a feeble-minded tavern girl

He married a worthy Quakeress

She bore a son known as "Old Horror" who had ten children

She bore seven upright worthy children

From "Old Horror's" ten children came hundreds of the lowest types of human beings

From these seven worthy children came hundreds of the highest types of human beings

Figure 4.3 The influence of heredity as demonstrated by the "good" and the "bad" Kallikaks. (*Source:* Henry E. Garrett, *General Psychology* [New York: American Book Company, 1955], p. 65. Reprinted by permission.)

which followed the Kallikak format and claimed to document extensive pedigrees of degeneracy. These investigations played an important role in biasing scholars, as well as the general public, toward the "bad seed" philosophy. Among these popular studies were: *The Ishmaelites* (Estabrook), *The Dack Family* (Finlayson), *The Hill Folk: Report on a Rural Community of Hereditary Defects* (Danielson and Davenport), *The Nam Family: A Study in Cacogenics* (Estabrook and Davenport), and the *Mongrel Vir-*

ginians (Estabrook and McDougle). However, it was the study of the Kallikak family that took the lead and provided material for frequent lectures and subject matter for many basic psychology courses. The history was discussed in psychology textbooks and appeared as recently as the mid-1950s in at least one popular psychology text.

While the theme of family degeneracy was a popular subject, it was probably not a major influence in the decision by American psychologists to support eugenic programs. But several outstanding psychologists of this period did contribute leadership and intellectual support to the race-betterment movement, and these advocates strongly influenced generations of students, colleagues, and other followers. Among these leaders were G. Stanley Hall and Edward L. Thorndike.

G. Stanley Hall

Granville Stanley Hall (1846–1924) was unquestionably a pioneer in American psychology. Among his achievements were the creation of two psychology journals and the establishment of the American Psychological Association. His intellectual banter extolling Darwinian theory quickly led him on to accept the belief that individual growth, both intellectual and physical, progressed through evolutionary stages. The "recapitulation theory" strongly influenced his psychological theories, and they in turn frequently led him to racist conclusions and statements. In *Adolescence* (1904) he described Africans, Indians, and Chinese as members of "adolescent races" in a stage of incomplete growth. Extending this view, Hall wrote that "every child, from conception to maturity, recapitulates every stage of development through which the human race from its lowest animal beginning has passed."[25] Therefore, individuals who were judged as incompetent, for one reason or another, simply had not "recapitulated" beyond an inferior stage. In order to prevent these "unfortunates" from reproducing their kind, Hall endorsed the eugenicists' program of sterilization. Ultimately, Hall felt, society should be ruled by the "innately superior," leaving the "inferior" to assume roles of subservience.

Even as a strong proponent of formal education, a mechanism designed to improve all elements of American society, Hall felt that heredity was the dominant factor determining an individual's capacity to benefit from a formal education. The logical consequence of Hall's philosophies and theories was eugenics. His strong belief in the importance of country living was frequently expressed; he felt that modern cities "abound in people really lower and far more degraded than those we call savages."[26] So significant was his belief in the virtues of rural living that he included the "love of nature" among eight factors necessary for human character building.[27] For Hall, the combination of "good ancestry" and country living produced the most desirable citizen. Interestingly, Hall's belief in "the white man's burden" led him to train several black scholars in psychology and to play a major role in the admission of black graduate students to sociology as well as psychology studies at Clark University.

Edward L. Thorndike

Edward L. Thorndike (1874–1949), another leader in American psychology, has been credited with several specific contributions to educational psychology. He invented the puzzle-box to investigate how cats and dogs solve problems; he found that being told that one was right helped a student to retain a correct response; he devised numerous tests designed to measure learning and aptitude and was one of the most vocal intellectual leaders of American eugenicists. As early as 1913, in a lecture at Columbia University, Thorndike clearly stated his position with regard to the nature versus nurture debate:

> Long before a child begins his schooling, or a man his work at trade or profession, or a woman her management of a home—long indeed before they are born—their superiority or inferiority to others of the same environmental advantages is determined by the constitution of the germs and ova whence they spring, and which, at the start of their individual lives, they are.[28]

His emphasis on the importance of heredity led Thorndike to adopt several prominent theoretical positions in regard to eugenics. One of his premises held that man's "original nature" had selective powers over his environment and that man would choose and reject, exploit or be exploited by elements in the environment according to his capacity. Thorndike's explanation for the subjugation of individuals or groups was based upon this view; thus the institution of American slavery existed because the black man's original nature was conducive to exploitation by the white man. Thorndike held that eugenic programs not only promised intellectual improvements, but insured dominance of the ruling class for both black and white populations as well. As late as 1940, Thorndike added to this view: "Improvement of the human genes produces indirectly better customs and institutions; it is an insurance against the deterioration of good customs and institutions."[29]

In addition to calling for sterilization to eliminate bad genes and decrease the numbers of the "socially and mentally" unfit, he advocated financial "allowances for children of men of very high intelligence and achievement during the age of 21 to 30 to reproduce their kind."[30] Thorndike felt that all developing professionals should be exposed to eugenic principles: "eugenics in the case of intellect, morals and skill . . . should soon be in every primer of psychology, sociology, and education. . . ."[31]

Like G. Stanley Hall, Thorndike never equivocated from his belief in hereditary determinism.

> It may interest you to know that the first (postwar) problem chosen for investigation by the Division of Psychology and Anthropology of the National Research Council is the problem of the mental and moral qualities of the different elements of the population of the United States. What does this country get in the million or more Mexican immigrants of the last four years? What has it got from Italy, from Russia, from Scotland and Ireland? What are the descendants of the Puritans and Cavaliers and Huguenots and Dutch (like?); and what are they doing for America? Psychology will undertake to do its share in an inventory of the human assets and liabilities of the United States, whenever it is asked to do so.[32]

The popularity of eugenics and the support it had among many white educators and psychologists played a significant role in reinforcing the promise of psychology to understand, predict, and control human behavior. While the heredity-environment debates of the 1920s raged, eugenics was not interpreted in the same light by the emerging black academic world. On the contrary, conclusions reached by eugenicists were often declared invalid or meaningless or just ignored by black professionals. The reasoning was obvious: eugenicists most often appeared to be white supremicists using the concept of genetics as their weaponry. During this period, a sense of helplessness prevailed among black academicians whose voices of dissent made little or no impact on the white research community. The armchair speculations made by eugenicists were disregarded by black scholars and as a result, psychological science, sans eugenics indoctrination, was the thrust in the training of prospective black teachers and ministers.

Notes

1. Plato, *Republic,* trans. Paul Shorey, The Loeb Classical Library (New York: Putnam, 1935) p. 30.
2. T. R. Malthus, *An Essay on the Principle of Population* (London: J. Johnson Company, 1803).

3. A. H. Hersh, "Eugenics," *The Encyclopedia Americana:* 10 (New York: 1969), p. 567.

4. Madison Grant, Irving Fisher, Fairfield Osborne, and Henry Crampton joined Laughlin in establishing the American Eugenic Society. These men felt that the white race was superior to other races and that the "Nordic" white was superior to other whites.

5. H. H. Laughlin, *Eugenics Record Office* (Cold Spring Harbor, New York, June 1913), vol. 1.

6. C. B. Davenport, *Heredity in Relation to Eugenics* (New York: Arno Press, 1972 [1911]).

7. The American Breeders Association (later called the American Genetics Association) was organized to bring together animal and plant breeders to realize the importance of the laws of heredity. The Committee on Eugenics of this organization included psychologists Robert M. Yerkes, Harvard University; Madison Bentley, Cornell University; and psychiatrist Adolf Meyer, Johns Hopkins University.

8. Laughlin, *op. cit.*

9. C. B. Davenport, *The Trait Book, Eugenics Record Office* (Cold Spring Harbor, New York, February 1912), vol. 6, p. 3.

10. Laughlin, *op. cit.*, p. 4.

11. D. W. LaRue, "Teaching Eugenics," *Eugenical News* (August 1917), p. 62.

12. This view was also called the *biogenetic law.*

13. J. C. Flugel and D. J. West, *A Hundred Years of Psychology* (New York: Macmillan, 1934) p. 113.

14. During this era, social misfits were classified as the 5 Ds: *dependent,* a tramp or pauper; *defective,* manic-depressive or the senile dement; *deficient,* idiot or imbecile; *delinquent,* thief or truant; and *degenerate,* sadist or moral imbecile.

15. H. Laughlin, *Report of the Committee to Study and to Report on the Best Practical Means of Cutting Off the Defective Germ-Plasm in the American Population. 1. The Scope of the Committee's Work.* Bulletin 10A, *Eugenics Record Office* (Cold Spring Harbor, New York, February 1914), p. 7.

16. *Buck v. Bell,* Superintendent, 274 US 200, United States Supreme Court, 1927.

17. R. C. Tryon, "Genetic Differences in Maze Learning in Rats," *National Society for the Study of Education, Intelligence: Its Nature and Nurture,* Thirty-Ninth Yearbook, Part 1 (Bloomington, Illinois: Public School Publishing Company, 1940) pp. 111–119.

18. M. Burlingame and C. P. Stone, "Family Resemblance in Maze-Learning Ability in White Rats," *National Society for the Study of Education, Nature and Nurture, Their Influence Upon Intelligence,* Twenty-Seventh Yearbook, Part 1 (Bloomington, Illinois: Public School Publishing Company, 1928) pp. 89–99.

19. Tryon, *op. cit.*, p. 112.

20. L. V. Searle, "The Organization of Hereditary Maze-Brightness and Maze-Dullness," *Genetic Psychology Monograph,* 39, 1949, pp. 279–325.

21. Davenport, *op. cit.*, p. 207.

22. "Selection of Negroes," *Eugenical News,* 2 (March 1917), p. 24.

23. R. L. Dugdale, *The Jukes: A Study in Crime, Pauperism, Disease, and Heredity* (New York: Putnam, 1910), and A. H. Estabrook, *The Jukes in 1915* (Washington, D.C.: Carnegie Institution, 1916).

24. H. H. Goddard, *The Kallikak Family: A Study in the Heredity of Feeblemindedness* (New York: Macmillan, 1912).

25. G. S. Hall, *Adolescence* (New York: Appleton), 1904, p. 2.

26. Ibid., p. 4.

27. These factors were: (1) health; (2) second breath; (3) free mobilization up and down the pleasure-pain scale; (4) sympathy; (5) love of nature; (6) sublimation; (7) activity v. passivity; and (8) loyalty or fidelity.

28. E. L. Thorndike, "Eugenics: With Special Reference to Intellect and Character," *The Popular Science Monthly,* 83 (1913), p. 126.

29. E. L. Thorndike, *Human Nature and the Social Order* (New York: Macmillan, 1940) p. 453.

30. Ibid., p. 458.

31. E. L. Thorndike, "Eugenics: With Special Reference to Intellect and Character," *The Popular Science Monthly,* 83 (1913) p. 131.

32. G. Joncich, *The Sane Positivist: A Biography of Edward L. Thorndike* (Middletown, Connecticut: Wesleyan University Press, 1968) p. 375.

two
Psychology and Psychologists

5
Psychology and education in black colleges and universities

In the early 1500s, black slaves were brought to the New World when Spanish colonists from the West Indies attempted to establish sugarcane plantations on the southeastern coast of North America. However, disease and other ill fortune forced the Spaniards and most of the slaves to return to Hispanola. Almost a hundred years later, in 1619, ". . . a dutch man of warre docked at Jamestown, Virginia and sold twenty negars" as servants to English colonists, thereby marking the beginning of the struggle of black people for existence in the New World.[1]

Nearly two centuries later, when the cotton gin was perfected, the demand for black slaves in the South rose sharply, and what had been a small band of twenty African servants in Virginia in 1619 grew to a magnitude of over four million throughout North America.

As the black population increased, so did the number of slave revolts. Denmark Vesey's insurrection in South Carolina in 1822 and Nat Turner's revolt in Virginia in 1831 gained widespread attention. Nat Turner, by all accounts, was a brilliant slave preacher who sharpened his early reading skills through "sabbath schools" and Bible study. Denmark Vesey, likewise, was an intelligent man who acquired his basic skills in much the same way as Turner. Because leadership in these specific insurrections was traced to persons who could read and write, harsh laws forbidding the instruction of blacks in reading, writing, and arithmetic were passed as defensive measures throughout the South. These laws, commonly called the *black codes,* declared that black people were not to be regarded as *persons* but as *property.* For example, the rape of a black woman (by other than the slave master) was considered a crime only because it involved trespassing on and destroying personal property.[2]

Since these codes had statutes which specifically prohibited attempts to educate slaves, any white person convicted of teaching blacks faced heavy fines and imprisonment while the slave faced cruel punishments.[3] In order to oversee the slaves' leisure activities, all gatherings were monitored by whites and only oral communication between slaves was permissible. This latter restriction was often carried to incredible extremes; in Mississippi, for example, slaves were prevented from beating drums or blowing horns for fear of secret messages being transmitted. Generally, it was only in song that blacks could share and transmit a common philosophy, and even here the lyrics were restricted to expressions of religious ideals which promised freedom from trouble and misery in heavenly reward.

The restriction of educational pursuits in the nineteenth century caused slaves to regard reading and writing as forbidden fruit, and in many instances they stole away to secret places at night to study under the direction of friends. The black codes all but removed any hope for slaves to acquire formal education. In the North, a few freedmen did manage to obtain limited schooling, frequently while facing the possibility of physical harm. In a number of instances, prejudice against freedmen trying to secure an education led to acts of violence on the part of "loyal white citizens." Historical accounts reveal cases in which black children were stoned on their way to and from school and their teachers publicly whipped. Teaching materials were scant in the makeshift freedmen schools; publications of northern tract societies, Bibles, miscellanies from New England attics, and similar materials furnished by benevolent organizations substituted for textbooks and other conventional teaching aids. In a few cases, freedmen sailed to England and Scotland to become college educated while some attended liberal American institutions. Berea College in Kentucky and Oberlin College in Ohio were the principal liberal schools of this period.

In 1862, John Brown Russworm at Bowdoin College (Massachusetts), Edward Jones at Amherst College (Massachusetts), and later Mary Jane Patterson at Oberlin became the first blacks in the United States to receive college degrees. By the time of the Emancipation Proclamation, approximately forty black men and women had managed to earn college degrees.

During the Civil War, the combination of warfare and the quest for learning by black soldiers produced some remarkable scenes:

> Passing through a sally-port at Fort Hudson, a few days since, near that rugged and broken ground made memorable by the desperate charge of the colored regiments, June 14th, 1863, I met a corporal coming in from the outworks with his gun upon his shoulder, and hanging from the bayonet by a bit of cord a Webster's spelling-book. Already, hundreds in every regiment have learned to read and write. In almost every tent, the spelling-book and New Testament lie side by side with weapons of war. The negroes fight and the negroes read.[4]

In the months and years that immediately followed the war, formal schools for black people were created and higher education for blacks had its beginnings.

The Birth of Black Colleges

Following the war, the old secret night schools for slaves were converted to open day schools as federal efforts, missionary associations, and aid societies vigorously began to establish learning centers for the "black refugees." Religion was emphasized in these schools because most of the teachers were missionary representatives of benevolent and religious orders.

In 1854, Lincoln University in Pennsylvania became the first American institution for blacks chartered to grant higher degrees. Two years later, Wilberforce University was established in Ohio. In the next fifteen years, Shaw University (1865), Fisk University (1866), Talladega College (1867), Howard University (1867), Tougaloo College (1869), and Benedict College (1871) were all founded. In 1866, Missouri became the first state to establish a separate public college for blacks. By 1885, Atlanta had become the home of five black institutions: Morehouse College, Clark

College, Spelman College, Morris Brown College, and Atlanta University. By 1940, more than one hundred black colleges and universities were located in seventeen southern states, enrolling most of their students from the South's segregated public school system (Table 14).

Serving purposes unprecedented in the annals of American education, these physically inadequate colleges embarked on their mission to train needed educators and physicians for black communities. Often located in the same vicinity as a large, well-to-do, all-white college, the small black college struggled to provide an environment of instruction and inspiration. It was clear that the black schools, with their limited facilities, understaffing, and inadequate funding, were never intended to be on a par with the white institutions; financial contributions were grossly inadequate in supplementing meager state appropriations. As the number of black faculty members increased to meet the growing student enrollments, teachers faced heavy teaching loads with few benefits.[5] Most teachers were flagrantly underpaid.[6] Yet, in spite of these debilitating circumstances, the black colleges became spawning grounds for black professionals and scholars for decades to come.

Psychology Courses in Black Colleges

Most of the subject matter taught in the early days of the black schools consisted of classical discourses requiring only classroom space and minimal equipment. Very little attention was paid to the teaching of science; "the Latin, Greek, geometry, logic, and philosophy already stereotyped in white colleges of the South, became the curriculum of the Negro colleges."[7] The urgent need for elementary and secondary schoolteachers, preachers, and trade workers led to a type of academic training which deemphasized the scientific curriculum. This had a direct effect on the content of psychology courses; the German influence in American psychology (which had created the preoccupation with laboratory research in *reaction time, just-noticeable-differences,* and *memory* exercises) was virtually ignored in the black schools. While white institutions emphasized psychology as a laboratory science and made strenuous efforts for it to emulate the "hard" sciences, black institutions were forced to narrow the discipline to a practical and applied sphere. In subsequent years, the assignment of psychology courses within departments of education became a frequent practice. Still, as late as 1940, only four black schools offered psychology as an undergraduate major, a situation

Table 14 Establishment of Black Colleges and Universities (1854–1932)

Institution	Location	Year founded
1. Lincoln University	Chester County, Pa.	1854
2. Wilberforce University	Wilberforce, Ohio	1856
3. Atlanta University	Atlanta, Ga.	1860
4. Shaw University	Raleigh, N. C.	1865
5. Virginia Union University	Richmond, Va.	1865
6. Fisk University	Nashville, Tenn.	1865
7. Lincoln University	Jefferson City, Mo.	1866
8. Howard University	Washington, D. C.	1867
9. Talladega College	Talladega, Ala.	1867
10. Morehouse College	Atlanta, Ga.	1867
11. Johnson C. Smith University	Charlotte, N. C.	1867
12. Saint Augustine's College	Raleigh, N. C.	1867
13. Roger Williams University	Nashville, Tenn.	1867
14. Storer College	Harper's Ferry, W. Va.	1868
15. Hampton Institute	Hampton, Va.	1868
16. Straight College	New Orleans, La.	1868
17. New Orleans University	New Orleans, La.	1869
18. Tougaloo College	Tougaloo, Miss.	1869
19. Claflin University	Orangeburg, S. C.	1869
20. LeMoyne College	Memphis, Tenn.	1870
21. Allen University	Columbia, S. C.	1870
22. Benedict College	Columbia, S. C.	1870
23. Barber-Scotia College	Concord, N. C.	1870
24. Leland University	Baker, La.	1870
25. Clark University	Atlanta, Ga.	1870
26. Alcorn A. & M. College	Alcorn, Miss.	1871
27. Knoxville College	Knoxville, Tenn.	1872
28. Brewer Junior College	Greenwood, S. C.	1872
29. Wiley College	Marshall, Texas	1873
30. Alabama State Teachers College	Montgomery, Ala.	1874
31. Alabama State A. & M. Normal	Huntsville, Ala.	1875
32. Arkansas A. M. & N. College	Pine Bluff, Ark.	1875
33. Morgan College	Baltimore, Md.	1876
34. Philander Smith College	Little Rock, Ark.	1877
35. Western University	Kansas City, Kans.	1877
36. Jackson College	Jackson, Miss.	1877
37. State Normal School	Fayetteville, N. C.	1877
38. Tillotson College	Austin Texas	1877
39. Selma University	Selma, Ala.	1878
40. Lane College	Jackson, Tenn.	1878
41. Voorhees N. & I. School	Denmark, S. C.	1879
42. Tuskegee N. & I. Institute	Tuskegee, Ala.	1881
43. Spelman College	Atlanta, Ga.	1881
44. Southern Christian Institute	Edwards, Miss.	1881
45. Bettis Academy	Trenton, S. C.	1881
46. Morristown N. & I. College	Morristown, Tenn.	1881
47. Bishop College	Marshall, Texas	1881
48. Paul Quinn College	Waco, Texas	1881
49. Paine College	Augusta, Ga.	1882
50. Livingstone College	Salisbury, N. C.	1882
51. Edward Waters College	Jacksonville, Fla.	1883
52. Swift Memorial College	Rogersville, Tenn.	1883
53. Virginia State College	Petersburg, Va.	1883
54. Arkansas Baptist College	Little Rock, Ark.	1885
55. Morris Brown College	Atlanta, Ga.	1885
56. Natchez College	Natchez, Miss.	1885
57. Kittrell College	Kittrell, N. C.	1885
58. Shorter College	North Little Rock, Ark.	1886
59. Princess Anne Academy	Princess Anne, Md.	1886
60. Rust College	Holly Springs, Miss.	1886

Table 14 Continued

Institution	Location	Year founded
61. Mary Allen Seminary	Crockett, Texas	1886
62. Prairie View State College	Prairie View, Texas	1886
63. Florida A. & M. College	Tallahassee, Fla.	1887
64. Guadalupe College	Seguin, Texas	1887
65. St. Paul N. & I. College	Lawrenceville, Va.	1888
66. Virginia College & Seminary	Lynchburg, Va.	1888
67. State Normal School	Elizabeth City, N. C.	1889
68. Georgia State Ind. College	Savannah, Ga.	1890
69. Coleman College	Gibsland, La.	1890
70. Stowe Teachers College	St. Louis, Mo.	1890
71. State College for Colored Youth	Dover, Del.	1891
72. The A. & T. College	Greensboro, N. C.	1891
73. West Virginia State College	Institute, W. Va.	1891
74. Florida N. & I. College	St. Augustine, Fla.	1892
75. Fort Valley N. & I. School	Fort Valley, Ga.	1893
76. Texas College	Tyler, Texas	1894
77. Brick Junior College	Bricks, N. C.	1895
78. State A. & M. College	Orangeburg, S. C.	1895
79. Kentucky State Ind. College	Frankfort, Ky.	1896
80. Colored A. & N. University	Langston, Okla.	1897
81. St. Phillips Junior College	San Antonio, Texas	1898
82. Central City College	Macon, Ga.	1899
83. Samual Houston College	Austin, Texas	1900
84. Miles Memorial College	Birmingham, Ala.	1902
85. Coppin Normal School	Baltimore, Md.	1902
86. Bethune Cookman College	Daytona Beach, Fla.	1904
87. Georgia N. & A. College	Albany, Ga.	1905
88. Louisiana N. & I. College	Grambling, La.	1905
89. Morris College	Sumter, S. C.	1905
90. Butler College	Tyler, Texas	1905
91. Mississippi Industrial College	Holly Springs, Miss.	1906
92. Jarvis Christian College	Hawkins, Texas	1909
93. West Kentucky Ind. College	Paducah, Ky.	1910
94. Maryland Normal School	Bowie, Md.	1911
95. Lincoln Institute	Lincoln Ridge, Ky.	1912
96. Tennessee A. & I. College	Nashville, Tenn.	1912
97. Cheyney Training School	Cheyney, Pa.	1913
98. Southern University	Scotlandville, La.	1914
99. Xavier University	New Orleans, La.	1915
100. Bluefield St. Teachers College	Bluefield, W. Va.	1921
101. N. C. College for Negroes	Durham, N. C.	1925
102. Winston-Salem Teachers College	Winston-Salem N. C.	1925
103. Bennett College	Greensboro, N. C.	1926
104. Houston Junior College	Houston, Texas	1927
105. Dunbar Junior College	Little Rock, Ark.	1929
106. Miner Teachers College	Washington, D. C.	1929
107. Louisville Municipal College	Louisville, Ky.	1931
108. Dillard University	New Orleans, La.	1935
109. State Teachers & Agri. College	Forsyth, Ga.	Unknown

SOURCE: D. O. W. Holmes, *The Evolution of the Negro College* (New York: Teachers College, Columbia University, 1934). Reprinted by permission.

that not only limited the opportunities for blacks to earn a degree in the subject but influenced the popularity of educational psychology courses as well. Instruction in experimental psychology and methodology courses was found lacking in many programs.

West Virginia State College, an early leader in educational research efforts, initiated a number of interesting investigations during the 1930–1940 period. Among these were a series of studies designed to survey the "status of curricula offerings and aspects of curriculum in colleges for Negroes." The first of these studies was *Psychology in Negro Institutions,* in which Herman G. Canady, chairman of West Virginia's psychology department, set out to obtain information concerning: (a) the status of psychology in the curriculum, (b) the nature of the introductory course in psychology, (c) undergraduate courses in psychology, (d) provisions for laboratory work, (e) library equipment, (f) teaching personnel, and (g) research in psychology,[8] in America's black colleges. Canady's data were derived from analyses of a questionnaire sent to fifty black colleges in 1936.

Canady's survey revealed that only fourteen institutions, out of the total of fifty, had departments of psychology and that only four of these schools offered psychology as a major subject. In spite of this lack of formal attention to the field, psychology courses were viewed as a popular subject by many black students. Several other studies corroborated this finding in appraising the popularity of various courses[9] (Table 15).

Typically, the colleges surveyed by Canady emphasized basic and applied courses in psychology. These courses were usually one semester in duration and were taught by the lecture-discussion method. Few practicum existed and laboratory courses were rare, although most professors at these schools indicated they would have offered laboratory experiences if the equipment and space were available.[10] Canady also reported that a total of twenty-eight different courses in psychology were taught during the 1940s (Table 16). He specifically drew attention to the absence of certain courses:

> It is of interest to note the larger number of courses of an applied nature and the relatively few in pure and theoretical psychology; also, that no institution offers a course in *race psychology* and that no institution offers a course with the distinct title of "The Psychology of the Negro."[11]

It appears that Canady had called for the first black psychology course as early as the 1930s.

Library and Research Facilities in Black Colleges

The construction of physical plants and provisions for general library holdings were frequently made possible through donations by Northern philanthropists. Notable in these efforts was

Table 15 Choice of Significant Subjects or Activities Expressed by Undergraduate and Graduate Students in Black Colleges (1936)

Significant Subject	Atlanta U.G.	Atlanta G.	Fisk U.G.	Fisk G.	Hampton U.G.	Hampton G.	Howard U.G.	Howard G.	Prairie V. U.G.	Prairie V. G.	Va. State U.G.	Va. State G.	Xavier U.G.	Xavier G.	Total U.G.	Total G.
Social Science	18	24	18	11	7	9	38	27	:	1	6	3	:	1	87	76
Education	10	6	12	15	6	10	21	23	3	3	3	3	3	4	58	64
Science	13	10	9	7	6	7	15	10	:	:	1	1	:	:	44	35
English	10	8	3	3	12	1	9	11	:	:	:	:	3	5	37	28
Research	:	4	:	4	:	5	:	5	:	:	:	1	:	:	:	19
Miscellaneous	1	1	:	2	3	1	4	6	4	2	:	:	4	:	16	12
Psychology	**2**	**2**	**3**	**:**	**3**	**:**	**7**	**4**	**:**	**:**	**:**	**:**	**:**	**1**	**15**	**7**
Mathematics	3	1	:	:	3	:	5	4	:	:	:	:	:	:	11	5
Foreign Language	2	1	3	3	:	:	5	2	:	:	1	:	1	:	9	3
Music	1	:	:	:	2	:	2	:	:	:	1	:	1	:	9	3
Social Work	:	:	:	:	:	:	:	7	:	:	:	:	:	:	:	7
Business Administration	4	4	1	:	:	1	1	1	3	1	1	:	:	:	6	6
Agriculture	:	:	:	:	:	:	:	:	:	:	:	:	:	:	4	1
Home Economics	:	:	1	:	:	:	2	:	:	:	:	:	:	:	3	:
Library Science	:	:	1	2	:	:	:	1	:	3	:	:	:	:	1	3
Rural Work	:	:	:	:	:	:	:	:	:	:	:	:	:	:	:	:
Total	64	61	51	47	42	34[a]	109	101	10	10	12	8	12	11	300	272

SOURCE: Fred McCuistion, *Graduate Instruction for Negroes in the United States* (Nashville: George Peabody College for Teachers, 1939), p. 79. Reprinted by permission.
[a] Summer session only.

Table 16 Courses Offered in Psychology in Black Institutions (1936)

Name of course	Times offered
Educational Psychology	41
General Psychology	40
Child Psychology	30
Social Psychology	22
Adolescent Psychology	22
Abnormal Psychology	14
Experimental Psychology	7
Statistical Methods	5
Applied Psychology	4
Psychology of Religion	4
Psychological Test	3
Differential Psychology	3
Race Psychology	2
Genetic Psychology	2
Business Psychology	2
Psychology of Learning	2
Recent Schools of Psychology	2
Clinical Psychology	2
Elementary Psychology for Nurses	1
Medical Psychology	1
Legal Psychology	1
Psychological and Psychiatric Social Work	1
Psychology of Personal Adjustment	1
Psychology of Selling and Adjusting	1
Mental Psychology	1
Human Behavior	1
Nations Psychology	1
Comparative Psychology	1

SOURCE: H. G. Canady, "Psychology in Negro Institutions," *West Virginia State Bulletin*, 3 (June 1939).

Julius Rosenwald, a Chicago merchant who began in 1911 by providing funds to assist in the construction of buildings at black schools. The Rosenwald funds were devoted to the construction of total physical plants, and these efforts drew attention to and greatly stimulated the development of libraries at many colleges. Around 1915, the Carnegie Corporation earmarked funds specifically for the development of libraries and library service in a number of these schools. However, even with this financial assistance, library facilities continued to be grossly inadequate in meeting the needs of the students.

A total of twenty-six different psychology periodicals were subscribed to by the libraries at the black schools. (The most popular journals were: *American Journal of Psychology, Journal of Social Psychology, Journal of Educational Psychology,* and *Mental Hygiene.* The less popular journals were *Journal of Comparative Psychology, Journal of Genetic Psychology,* and the *Psychological Bulletin.*)[12]

Only eight psychology professors (three of whom were white) out of a total of eighty-eight in the black colleges reported having published research during the period 1931–1936.[13] The heavy

Table 17 Major Fields of Graduate and Undergraduate Training and Highest Degree Held by Psychology Instructors in Black Colleges (1936)

Major field of training	No. of instructors	Highest degree held			
		Ph.D. Ed.D.	M.A. M.S.	B.A. B.S. Ph.B.	B.D.
Psychology	20	5[a]	13	2	
Ed. Psychology	7	2	5		
Education	38	5	28	5	
Philosophy	5	2	2		1
Sociology 7)					
Theology 1)	10		8		
Relig. Ed. 1)					
Spanish 1)					
Dept. Omitted	2		2		
Degree Omitted	6				
Totals	88	16	58	7	1
Trained in approved fields	27	7	18	2	

SOURCE: H. G. Canady, "Psychology in Negro Institutions," *West Virginia State Bulletin*, 3 (June 1939).
  [a] Three of these are white.

commitment to teaching responsibilities and the lack of graduate training undoubtedly contributed to this situation. (Table 17 describes the educational training of the professors by listing their highest degree held in 1936.)

Employment Opportunities in Psychology

The limited number of black role-models in psychology and a lack of encouragement from the employment field presented a persistent problem in the recruitment of students for careers in psychology. In order to offset the lack of information about employment opportunities, college catalogs frequently described employment possibilities, but this practice was inadequate in providing answers to questions of whether job opportunities for black graduates existed and what specific areas of psychology offered the best chances for jobs.

Lily Brunschwig, one of a few white psychology professors in black colleges during the late 1930s, called attention to the growing interest her undergraduate students had expressed in choosing psychology as a career. In 1939, to gain information about employment opportunities, she dispatched a questionnaire to black psychologists and other blacks trained in the field of psy-

Table 18 Major Activities of Black Psychologists (1940)

Activity	Number of individuals
Teacher of Psychology—Full Time	8
Teacher of Psychology—76 to 95% of the Time	8
Teacher of Psychology—51 to 75% of the Time	16
Teacher of Psychology—10 to 50% of the Time	14
Psychological Research: School Psychologist	6
Clinical or Consulting Psychologist	1
Psychologist in Nursery School	1
Vocational Guidance, Student Personnel	0
Administrator, College or High School	3

SOURCE: Lily Brunschwig, "Opportunities for Negroes in the Field of Psychology," *Journal of Negro Education*, October 1941, p. 666. Reprinted by permission of the publisher.

chology. She asked, "What vocational opportunities are or will be available for Negro students wishing to prepare for psychology as a career?" While her study was not intended to provide a complete census of black psychologists, it did offer an interesting sample of the activities of black professionals trained in psychology at that time (Table 18).

By far the largest number of psychologists who took part in the Brunschwig study described themselves as teachers of psychology.[14] (This finding was to be expected; college teaching was the chief avenue of employment in all fields for the highly trained black.) Of the total number in the Brunschwig study, only seven were engaged in activities such as research, clinical work, and school psychology. The study did note that a substantial representation of black women had employment in the profession of psychology at that time. (This was to be expected; a larger number of black women graduated from college than did black men.) An interesting sidelight of this study was the inclusion of a statement from a young black psychologist who had secured employment in the face of "vigorous discouragement":

> In reply to your letter and questionnaire regarding vocational opportunities for Negroes in the field of psychology, I can sum up my own opinions by saying that Negroes who think of psychology in terms of their life work are preparing for a nonexistent field. But I say, go on and prepare for it. The demand for real psychology will inevitably develop—and it should begin within the next few years. . . . The trick in securing work in psychology lies in keeping body and soul together until a job breaks. I did it by three years of social work. Then, in the summer of 1938 I learned that the new director of the clinic of [   ] might receive favorably an application from me. There were many difficulties involved in the acceptance of my application. There had never been a Negro in the clinic; there were white boys as well as Negro boys to be tested; they were not sure that a Negro could adjust to the social conditions of the institution; they were not certain that a Negro employee would

be received as apartment mate by a white employee; and so on. . . . Finally, all mental resistance to my application was broken down and I came to intern. . . . After interning from October to June, I was offered my present position. The vacancy thus created in the clinic made it possible for another Negro to intern. A third Negro, from Howard University, worked under my direction last summer. So this institution may be considered one place where there are opportunities for internship.

One of your questions deals with opportunities for advancement in the field. They are not too good. And this is not a racial problem. The psychologists who are making money are those who have left the field of applied psychology. . . . I'd say that opportunities are better for Negroes than for whites, but that isn't saying much. We have white interns now who float from one institution to another as interns—some with three years of experience. There are too many white psychologists for the present demand; Negroes have no place in psychology, as was pointed out to me some time ago, because jobs have not yet opened in Negro institutions. When there are jobs, and this should be rather soon, they will go to those who are prepared for them. . . .[15]

The immediate employment picture was dismal, but prospects for the future expressed by many of the professionals were encouraging, leading Brunschwig to conclude that "vocational opportunities for Negro psychologists will increase" in spite of the "period of social change and uncertainty."[16]

Table 19 Major Fields of Graduate Students in Black Colleges (1919–1938)

Field	Atlanta	Fisk	Hampton	Howard	Virginia State	Xavier	Total
Anthropology ..	..	1	..	..	..	..	1
Biology	14	6	..	..	..	..	20
Botany.........	..	..	..	7	..	..	7
Chemistry	10	12	..	18	..	..	40
Economics	20	..	..	4	..	..	24
Education	46	43	23	60	5	3	180
English	18	26	..	49	..	1	94
Foreign Language	11	..	..	25	..	..	36
History	26	1	..	55	..	4	86
Mathematics ...	19	4	..	21	..	..	44
Music	..	7	..	..	..	..	7
Philosophy	..	..	..	1	..	1	2
Physics	..	..	..	7	..	..	7
Psychology	..	..	..	**20**	..	..	**20**
Religion	..	..	..	5	..	..	5
Social Work	..	..	..	1	..	..	1
Sociology	22	16	..	3	..	..	41
Political Science	..	..	..	1	..	..	1
Zoology	..	..	..	18	..	..	18
Not Given	..	..	..	1	..	..	1
Total	186	116	23	296	5	9	635

SOURCE: Fred McCuistion, *Graduate Instruction for Negroes in the United States* (Nashville: George Peabody College for Teachers, 1939), pp. 43–44. Reprinted by permission.

Howard University

Howard University (Washington, D.C.) was the leading black school providing graduate and undergraduate training in psychology. Between 1919 and 1938, twenty students enrolled in graduate studies in psychology at Howard (Table 19).

The importance of the Howard University psychology program may be seen in the finding that only 36 black students were enrolled in graduate studies in psychology in institutions outside the South between 1930 and 1938 (Table 20).

The uniqueness and strength of Howard's program in psychology must be attributed to the leadership of Francis C. Sumner. In 1928, Sumner, who had just left a successful chairmanship of West Virginia State College's psychology department, placed

Table 20 Black Graduate Students in Institutions Outside the South: Major Fields of Study and Enrollment (1930–1938)

Major field	Enrollment		
	1930–1936	1938–1939	Total
Health	33	20	53
Home Economics	32	19	51
Zoology	29	16	45
Science—General	29	14	43
Music	23	20	43
Economics	31	11	42
French	37	5	42
Psychology	**31**	**5**	**36**
Business	17	9	26
Physics	14	9	23
Fine Arts	10	12	22
Biology	7	11	18
Political Science	10	6	16
Agriculture	7	5	12
Foreign Language	10	2	12
Latin	7	1	8
Law	8	..	8
Unclassified	3	5	8
Bacteriology	4	3	7
Classics	5	1	6
Library Science	5	1	6
Engineering	4	2	6
German	3	2	5
Anthropology	4	..	4
Industrial Arts	2	2	4
Philosophy	2	2	4
Botany	2	..	2
Dramatics	..	2	2
Journalism	1	..	1
Physiology	..	1	1
Total	1,084	663	1,747

SOURCE: Fred McCuistion, *Graduate Instruction for Negroes in the United States* (Nashville: George Peabody College for Teachers, 1939), pp. 57–58. Reprinted by permission.

Table 21 Courses of Instruction for the Beginning Psychology Sequence at Howard University (1932–1933)

Psychology 1, 2, and 4 form the natural approach to all advanced courses in Psychology and are a definite requirement of all students who major in Psychology.

Psychology 1. *General Psychology 1.* An introduction to psychology from the behavioristic, introspective, and dynamic standpoints. Lectures, collateral readings, and demonstration. Credit for Psychology 1 will not be given until Psychology 2 is completed. (Mr. Sumner, Mr. Meenes)

Psychology 2. *General Psychology 2.* A continuation of Psychology 1. (Mr. Sumner, Mr. Meenes)

psychology 4. *Experimental Psychology.* An elementary laboratory course in psychology. (Mr. Meenes)

SOURCE: *Howard University Catalog—Undergraduate, 1932–1933* (Washington, D.C.: Howard University, 1932).

an immediate priority on building a strong program in psychology at Howard. In order to give students a firm foundation in the field, a department of psychology with a strong experimental orientation was established. Two years later, Max Meenes, a white associate professor trained as a "brass instrument psychologist," joined Sumner and graduate student Frederick Watts to form a three-man department. Meenes, commenting in 1972 on Sumner's program for Howard psychology majors, outlined the introductory course sequencing during the 1930s (Table 21):

> The first course in psychology ran through three quarters. It was unique in a sense that the first quarter was psychology according to Titchener and we used Titchener's book. The second quarter, we were teaching psychology from the point of view of behaviorism. We used Watson's book. The third quarter, we were interested in dynamic psychology and we used McDougall and Freud. The major had to have all three of these basic courses.[17]

Describing other courses in the Howard psychology program, Meenes continued:

> In addition to the usual run of courses in those days, we had courses in learning, personality, mental hygiene, and so on. Dr. Sumner was very much interested in the psychology of religion, so we provided such a unique course. We emphasized the laboratory-experimental aspect of psychology. In that way, we were different from all the other black schools.[18]

Howard's graduate courses in psychology were equally outstanding for that time and were specifically designed to enable graduates to succeed in pursuing their doctorates at the large white universities (Table 22).

> Now at the graduate level we went only into the master's degree; we didn't want to issue any doctorates here because we thought our students should go elsewhere. . . . We didn't want them to be ingrown. Our graduate work was perhaps a little bit unusual too; we had two courses designed to enable our students to pass the

Table 22 Advanced Courses in Psychology at Howard University (1932–1933)

Psychology 212. *Psychological Journals.* A systematic study of current psychological journals.
Psychology 213. *Reading of French Psychology.* A reading of several psychological works in French. Prerequisites: eight courses in Psychology and a reading knowledge of French.
Psychology 214. *Reading of German Psychology.* A reading of several psychological works in German. Prerequisites: eight courses in Psychology and a reading knowledge of German.

SOURCE: *Howard University Catalog—Undergraduate and Graduate, 1932–1933* (Washington, D.C.: Howard University, 1932).

language exams for the doctorate. One was readings in German psychology and the other was readings in French psychology.[19]

Discussing the successes of the Howard program and the subsequent pursuit of the doctorate by Howard graduates, Meenes described the apprehensions of students who were competing in a society that was more often than not unreceptive to black graduate students:

Our students were a little bit reluctant to face the outside competition. They worried that they might not have an adequae background. But we saw to it that they did get it. And then they came back to us, frequently quite surprised, to say, "you know, I am getting along fine. As fine as anybody." These were students who went on to Columbia, Minnesota, Wisconsin, California, and so on. Yes, they did have a good background. It really made us feel proud.[20]

On April 30, 1935, a new classroom building on the Howard campus was formally opened, providing a "spacious and modernly appointed unit" for the psychology department.[21] The new facility was the only unit in any black institution at that time designed specifically for psychology; it compared favorably with facilities at many of the leading institutions in America (Figure 5.1).

In 1938, Sumner outlined three objectives for the psychology department:

A. Servicing of students preparing for various professional lines such as business, education, law, medicine, religion, music, art, clinic work and nursing. A certain amount of scientific psychological knowledge is requisite in all these professional lines which involves the interplay of human beings. In many instances certain course requirements in psychology are definitely stated as preparatory prerequisites. In other instances, courses in psychology are recommended although not definitely prescribed.

B. Cultural significance of psychology is stressed by the Psychology Department and this appeals to a large number of students. Here a knowledge of psychology is of importance for the deeper understanding of literature, religion, philosophy, art, crime, genius, mental derangement, history, biography and all other creations of the human mind.

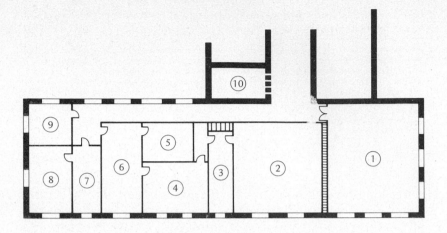

Figure 5.1 Psychology Unit, Douglass Memorial Hall, Howard University, Washington, D.C.: (1) a large undergraduate laboratory which seats 30 students and which has concealed cabinets for storage of apparatus, (2) a lecture room seating 48 students, (3) office of the department head, (4) a small lecture room and laboratory for graduate students, (5) a dark room furnished with a number of daylight lamps, work-benches, etc., (6) a machine shop containing a metal lathe, a wood lathe, a jig-saw, electric drill, work benches and tools, (7), (8), and (9) small laboratories for professors and graduate students. (*Source:* F. C. Sumner, "The New Psychology Unit at Howard University," *Psychological Bulletin*, 1935, p. 860. Copyright 1935 by the American Psychological Association. Reprinted by permission.)

> C. The preparation of a few select students for scientific pursuit of psychology in graduate study leading to the Master's and Doctor's degree.[22]

In 1943, the annual award of a Gold Key was established for the Howard University senior completing a major in psychology with exceptional distinction. This award, later called the Dodson Award after its benefactor, Mrs. Willie A. Dodson, was designed to provide an incentive for achievement among students in the department. The first recipient of the award was Mrs. Mauvice Winslow Brett of the Class of 1944.

Not only was Howard University producing outstanding scholars in psychology, but the popularity of the department led Sumner, in 1947, to announce:

> During the year 1946–47 the enrollment at the graduate and undergraduate levels was the highest in the history of the Psychology Department. The scholastic ability of the undergraduate students in psychology was on the whole higher than usual.[23]

Max Meenes (left) with his former students Mamie and Kenneth Clark in 1957. A native of Poland, Professor Meenes came to the United States as a child. He earned B.A. and Ph.D. degrees at Clark University and an M.A. at Princeton. He was head of the Howard University psychology department from 1956 to 1966 and published several books and studies. Professor Meenes died in 1973. The Clarks, holders of Ph.D.s from Columbia University, had received B.A.s and M.A.s at Howard.

Finally, on June 2, 1947, the Howard University chapter of Psi Chi, the national honorary society for psychology, was installed:

> Dr. Max Meenes served as Installation Officer and Dr. F. C. Sumner as Sponsor. Fourteen students were initiated as chartered members. Edward Brock, a Junior, was installed as Chapter President. This Chapter is the first one of Psi Chi to be established in a Negro school.[24]

It was clear that Howard's psychology department was the leading institution for the training of black psychologists in this country.

Black Psychologists Organize

In 1938, Herman Canady of West Virginia State College led a vigorous effort to organize black professionals in psychology. The effort was made in conjunction with the 1938 American Teachers Association (ATA) annual convention, held at Tuskegee Institute in Alabama. (The racial discrimination of the 1930s prevented

115

black educators from joining southern chapters of the National
Education Association (NEA); consequently, the all-black American Teachers Association became the chief professional organization for most black educators.) The ATA membership included
most of the black psychologists of this period, and annual meetings of the ATA often found these psychologists in caucuses, discussing common interests and concerns. It was within this context
that Herman Canady attempted to organize black psychologists.
To this end, he mailed "A Prospectus of an Organization of Negroes Interested in Psychology and Related Fields" to those members of the ATA who were interested or worked in the area of
psychology.

**A PROSPECTUS OF AN ORGANIZATION OF NEGROES
INTERESTED IN PSYCHOLOGY AND RELATED FIELDS**

Name Psychology Section of A.T.A., or ????

**Major
Objective** To advance, promote and encourage the teaching
and application of the science of psychology and
related fields, particularly in Negro institutions.

**Specific
Purposes** To set up qualifications for teachers of psychology
in Negro institutions and to maintain a list of
institutions that meet the standards determined by
the association.

To assist Negro institutions in the training and
selection of psychologists.

To bring to the section outstanding persons of
the nation for general and specific enlightenment
on current trends in psychology, cognate subjects
and in research techniques.

To discuss outstanding research efforts in Negro
institutions and elsewhere.

To offer counsel and advice to members of the
association in selecting and conducting research
programs.

To assist in securing financial aid for members who
are working on projects which call for expenditures
which exceed the resources of the average
individual.

To stimulate the study and research of psychological problems as a basis for understanding behavior
problems of Negroes.

To create genuine interest in scientific psychology
in institutions of higher learning for Negroes.

> To keep members in touch with major studies, surveys, etc., being carried on in the country in which trained and qualified Negroes might participate.
>
> To represent to research workers and teachers of other subjects the highest ideals of both synthetic and analytic research.
>
> To look forward to the publication of a quarterly having some such title as Human Psychology, or Racial Psychology, or etc.
>
> **Membership** Membership shall be open to persons who are interested in the teaching, application and advancement of the science of psychology and related fields.
>
> **Officers** There shall be three officers: namely, Chairman, Vice-Chairman, Secretary.
>
> **Meeting** Meeting shall be held at the time and place of the convening of A.T.A., or ????

The 1938 ATA Convention at Tuskegee provided a two-day program allowing psychologists to discuss the proposed formation of their group and to contribute to the convention's theme, "The Negro Youth Looks at Occupations in America."

> **AMERICAN TEACHERS' ASSOCIATION**
> Tuskegee Convention of July 26–29, 1938
>
> ---
>
> Program for the Psychology Section for Thursday Afternoon, July 28, 1938   2:15–4:15 p.m.
>
> CONVENTION THEME:
> **THE NEGRO YOUTH
> LOOKS AT OCCUPATIONS IN AMERICA**
>
> **Presiding:** Dr. Oran W. Eagleson, Department of Psychology, Spelman College, Atlanta, Ga.
>
> **Topic:** *The Services of Psychology to Education and the Social Order*
> (This involves primarily a consideration of the application of psychology to the solution of many of the social, educational and political problems of the Negro. Consideration might also be given to the following questions: To what extent would research in psychology in Negro institutions serve as a basis for understanding behavior problems of Negroes? What are some psychological problems that need investigation?)

Panel Jury: (1) *To Education,* Dr. Martin D. Jenkins, Dean, Cheyney Teachers' College, Cheyney, Pa.
(2) *To Vocational Guidance,* Dr. Charles L. Cooper, Department of Industrial Education, A & T College, Greensboro, N.C.
(3) *To the Public School,* Dr. Howard H. Long, Assistant Superintendent of Schools, Washington, D.C.
(4) *To Student Personnel Work,* Dr. Ambrose Caliver, U.S. Office of Education, Washington, D.C.
(5) *To Medicine,* Dr. George Branche, U.S. Veterans Hospital, Tuskegee, Ala.
(6) *To the Social Sciences,* Dr. Bertram W. Doyle, General Secretary, Board of Education, C.M.E. Church, Nashville, Tenn.

AMERICAN TEACHERS' ASSOCIATION
Tuskegee Convention of July 26–29, 1938

Program of the Psychology Section for Wednesday Afternoon, July 27, 1938   2:15–4:15 p.m.

CONVENTION THEME:
THE NEGRO YOUTH
LOOKS AT OCCUPATIONS IN AMERICA

Part I (60 minutes)

Presiding: Herman G. Canady, Department of Psychology, West Virginia State College, Institute, W.Va.

Topic: *Consideration of the Prospectus of the Psychology Section and the Formation of a Permanent Organization*

Part II (60 minutes)

Presiding: Dean J. Otis Smith, Alcorn A & M, Alcorn, Miss.

Topic: *Psychology in Negro Institutions—Undergraduate and Graduate Curricula*
(This discussion will concern itself with personnel, courses, equipment and library facilities; also, the problems of instruction and the improvement of the teaching of psychology.)

Speakers: Herman G. Canady, Department of Psychology, West Virginia State College, Institute, W.Va.
Dr. F. C. Sumner, Department of Psychology, Howard University, Washington, D.C.

Enthusiasm was evident: it was unanimously voted to organize the group. While a separate organization of psychologists did not materialize, Division 6, Department of Psychology of the

ATA was established. The first elected officers of this division were: Herman G. Canady, Chairman; Howard H. Long, Vice-Chairman; and Oran W. Eagleson, Secretary.

Notes

1. E. Arber and A. G. Bradley, eds., *Travels and Works of Captain John Smith* (Edinburgh, 1910) vol. 2, p. 541.
2. J. H. Franklin, *From Slavery to Freedom: A History of Negro Americans*, 3rd ed. (New York: Knopf, 1967), p. 188.
3. The early education of blacks during the 1700s was limited to a few scattered schools. The Society for the Propagation of the Gospel in Foreign Parts, organized in 1701, established a school for Negroes in Charleston, South Carolina in 1745 and another in North Carolina in 1763. The New York African Free School, established by the Society in 1786, became the first public school for blacks. Other schools were established in Henrico County, Virginia; Washington, D.C.; Georgetown; Cincinnati; and New York City.
4. M. F. Armstrong and H. W. Ludlow, *Hampton and Its Students* (New York: Putnam, 1875), p. 121.
5. See A. P. Davis, "The Negro Professor," *The Crisis* (April 1936), pp. 103–104, for an interesting account of the plight of black professors during the 1930s.
6. "Survey of Negro Colleges and Universities," United States Department of the Interior, Bureau of Education Bulletin (1928), 7, p. 45.
7. F. McCuistion, *Graduate Instruction for Negroes in the United States* (Nashville, Tennessee: George Peabody College for Teachers, 1939) p. 12.
8. H. G. Canady, "Psychology in Negro Institutions," *West Virginia State Bulletin,* 3 (June 1939).
9. McCuistion, *op. cit.,* p. 79.
10. Canady, *op. cit.,* p. 167.
11. Ibid., p. 168.
12. Ibid., p. 168.
13. Ibid., p. 168.
14. L. Brunschwig, "Opportunities for Negroes in the Field of Psychology," *Journal of Negro Education* (October 1941), pp. 664–676.
15. Ibid., p. 675.
16. Ibid., p. 676.
17. From taped interview conducted by the author with Max Meenes at Howard University on November 28, 1972.
18. Ibid.
19. Ibid.
20. Ibid.
21. F. C. Sumner, "The New Psychology Unit at Howard University," *Psychological Bulletin* (1935), pp. 859–860.
22. F. C. Sumner, Howard University Annual Reports, 1938–1940, Department of Psychology, F. C. Sumner, pp. lxxiii–lxxiv.
23. Ibid., 1946–1947, pp. 212–213.
24. Ibid., p. 213.

6
Early black psychologists

While Europe served as the training area for many early white psychologists, America was the spawning ground for black psychologists. Hall at Clark, Cattell at Columbia, and Titchener at Cornell received their early psychological training at Leipzig, Germany; each of these scholars became a leader in psychology and actively engaged in research, publishing, and the training of future psychologists. On the other hand, such scholars as Sumner at Howard, Eagleson at Spelman, and Canady at West Virginia State were trained at major universities in the United States, where they received little or no encouragement to continue in the experimental side of psychology. They performed research, but their overall efforts were lessened by this lack of encouragement. Private foundations and federal sources consistently overlooked the black colleges; consequently, financial assistance for research projects was scarce or generally unavailable.

Charles R. Drew, famed physician-researcher, expressed his feelings about the difficulties of black scholars attempting scientific research during the 1930s in these terms:

> While one must grant at once that extraordinary talent, great intellectual strength and unusual opportunity are necessary to break out of this prison of Negro problem . . . the walls here in America are at times too thick to breach and too high to climb.[1]

Clearly the atmosphere of racism and discrimination that existed then contributed to the absence of blacks from the recorded history of American psychology. Popular procedures for determining historical eminence (names of candidates must be meaningful to white judges) contributed further to the omission—an omission not of intent, but of ignorance.

Graduate Training in Psychology

The struggle for blacks to attain graduate-level training in psychology was extremely difficult during the 1910s and success was largely a result of the individual's own initiative. Other than Oberlin College (Ohio), only a few northern white universities accepted and encouraged black students. Clark University (Massachusetts) was one institution that encouraged the enrollment of black graduate students by allowing their entrance examinations to be administered in black colleges. In attendance at Clark during the 1915–1920 period were Howard Long (M.A., psychology, 1916), Francis Sumner (Ph.D., psychology, 1920), J. Henry Alston (M.A., psychology, 1920), E. Franklin Frazier (M.A., sociology, 1920), and Thomas Brown (Ph.D., sociology, 1920).

Recruitment policies, teaching assistantships, and other inducements were rarely directed at black students. Since the majority of black college graduates lived in the South and southern white universities denied them admission, it is obvious why the total number of black graduate students was limited. Geography became a major factor in determining whether one would attend graduate school, and a negative correlation existed between the distance from the North that a black college graduate lived and his chances for enrollment. Even when the decision was made to attend graduate school, the cost of out-of-state fees, tuition, relocation, and minimal maintenance forced most potential black graduate students to delay their training for many years until sufficient money had been saved. This delay elevated the median age

J. Henry Alston

of black graduate students, especially those from the South, 10 to 15 years above that of their white counterparts. A more tragic result of this situation was that untold numbers of black college graduates abandoned their vocational goals to accept employment, often below the level of their formal education, that offered decent wages, retirement programs, and other fringe benefits. Post Office and railroad jobs were available to blacks and were therefore frequently sought after.

There were a few cases of black psychologists who were unable to find jobs in psychology and went into other professional fields. One of these was J. Henry Alston, the first black American to publish an original research effort in an APA journal.[2] Alston studied under G. Stanley Hall at Clark and became fascinated with neurology and experimental psychology. His 1920 research publication, "Psychophysics of the Spatial Conditions for the Fusion of Warmth and Cold into Heat," was received with much praise by E. G. Boring and other leading researchers. However, after receiving his M.A. in experimental psychology, he switched his academic interest to education and administration because of the lack of job opportunities in experimental psychology. Alston later recalled: "After writing several schools, I found that they did not need or feel the need of persons in pure psychology so I was forced by circumstances to change to education as most of our colleges were then teacher training institutes."[3] Altson eventually became a minister and presiding elder in the Christian Methodist Episcopal Church.

Even when job opportunities were available in academia, the prospect of struggling to earn an advanced degree in order to become a college professor, when most black colleges offered poor salaries, little job security and no retirement plans, was not encouraging. One writer offered this view of the situation in 1936:

> [The black college professor] is criminally underpaid. Having slaved at the most menial and humiliating work for a period of five to ten years in order to get his degrees from a high-priced northern university, he comes out finally with a body often impaired in health and practically always a large debt to repay . . . money he has had to borrow to supplement that which he so painfully earned. He is then ready to go to work; and if he is fortunate enough to get a position, he can look forward to an average salary of less than *two thousand dollars a year.* . . . He teaches from eighteen to twenty-one hours a week . . . and has been educated above his means, because the average American white man of his economic status would not have gone as far in education as he has.[4]

The author, Arthur P. Davis, himself a college professor, continued to paint a disheartening picture:

> Lack of money, over-work, and other unpleasant factors make it practically impossible for him to do anything outstanding in the field of pure scholarship. He cannot buy books on a large scale himself, and he cannot get them at his school libraries, because there are no really adequate libraries in the Negro schools. Probably the worst handicap of all is the lack of a scholarly atmosphere about him. There is no incentive, and, of course, no money for research in most schools.[5]

In spite of this discouraging employment situation, a few scholars remained in psychology and earned their doctorates.

Black Holders of Psychology Doctorates

There were several instances in which black Americans traveled to Europe to obtain graduate training. One of these was the savant Gilbert Haven Jones, who earned his Ph.D. degree in philosophy in 1901 at the University of Jena in Germany and later studied at the University of Gottingen in Germany. A philosopher, Jones was the first black person with an earned doctorate to teach psychology in the United States. (At the time of Jones's graduate work, psychology was not yet a separate field of study in most universities, and the subject was covered under the broad category of philosophy.) Jones, born in Fort Mott, South Carolina, in 1883, was a professor of philosophy and education at St. Augus-

Table 23 Source and Output of Black Doctorate Holders in Psychology and Educational Psychology (1920–1950)

University	Year of award
Clark University	1920
University of Chicago	1925, 1939
New York University	1930, 1948, 1949, 1950
Columbia University	1932, 1937, 1940, 1944
University of Cincinnati	1933
Harvard University	1933, 1939
University of Minnesota	1934, 1944, 1947
Indiana University	1935
Northwestern University	1935, 1941, 1942
Ohio State University	1937, 1946
Temple University	1937, 1939
University of California (Berkeley)	1938, 1948
University of Pennsylvania	1941, 1943
Pennsylvania State University	1946
University of Michigan	1949

tine College in North Carolina, A & M University in Oklahoma, and Wilberforce University in Ohio (where he was later appointed Dean, then Vice-President).

In the United States, the training of black scholars in psychology was minuscule. The Committee on Equality of Opportunity in Psychology (APA) reported that the ten most prestigious departments of psychology in the United States[6] granted only eight Ph.D.s in psychology to black candidates between 1920 and 1966 while granting a total of 3,767 Ph.D.s during this same period; six of these leading departments had not had a single black Ph.D.[7] (The source and numbers of black Ph.D.s in the fields of psychology and educational psychology at *all* American universities for the period 1920–1950 are shown in Table 23.)

The balance of this chapter recounts the personal histories and careers of the black women and men who earned doctorates in psychology and educational psychology at American colleges and universities during the years 1920–1950. (Table 24 gives a complete listing of these individuals and their academic degrees.)

Table 24 Individuals Granted Doctorates in Psychology and Educational Psychology (1920–1950)

Name	Institutions; Bachelor's and master's degrees		Doctorate degree institution	Major subject	Year	Degree	Dissertation title
1. Francis Cecil Sumner	Lincoln University (Pa.) Clark University (Mass.) Clark University (Mass.)	B.A. B.A. A.M.	Clark University (Mass.)	Psychology	1920	PhD	Psychoanalysis of Freud and Adler
2. Charles Henry Thompson	Virginia Union University University of Chicago	B.A. M.A.	University of Chicago	Educational Psychology	1925	PhD	An Objective Determination of a Curriculum for Kindergarten Teachers
3. Albert Sidney Beckham	Lincoln University (Pa.) Ohio State University Ohio State University	B.A. B.A. M.A.	New York University	Educational Psychology	1930	PdD	The Provisions for High School Opportunity for Negro Pupils in Kentucky
4. Robert Prentiss Daniel	Virginia Union University Teachers College-Columbia	A.B. A.M.	Columbia University	Educational Psychology	1932	PhD	A Psychological Study of Delinquent and Non-Delinquent Negro Boys
5. Inez Beverly Prosser	Prairie View College Samuel Huston College University of Colorado	B.A. M.A.	University of Cincinnati	Educational Psychology	1933	PhD	Non-Academic Development of Negro Children in Mixed and Segregated Schools
6. Howard Hale Long	Howard University Clark University	B.S. M.A.	Harvard University	Educational Psychology	1933	EdD	Analysis of Test Results from Third Grade Children Selected on the Basis of Socio-Economic Status
7. Ruth Howard Beckham	Simmons College (Mass.) Columbia University	B.S. M.S.	University of Minnesota	Psychology	1934	PhD	A Study of the Development of Triplets
8. Oran Wendle Eagleson	Indiana University Indiana University	B.A. A.M.	Indiana University	Psychology	1935	PhD	Comparative Studies of White and Negro Subjects in Learning to Discriminate Visual Magnitude
9. Martin David Jenkins	Howard University Indiana State	B.S. M.S.	Northwestern University	Educational Psychology	1935	PhD	A Socio-Psychological Study of Negro Children of Superior Intelligence
10. Frank Theodore Wilson	Lincoln University Columbia University	B.A. A.M.	Columbia University	Educational Psychology and Religious Education	1937	EdD	A Program of Religious Education in the Liberal Arts College at Lincoln University
11. Alberta Banner Turner	Ohio State University Ohio State University	B.S. M.S.	Ohio State University	Psychology	1937	PhD	The Effects of Practice on the Perception and Memorization of Digits Presented in Single Exposure
12. John Henry Brodhead	Temple University Temple University	B.S. M.S.	Temple University	Psychology	1937	EdD	Educational Achievement and Its Relationship to the Socio-Economic Status of the Negro in the High School of Philadelphia

Table 24 Continued

Name	Institutions; Bachelor's and master's degrees		Doctorate degree institution	Major subject	Year	Degree	Dissertation title
13. Carlton B. Goodlett	Howard University	B.A.	University of California Meharry Medical College (M.D.)	Psychology	1938	PhD	A Comparative Study of Adolescent Interests in Two Socio-Economic Groups
14. Carol Blanche Cotton	Oberlin College	—	University of Chicago	Psychology	1939	PhD	A Study of the Reactions of Spastic Children to Certain Test Situations
15. James Duckery	University of Pennsylvania	—	Temple University	Psychology	1939	EdD	An Intensive Survey of a Negro Special Class School
16. Rose Butler Browne	Rhode Island State College	—	Harvard University	Educational Psychology	1939	EdD	A Critical Evaluation of Experimental Studies of Remedial Reading
17. Kenneth Bancroft Clark	Howard University Columbia University	B.A. M.S.	Columbia University	Psychology	1940	PhD	Some Factors Influencing the Remembering of Prose Materials
18. Herman George Canady	Northwestern University Northwestern University	B.A. A.M.	Northwestern University	Psychology	1941	PhD	Test Standing and Social Setting
19. Frederick Payne Watts	Howard University Howard University	B.A. A.M.	University of Pennsylvania	Psychology	1941	PhD	A Comparative and Clinical Study of Delinquent and Non-Delinquent Negro Boys
20. James Thomas Morton, Jr.	University of Illinois Northwestern University	B.A. M.A.	Northwestern University	Psychology	1942	PhD	The Distortion of Syllogistic Reasoning Produced by Personal Convictions
21. James Arthur Bayton	Howard University Howard University Columbia University	B.A. M.S.	University of Pennsylvania	Psychology	1943	PhD	Interrelations Between Levels of Aspiration, Performance, and Estimates of Past Performance
22. Mamie Phipps Clark	Howard University Howard University	B.A. M.A.	Columbia University	Psychology	1944	PhD	Changes in Primary Mental Abilities with Age
23. Shearley Oliver Roberts	Brown University Brown University	B.A. A.M.	University of Minnesota	Psychology	1944	PhD	The Measurement of Adjustment of Negro College Youth
24. Roger Kenton Williams	Claflin College Claflin College	B.A. M.S.	Pennsylvania State University	Psychology	1946	PhD	A Comparison of College Students Classified by a Psychological Clinic as Personality Maladjustment Cases and as Vocational Guidance Cases
25. Howard Emery Wright	Lincoln University Ohio State University	B.A. M.A.	Ohio State University	Psychology	1946	PhD	Racial Humor: A Value Analysis

#	Name	Undergraduate / Graduate Institution	Degrees	Doctoral Institution	Field	Year	Degree	Dissertation
26.	Alonzo Davis	Howard University / Howard University	B.S. / M.S.	University of Minnesota	Psychology	1947	PhD	Status Factors in Personality Characteristics of Negro College Students
27.	Mae Pullins Claytor	Howard University / New York University	B.A. / M.A.	New York University	Educational Psychology	1948	EdD	The Construction of a Home Adjustment Questionnaire Which May Be Used as an Aid in the Detection of Symptoms of Juvenile Delinquency
28.	Mildred McK. Statterwhite			University of California	Educational Psychology	1948	PhD	The Vocational Interests of Negro Teachers and College Students
29.	George Thomas Kyle	University of Illinois / University of Illinois	B.A. / M.A.	New York University	Psychology	1949	PhD	A Comparison of Normal and Schizophrenic Subjects in Level of Aspiration, Frustration, and Aggression
30.	Roderick Wellington Pugh	Fisk University / Ohio State University	B.A. / M.A.	University of Chicago	Psychology	1949	PhD	An Investigation of Some Psychological Processes Accompanying Concurrent Electric Convulsive Therapy and Nondirective Psychotherapy with Paranoid Schizophrenia
31.	Herman Hodge Long	Talledega College / Hartford School of Religion	B.A. / M.A.	University of Michigan	Educational Psychology	1949	PhD	Sensitivity Response Patterns of Negro and White Groups to Anger-Producing Social Stimuli
32.	Montraville Isadore Claiborne	Fisk University / University of Michigan	B.A. / M.A.	New York University	Psychology	1950	PhD	Classroom Mental Hygiene Practices of Teachers in Negro Public Schools and the Relation between These Practices and Certain Factors Which Influence the Quality of Teaching

CHARLES HENRY THOMPSON (1896–1975)

Charles H. Thompson, the son of Patrick Henry and Sara Estelle (Byers) Thompson, was born in Jackson, Mississippi, where both of his parents were teachers at Jackson College. His father, a graduate of Wayland Theological Seminary (later Virginia Union University) sent his son to Wayland Academy in Virginia to complete his high school education. After graduation in 1914, Thompson enrolled at Virginia Union University and, by doubling his course enrollments, was graduated in 1917 with a B.A. degree.

Following a brief period as an army cadet at the army training camp in Des Moines, Iowa, he enrolled at the University of Chicago, completing a second undergraduate degree in 1918. He was then drafted into the army and stationed at Camp Grant (Illinois) and later in France. He remained in the army for nineteen months as an Infantry Personnel Regimental Sergeant Major. Upon discharge, Thompson returned to the University of Chicago. Carrying a double major in education and psychology, he was awarded the master's degree in 1920 and his Ph.D. in 1925. At Chicago Thompson studied under William Scott Gray, Harvey Carr, and C. H. Judd.

Thompson, the first black American to receive a doctor's degree in educational psychology, had a strong desire to become a psychiatrist, but he decided on the study of educational psychology because he did not know of any black person who was a psychiatrist at that time.

From 1920 to 1921, Thompson was an instructor in psychology at Virginia Union University. From 1922 to 1924, he was Director of Instruction at Alabama State Normal School. From 1925 to 1926, he was an instructor in psychology and social science at Sumner High School and Junior College in Kansas City, Kansas. In 1926 he began a lifelong association with Howard University, where he held positions as professor of education, Dean of the College of Liberal Arts, and Dean of the Graduate School. For more than thirty years, Dr. Thompson was editor-in-chief of the *Journal of Negro Education*. With his leadership, the journal grew to become a highly prestigious periodical; as editor, Dr. Thompson wrote more than one hundred articles and editorials.

Dr. Thompson has served on a number of national and international committees on education. He is a fellow of the American Association for the Advancement of Science and holds membership in a number of professional organizations.

128

ALBERT SIDNEY BECKHAM (1897–1964)

A native of Camden, South Carolina, Albert Beckham was born to Calvin Albert and Elizabeth (James) Beckham on September 21, 1897. His father was a merchant and businessman in Camden. Beckham received his early education in the Presbyterian schools of Camden and was privately tutored. He attended Pennsylvania's Lincoln University and graduated with a B.A. degree in 1915. He then enrolled at Ohio State University and earned a second bachelor's degree in 1916. The following year, the twenty-year-old Beckham was awarded the M.A. degree in psychology.

As America was then embroiled in World War I, Beckham applied for duty in the Air Corps. But he was refused training and told that he could contribute to the war effort by teaching psychology at a college. As a result, Beckham was assigned to the Sergeant's Army Training Corps (SATC) from 1917 to 1918 as a war professor in psychology at Wilberforce University in Ohio. He remained at Wilberforce as assistant professor of psychology until 1920.

When Beckham's parents moved from South Carolina to New York City, he joined them in New York, and in 1921 and 1922 he was editor of the New York City Dispatch until he became a Jay Gould Fellow in Psychology at New York University. In 1924 he accepted an instructorship at Howard University; from 1925 to 1928, he was an assistant professor of psychology. During this period, he founded the psychological laboratory at Howard, the first of its kind in a black institution of higher learning. In 1928 he returned to New York and continued psychological study at NYU, where in 1930 he received a Ph.D. in psychology.

A Fellow of the National Committee for Mental Hygiene at the Illinois Institute for Juvenile Research from 1929 to 1930, Dr. Beckham also served as senior assistant psychologist at the institute from 1931 to 1935. There he conducted research and developed such reports as "Minimum Levels of Intelligence for Certain Occupations," which became a guide for state institutions for training the mentally handicapped.

Dr. Beckham was affiliated with Chicago's Board of Education, Bureau of Child Study, from 1935 to 1964. He served several school districts, but his longest term of service was spent as psychologist at DuSable High School. There he counseled thousands of black youths, many of whom today credit his guidance as a key factor in their later (and for some, distinguished) careers. At DuSable he innovated the services of a school psychology clinic and developed parent counseling groups in which the study of

adolescence helped mothers and fathers to deal understandingly with their children. The clinic reached into the community and brought together ministers whose parishes included families of DuSable students; for the first time in that community, a church-neighborhood-school relationship became viable.

Dr. Beckham continued to publish research throughout his career. Studies from the Institute for Juvenile Research in Chicago included "A Study of Race Attitudes in Negro Children of Adolescent Age" and "A Study of the Intelligence of Colored Adolescents of Different Social Economic Status in Typical Metropolitan Areas." The latter surveyed the largest number of black children to be included in one study.

While at DuSable High School, Dr. Beckham published sev-

131

eral psychological studies: "Incidence of Frustration in a Counseled and Non-Counseled High School Group," "Narcolepsy Among Negroes," and "Incidence of Albinism in Negro Families."

From 1960 to 1963, he was psychological consultant at Ada S. McKinley Community House, Chicago, where he evaluated retarded children, adults, and women in vocational training classes. Here, as at other sites, he combined research with psychological service. The unpublished "A Study of Retarded Children and Their Mothers" details physical handicaps of retarded children and the relation between child's and mother's tested intelligence.

With his wife, Dr. Ruth W. Howard, Dr. Beckham conducted a practice in clinical psychology known as The Center for Psychological Service; in this capacity, he serviced private and public agencies. At one time, he was consultant to the Civil Aeronautics Administration.

His professional affiliations included: Chicago Psychology Club, Illinois Psychological Association, American Psychological Association, American Association for the Advancement of Science, and Beta Kappa Xi scientific society. He was a board member of the Chicago Friends of the Mentally Ill and the People's Rehabilitation Foundation.

His civic affiliations included service as a board member of the Boy Scouts of Chicago, the Planned Parenthood Society, and the Grace Church Community Center. He was a member of Alpha Phi Alpha fraternity, the American Heritage Society and the American Forestry Association.

In 1945, he received an Honorary Doctor of Laws degree from Lincoln University.

ROBERT PRENTISS DANIEL (1902–1968)

Robert Daniel, the son of Charles James and Carrie (Green) Daniel, was born in Ettricks, Virginia. He graduated magna cum laude from Virginia Union University with a B.A. degree in 1924. Daniel received his master's degree in education in 1928 and his Ph.D. in educational psychology from Columbia University in 1932.

He was an instructor of mathematics at Virginia Union University from 1923 to 1925 and an instructor of English and education the following year. From 1926 to 1928, he was an assistant professor of education; from 1928 to 1936, he was professor of education and psychology and Director of the Extension Division at Virginia Union. In addition, from 1932 to 1936, Dr. Daniel was Director of the Division of Educational Psychology and Philosophy at Virginia Union, and in the summers of 1935 and 1936 he was a visiting professor of education at Hampton Institute in Virginia.

In 1936, Dr. Daniel was inaugurated as president of Shaw University in North Carolina. He remained in this capacity until 1950, when he assumed the presidency of Virginia State College, a position he held until his death in 1968.

Dr. Daniel was an ordained Baptist minister who served on numerous church governing boards and was active in many educational and psychological organizations. His professional affiliations included membership in the American Psychological Association, National Association for the Study of Negro Life, American Association of School Administrators, American Teachers Association, and the National Education Association. In 1953, he was nominated president of the Conference of Presidents of Negro Land Grant Colleges. His awards included the Distinguished Service Award in Education from the National Urban League in 1948.

Dr. Daniel was the author of "A Psychological Study of Delinquent Negro Boys" and of numerous other journal articles in the fields of psychology and education.

INEZ BEVERLY PROSSER (1897–1934)

Inez Beverly Prosser, born in Yoakum, Texas, in 1897, was the oldest daughter in a family of eleven brothers and sisters. Her father, Samuel Andrew Beverly, was a waiter, and her mother, Veola Hamilton Beverly, was a housewife. She attended public schools in Yoakum, graduating from high school in 1912. She was a very studious youngster who read constantly, and as a result her parents sent her to nearby Prairie View Normal College for teacher training. After graduation from Prairie View, she taught for a brief period in the Yoakum Colored Schools before accepting a teaching position in Austin, Texas. While teaching in Austin she attended Samuel Houston College and soon received her B.A. degree "with distinction" in education.

Following her marriage to Rufus A. Prosser, she attended the University of Colorado and earned a master's degree in educational psychology. Returning to Austin, she taught education courses at Tillotson College and became the dean and registrar of the college. During the 1929–1930 college year, Inez Prosser played a dominant role in a number of events at Tillotson, including the arrangement of the visit of Dr. George Washington Carver and the remodeling of several buildings. She received recognition as "an excellent teacher and leader."

In 1930 Inez Prosser accepted a teaching position and administrative duties at Tougaloo College in Mississippi. The award of a General Education Board Fellowship in 1931 provided her with the financial assistance to pursue further graduate studies in educational psychology at the University of Cincinnati. In 1933, Inez Prosser earned her Ph.D. in educational psychology, the first black American woman to receive this degree. Her dissertation, the "Non-Academic Development of Negro Children in Mixed and Segregated Schools," was one of the earliest investigations into the social domain of elementary school children. At her graduation, Dr. Prosser was remembered as a "small petite woman whose doctoral gown had simply engulfed her."

Dr. Prosser was devoted to helping her brothers and sisters to secure college educations. To this end, she provided encouragement and a "college fund" to assist whatever brother or sister wanted to attend college. All her brothers and sisters completed high school and six of them completed college.

She was a tireless scholar at a time of overwhelming odds against black people achieving such recognition as a doctor of philosophy degree. One year after receiving her doctorate, she

was killed in an automobile collision near Shreveport, Louisiana.

In 1968, at the HemisFair exposition in San Antonio, Texas, Dr. Prosser was cited for her contribution to Texas culture.

She was a member of Alpha Kappa Alpha sorority.

HOWARD HALE LONG (1888–1948)

Howard Long, the son of Thomas and Annie (Vassar) Long, was born in News Ferry, Virginia, and obtained his preparatory education at the Wayland Academy in Richmond, Virginia. He received his B.S. degree and the Bachelor's Diploma in Education from Howard University in 1915. As a graduate, Long studied experimental psychology under G. Stanley Hall at Clark University, where he was awarded a master's degree in 1916. From 1916 to 1917, he was a psychology instructor at Howard University. He then served during World War I as an infantry first lieutenant in Europe.

After the war, Long became Dean at Paine College in Georgia; in 1923, he was appointed Dean of the School of Education at Knoxville College. The following year, he accepted a position as Supervising Principal in the public school system of Washington, D.C. From 1925 until his retirement in 1948, he was an Associate Superintendent in Charge of Educational Research for the District of Columbia schools.

During this period, he published several research monographs in educational psychology and provided leadership for many research projects. His early publications, "An Analysis of Some Factors Influencing Alpha Scores by States" and "On Mental Tests and Racial Psychology" were documents frequently quoted in the field of psychometry. Howard Long received his Doctor of Education degree in educational psychology from Harvard University in 1933, the first graduate of Howard University to earn this degree.

After retiring from the District of Columbia school system, he became Dean of Administration at Wilberforce State College in Ohio. He was married to the former Ollie Mae Guerrant and was a member of Alpha Phi Alpha fraternity.

RUTH WINIFRED HOWARD (1900–   )

Ruth W. Howard became the first black woman in the United States to receive the highest academic degree in psychology when she was awarded a Ph.D. by the University of Minnesota in 1934.

Ruth Howard was the eighth child in the family of the Reverend and Mrs. William James Howard of Washington, D.C. Throughout her childhood, she was exposed to the social work attitude of her father's ministry at the Zion Baptist Church in Washington. This, coupled with an affinity for books and reading, soon led her to recognize a desire to work with people and to study human behavior. After graduation from Dunbar High School in 1916, she attended Simmons College in Boston under a National Urban League grant. Majoring in social work, she received her B.S. degree in 1921 and her M.S. degree in 1927. From 1923 to 1929, she practiced social work, first in community organization with the Cleveland Urban League and later in child welfare with the State Welfare Agency.

A strong desire for more knowledge of human dynamics led Ruth Howard to the study of psychology. Under a Laura Spelman Rockefeller Fellowship for Parent Education, she studied at Columbia University's Teachers College and School of Social Work in 1929–1930. Continuing under a second Rockefeller fellowship, she studied at the University of Minnesota from 1930 to 1934. There she collaborated in research in areas of child development at the University's Institute for Child Development. In 1934, she received her Ph.D. in psychology and child development at Minnesota. Her doctoral research, "A Study of the Development of Triplets," was the first published study of a sizeable group of triplets of varying ages from several ethnic groups.

Shortly after completing her doctoral work, she married psychologist Albert S. Beckham and settled in Chicago. Following a clinical internship at the Illinois Institute for Juvenile Research, she entered into private practice in clinical psychology.

From 1940 to 1964, Dr. Howard served with her husband as co-director for the Center for Psychological Services. Concurrent professional duties have involved her with several schools of nursing; from 1940 to 1964 she was psychologist for Chicago's Provident Hospital School of Nursing, and she consulted at schools of nursing in Kansas City, Missouri, and Jacksonville, Florida. She conducted clinics at Kentucky State College and Edward Waters College in Jacksonville. She was lecturer and consultant to adolescents for the Evanston (Illinois) public schools (1953–1955). In 1955 she was reading therapist at the University of Chicago's

Reading Clinic. From 1966 to 1968, she was a staff member for Worthington and Hurst Psychological Consultants. In 1964–1966, she was a psychologist for the McKinley Center for Retarded Children and, in 1968–1972, a psychologist for the Chicago Board of Health, Mental Health Division.

Dr. Howard has continued in private practice and currently is working as psychological consultant for children's programs at Abraham Lincoln Centre and as consultant for Daniel D. Howard Associates in Chicago.

Dr. Howard's publications include: "Fantasy and the Play Interview," "Intellectual and Personality Traits of a Group of Triplets," and "Developmental History of a Group of Triplets."

Her professional affiliations are: Chicago Psychology Club, Illinois Psychological Association, American Psychological Association, American Association for the Advancement of Science, and the International Reading Association.

Her civic affiliations including being a board member of: YWCA of Chicago, Women's International League for Peace and Freedom, American Association of University Women, and the National Association of College Women. She is a member of International House Association, Art Institute of Chicago, Hyde Park-Kenwood Community Conference, and Delta Sigma Theta sorority. Her current interests lie in mental retardation, child development and family counseling.

ORAN WENDLE EAGLESON (1910–   )

Oran Eagleson was born in Unionville, Indiana, but before he was one year old, his parents took him to Bloomington, Indiana, where he lived until a few months after completing work for the Ph.D. degree at Indiana University in 1935. It was at Indiana that he had also earned his B.A. (1931) and M.A. (1932) degrees.

The summer before entering the ninth grade, with both parents deceased, Eagleson went to work in a shoe repair shop to help out with the expenses being borne by his sister, Katie M. Eagleson, and brother, Halson V. Eagleson. (His brother later became a professor of physics at Howard University after several years on the faculty at Morehouse College.) Young Eagleson held the job as shoe shiner and shoe repair finisher through high school, college, graduate school, and even for about five months after receiving his doctorate.

At the beginning of his undergraduate training, Eagleson thought he would major in philosophy. But he found the course in introductory psychology, taught by S. L. Crawley, to be so interesting and challenging that he decided psychology would be his major subject and philosophy his minor. Both as undergraduate and graduate student, he was greatly impressed and influenced by psychologists J. R. Kantor, W. N. Kellogg, W. F. Book, and R. C. Davis (who served as chairman of his doctoral committee).

After receiving his Ph.D. in August 1935, Dr. Eagleson could not find employment in his new profession until February 1936, when he had a job offer from North Carolina College for Negroes in Durham. There he taught courses in psychology, sociology, economics, and philosophy until financial readjustments at the college and a pending salary reduction made Dr. Eagleson look elsewhere for employment. S. O. Roberts, later at Fisk University, had recently left Spelman, a woman's college in Atlanta, where he had initiated the first psychological laboratory in any of the institutions of the Atlanta University Center. His leaving vacated a teaching position in psychology that was then offered to Dr. Eagleson.

In September 1936, Dr. Eagleson accepted the Spelman College position. The new position not only paid a higher salary, but it also offered the opportunity to teach just psychology courses. At this period, psychology courses were for elective or supplementary purposes—not a field in which the administration encouraged students to major; it was not until a few years later that psychology was listed as a major field of study. Dr. Eagleson encouraged many students to consider psychology as a major field,

141

and gradually the number of psychology majors increased. In the early years of the major program, all but a few students were interested in teaching, social work, or homemaking, and their interest in psychology was in the application of the discipline to these areas or to the improvement of their everyday living patterns.

While teaching at Spelman, Dr. Eagleson also served as an exchange professor at Atlanta University, where he offered courses and directed theses for graduate students. His association with the supervision of theses was continued up to the time he assumed the duties of Dean of Instruction at Spelman in September 1954, a position he held until September 1970, when he was appointed Callaway Professor of Psychology.

Dr. Eagleson was associated with the research program of the Cooperative Experimental Summer School of the Atlanta University Center and was co-director of the Morehouse-Spelman Intensified Pre-College Program. He also served as special lecturer and consultant in orientation and training projects conducted by the Peace Corps, Head Start, and several school systems in Georgia.

Dr. Eagleson's early research interests lay in racial comparisons, puzzle solving, handwriting, and musical topics. His research articles include: "Comparative Studies of White and Negro Subjects in Learning to Discriminate Visual Magnitude," "The Success of Sixty Subjects in Attempting to Recognize Their Handwriting," and "Identification of Musical Instruments When Heard Directly and Over a Public-Address System."

Dr. Eagleson is presently concerned with human values, religious behavior, and the measurement of personality.

MARTIN DAVID JENKINS (1904–   )

Martin Jenkins, the son of David and Josephine Jenkins, was born in Terre Haute, Indiana. He attended the public schools of Terre Haute, graduating from Wiley High School in 1921. He attended Howard University in Washington, D.C., receiving his B.S. degree in mathematics in 1925. From 1925 to 1930, he was a highway bridge contractor, in partnership with his father, in the firm of David Jenkins and Son. During this time, Markin Jenkins attended Indiana State College (now University) and earned a second undergraduate degree in teacher education.

In 1930, John Grandy, president of Virginia State College, visited Terre Haute on a speaking engagement and offered Jenkins a teaching post. He accepted the appointment, becoming an instructor of education at VSC from 1930 to 1932, when he was awarded a fellowship to pursue graduate studies at Northwestern University. (This was the first award of its kind to be granted to a black American at Northwestern.) He was awarded a master's degree in 1933.

Jenkins remained at Northwestern, studied under Prof. Paul A. Witty, and received his doctorate in 1935. His dissertation, "A Socio-Psychological Study of Negro Children of Superior Intelligence," and subsequent studies, became classics in educational psychology. While many psychologists were debating the question of equality of black-white intelligence test scores during this period, Jenkin's investigation discovered that intelligence levels for blacks were as high as those recognized for the white population. Furthermore, he identified a representative sample of "superior" black students, one of whom had the highest IQ then on record.

From 1935 to 1937, Dr. Jenkins was registrar and professor of education at North Carolina Agriculture and Technical College. In 1937, he accepted the position of Dean of Instruction at Cheyney State Teachers College in Pennsylvania. From 1938 to 1948, Dr. Jenkins was a professor of education at Howard University with a one-year duty assignment as a Senior Specialist in Higher Education, Office of Education (HEW). In 1948, he assumed the presidency of Morgan State College in Maryland, a position he held until 1970. He was then Director, Office of Urban Affairs, American Council on Education (Washington, D.C.) from 1970 to 1974. He is currently a consultant in higher education.

Dr. Jenkins has published more than eighty books, monographs, and articles. He has lectured widely in the United States and abroad; under the auspices of the U.S. Department of State, he delivered lectures on educational psychology at colleges and uni-

versities in France, Norway, Sweden, Greece, Italy, and Lebanon.

Dr. Jenkins is a Diplomate in Clinical Psychology (ABEPP). He has been decorated by the Liberian Government as Knight of the Liberian Humane Order of African Redemption. His numerous other awards include the Andrew White Medal from Loyola College, the Department of the Army Outstanding Civilian Service Medal, and a Commendation for Model Cities activities by the Departments of Health, Education, and Welfare and Housing and Urban Development.

He has been awarded honorary doctor's degrees by the University of Liberia, Delaware State College, Howard University, Indiana State University, Johns Hopkins University, Lincoln University, and Morgan State College. He is a member of the Phi Beta Kappa honor society and the Kappa Alpha Psi and Sigma Pi Phi fraternities.

In 1974, the Martin David Jenkins Behavioral Science Center, at Morgan State College, was dedicated in his honor.

145

ALBERTA BANNER TURNER (1909–)

Alberta Turner, daughter of James L. and Mable Banner, was born in Chicago, Illinois, and moved to Columbus, Ohio, at a very early age. Her father was a cement contractor and her mother was a beautician who devoted her life to hard work in order to finance her daughter's college education. Alberta Turner attended the public schools of Columbus, graduating from East High School in 1925. At the age of sixteen, she enrolled at Ohio State University; she received her B.S. degree in Home Economics in 1929.

She had planned to continue as a graduate student at OSU but instead was persuaded to accept a position in the home economics department at Wilberforce University (now Central State College) in Xenia, Ohio. As head of the Department of Home Economics at Wilberforce, she attended Ohio State in the summer months and earned an M.S. degree in education in 1931. Her major field was child development and her graduate advisor was experimental psychologist S. Renshaw, who later became her doctoral dissertation advisor. In 1935, Alberta Turner received a Ph.D. in psychology from OSU.

From 1935 to 1936, she was head of the home economics department at Winston-Salem College in North Carolina. From 1936 to 1937, she was professor of psychology and head of the department of Home Economics at Lincoln University in Missouri. The years 1938 to 1939 found Dr. Turner head of the Department of Home Economics at Southern University in Louisiana. In 1939, she returned to North Carolina to head the home economics department at Bennett College for Women. She remained at Bennett until she returned to Columbus, Ohio in 1942 on maternity leave.

Unexpectedly in 1944, Dr. Turner was offered her first full-time employment in psychology as a clinician at the Ohio Bureau of Juvenile Research. For the next twenty-seven years, Dr. Turner worked at the bureau in a variety of positions, promoted from clinical psychologist to supervising psychologist and then to the position of chief psychologist. In 1963, she was promoted to the Central Administrative Office of the Ohio Youth Commission and became the Director of Research for the Ohio Youth Commission. She served in this capacity until her retirement in 1971.

During the period of her employment with the Commission, Dr. Turner found time to teach a variety of graduate courses at Ohio State University. She was also a psychologist at the Ohio Reformatory for Women. She served for four years as a member of the National Advisory Council for Vocational Rehabilitation and the Rehabilitation Institute of Chicago. She also served as a

146

member of the Regional Advisory Council for the Research and Training Center at Northwestern University's McGraw Medical Center. She is past president of the National Jack and Jill of America and past national program director for Links, Inc.

In 1971, a citation from the State of Ohio and the Ohio Youth Commission read, "Alberta Banner Turner, Ph.D., has been synonymous with mention of the field of juvenile rehabilitation and treatment in Ohio for 27 years. She has played a very active role in its history. . . ." After her retirement, she became administrative assistant to Weight Watchers of Central Ohio, a position in keeping with her research interest in the psychological aspects of obesity.

Dr. Turner's publications include "The Effects of Practice on the Perception and Memorization of Digits Presented in Single Exposure" and "The Psychologist at the Juvenile Diagnostic Center: Past, Present, and Future."

Her honors and awards include Gamma Psi Kappa, Ten Women of the Year by the Columbus Citizen Journal, Alpha Kappa Alpha Award for Community and Scholastic Endeavors, and Pi Lamda Theta Citation. She has served as a member of the Criminal Justice Supervisory Commission and the Ohio Society for Crippled Children and Adults.

Dr. Turner holds Diplomate status in Clinical Psychology (ABEPP) and is certified by the Ohio Psychological Association. She is married to John G. Turner, retired from the U.S. Department of Labor, and is the mother of two children. She resides in Columbus, Ohio, and Freeport, Grand Bahamas, and is currently working on a study of "Incest Cases of Female Adolescents."

JOHN HENRY BRODHEAD (1898–1951)

John Brodhead was born in Washington, New Jersey, the son of Robert and Elizabeth Brodhead. He was graduated from the West Chester State Normal School in Pennsylvania in 1919. In 1937, he received his Doctor of Education degree in educational psychology from Temple University.

Dr. Brodhead was a teacher and principal in the Philadelphia school system from 1919. During the 1940s, he was principal of Reynolds School, one of the largest schools in Philadelphia.

Dr. Brodhead was active in a number of educational movements and organizations. He was elected president of the American Teachers Association (ATA) in 1949. He served as president of the Association of Pennsylvania Teachers, the New Era Educational Association, and the Pennsylvania Educational Association. He was a charter member of the Philadelphia Commission on Participation of Negroes in National Defense and was a later organizer and chairman of the Citizens Committee for Integration of Negro Nurses. This committee ultimately led to the admittance of black nursing trainees into the Philadelphia General Hospital.

He was the author of "The Educational and Socio-Economic Status of the Negro in the Secondary Schools of Pennsylvania."

KENNETH BANCROFT CLARK (1914–   )

Kenneth Clark, born in the Panama Canal Zone, is the son of Arthur and Miriam (Hanson) Clark. At the age of seven he came to the United States and received his public school education in New York City. He enrolled at Howard University in 1929 and several years later became a naturalized citizen. He received his B.S. degree in psychology from Howard University in 1935 and the following year was awarded the M.S. degree. He enrolled at Columbia University and, while a graduate student, was a research assistant for the comprehensive study of Gunnar Myrdal, *An American Dilemma*. He was awarded the Ph.D. degree in psychology in 1940.

Dr. Clark has taught at Queens College (New York) and, since 1942, has been a professor of psychology at City College in the City University at New York. Dr. Clark is president of the Metropolitan Applied Research Center, which he founded in 1967 "as a catalyst for change and as an advocate for the poor and powerless in American cities." He has been a visiting professor at Columbia University, the University of California at Berkeley, and Harvard University. Dr. Clark has been a member of the New York State Board of Regents since 1966 and is a member of the Board of Trustees of the University of Chicago. He is also a member of the New York Urban Development Corporation.

Dr. Clark was awarded the Spingard Medal by the NAACP in 1961 and the Kurt Lewin Memorial Award by the Society for Psychological Study of Social Issues in 1966. Among the colleges and universities which have granted him honorary degrees are: Haverford College, Yeshiva University, Oberlin College, Johns Hopkins University, Amherst College, New York University, Columbia University, and the University of Massachusetts.

The U.S. Supreme Court cited Dr. Clark's work on the harmful effects of segregation in its 1954 decision, *Brown v. Board of Education*. He is the author of several books and articles, including *Prejudice and Your Child* (1955) and the prize-winning *Dark Ghetto: Dilemmas of Social Power* (1965). He is co-author, with Jeannette Hopkins, of *Relevant War Against Poverty* (1968) and co-editor, with Talcott Parsons, of *Negro American* (1968). His most recent work is *Pathos of Power* (1974).

Dr. Clark is past president (1970–1971) of the American Psychological Association (the first black to hold that office) and former president of the Society for the Psychological Study of Social Issues. His fraternal memberships include Sigma Xi and Phi

Beta Kappa. He recently announced plans to join Gunnar Myrdal for a new study of racial problems in the United States.

Dr. Clark is married to Dr. Mamie Phipps Clark and is the father of two children.

CARLTON BENJAMIN GOODLETT (1914–   )

Carlton B. Goodlett, the son of Mr. and Mrs. A. R. Goodlett, was born in the black community of Orange Hill at the outskirts of Chipley, Florida. His mother received a teaching credential from Florida A & M College, and his father completed night high school in Omaha, Nebraska, where the family had then moved. Young Goodlett attended the public schools of Omaha, graduating from Central High School in 1931. While a high school student, he "discovered what it meant to be a black person in the white man's world." As a result, he identified strongly with his blackness and decided to attend a black university in spite of the opportunities he had to enroll in several white universities.

Armed with a national Alpha Phi Alpha fraternity scholarship, he began studies at Howard University in Washington, D.C., then an extremely segregated city. The proud seventeen-year-old from the midwest ran head-on into the realities of racism; the accumulation of his experiences led Goodlett to devote his life's work to fighting racism and its by-products.

Receiving his B.S. degree in psychology under the tutelage of Francis C. Sumner, he proceeded to the University of California at Berkeley to earn a master's degree in abnormal psychology and made plans to attend medical school. However, several events altered his plans as well as his goals. The first black person to study psychology in the graduate division at the University of California, Goodlett met and became the protege of Harold and Mary Jones. The Joneses, who had established several institutes of child welfare in the United States, persuaded Goodlett to work at the Berkeley Institute as a graduate student. His efforts at the Berkeley Institute eventually became the basis of his Ph.D. dissertation, "A Comparative Study of Adolescent Interests in Two Socio-Economic Groups." In 1938, he was awarded a Ph.D. in psychology at the University of California.

In 1938, Dr. Goodlett joined the faculty of West Virginia State College and taught educational psychology, learning, and statistics. While at WVSC, Goodlett attempted to organize an Institute for the Study of the Negro Child, but he could not obtain funding from the General Education Fund Foundation, which had previously funded and established child study institutes in several major white universities. He also worked with Herman Canady in an attempt to organize professional blacks in psychology during the late 1930s (see Chapter 5).

Dr. Goodlett went on to author several articles and monographs, including "The Mental Abilities of Twenty-Nine Deaf and

Partially Deaf Negro Children" and "The Reading Abilities of the Negro Elementary Child in Kanawha County, West Virginia." After two years of teaching at West Virginia State College, Goodlett enrolled in Meharry Medical College in Tennessee in 1940 to study medicine. While a student at Meharry, he taught courses in psychology at Meharry Medical College, Fisk University, and Tennessee Agricultural and Industrial College. The energetic Dr. Goodlett also found time to teach courses at Fort Valley State College in Georgia during two summer vacations.

After receiving his M.D. degree, he interned at Homer G. Phillips Hospital in St. Louis and then did a brief stint as a house physician at Maury County Colored Hospital in Columbus Tennessee, before returning to northern California in 1945. Since that time, Dr. Goodlett has been involved in community action programs and has served as a catalyst in many civil rights efforts. In 1947 he became co-publisher of the San Francisco *Sun Reporter* and in 1951 publisher; he is currently serving as president of the National Newspaper Publishers Association—The Black Press of America.

Dr. Goodlett has been president of the San Francisco NAACP, is president of the San Francisco Foundation to Study our Schools, is a director of the San Francisco Council of Boy Scouts of America, and is a member of the Society of Sigma Xi and the National Committee on Africa. He is also chairman of the California Black Leadership Conference, a trustee of the Third Baptist Church, and former vice president of the San Francisco Council of Churches.

In 1966 Dr. Goodlett ran in the gubernatorial primary election in California and came in third in a field of six Democrats. In 1967–1968 he taught a course at San Francisco State College entitled "Group Conflict in Urban America."

Dr. Goodlett maintains that there are two deadly menaces to the survival of black people in America: racism and the effects of alcohol and drug adiction. Under his sponsorship, a three- to five-year study is projected, to examine "The Role of Alcohol, Hard Drugs and Narcotics on the Black Experience," by four national black organizations: National Newspaper Publishers Association, National Bar Association, National Business League and National Medical Association.

Dr. Goodlett believes that blacks in the behavioral sciences, particularly in psychology, sociology, and psychiatry, have a special responsibility to study in depth the role of racism on the quality of the black experience in the nation and a further responsibility to lead in the development of techniques for the eradiction of racism in America.

HERMAN GEORGE CANADY (1901–1970)

Herman G. Canady, the son of Rev. Howard T. and Mrs. Anna (Carter) Canady, was born in Okmulgee, Oklahoma. He attended Douglass Elementary School and Favor High School in Guthrie, Oklahoma. In 1922, he graduated from the high school department of George R. Smith College in Sedalia, Missouri.

In the fall of 1923, with the assistance of a Charles F. Grey scholarship, Canady enrolled at Northwestern University's Theological School with the intention of becoming a minister. There he discovered an intense interest in the behavioral sciences and he decided to major in sociology. Throughout his undergraduate years, he worked at odd jobs around Evanston, Illinois, to pay his living expenses.

In June 1927, he graduated from Northwestern with a B.A. in sociology and a minor in psychology. He remained at Northwestern and the following year was awarded the M.A. degree in clinical psychology. Canady's master's thesis, "The Effects of Rapport on the IQ: A Study in Racial Psychology," criticized the neglect of the importance of the race of the examiner in establishing testing rapport and offered suggestions for establishing an adequate environment. This document became a historical treatise and a classic in its field.

In September 1928, after the departure of Francis Sumner from West Virginia Collegiate Institute (now West Virginia State College), Canady accepted an offer to join that faculty and assume the vacant chairmanship of the psychology department. Under Canady's vigorous leadership, WVSC became the nation's leading black college in psychological research. During a three-year period, 1936–1939, Canady conducted a host of social-psychological research projects and published many journal articles. Of these studies, "Adapting Education to the Abilities, Needs and Interests of Negro College Students" and "Individual Differences and Their Educational Significance in the Guidance of the Gifted and Talented Child" became significant resources for many black educational institutions. His "Psychology in Negro Institutions" was the only published research effort that evaluated the status, training, and research efforts of early psychologists in black colleges and universities.

In 1939, Canady was awarded a General Education Board fellowship which allowed him to take a leave of absence from West Virginia in 1939 and 1940 to return to Northwestern and complete his Ph.D. studies. In June 1941, he was awarded a doctorate in psychology. His dissertation, "Test Standing and Social Setting:

A Comparative Study of the Intelligence-Test Scores of Negroes Living Under Varied Environmental Conditions," became a widely-quoted study in sociology as well as in psychology.

Upon his return to West Virginia, Dr. Canady again assumed a research leadership posture and conducted a series of significant studies in social psychology. His record as a psychologist and researcher was eminent.

Dr. Canady was a visiting lecturer to schools and colleges under the auspices of the American Friends Service Committee (1946) and consultant to the Pacific Coast Council on Intercultural Education and Intercultural Projects of the San Diego City Schools (1947). He was a part-time clinical psychologist for the Mental Health Unit, Veterans Administration, Huntington, West

Virginia (1948–1953) and for the West Virginia Bureau of Mental Hygiene (1947–1968).

In 1950, Dr. Canady was designated Diplomate, American Board of Examiners in Professional Psychology. His awards included Man of the Year, 1949, from Alpha Chapter of Omega Psi Phi fraternity, and Middle-Eastern Provincial Achievement Award, 1951, from Kappa Alpha Psi fraternity. He held fraternal memberships in Sigma Xi, Alpha Kappa Delta, and Kappa Alpha Psi. His professional memberships included: Fellow of the American Association for the Advancement of Science, Fellow of the American Psychological Association, American Teachers Association (Chairman of the Department of Psychology, 1938–1945), American Association of University Professors, West Virginia State Psychological Association (President, 1954–1955), West Virginia Academy of Science (Chairman of the Department of Psychology, 1952–1953 and 1955–1956), and the West Virginia State Teachers Association.

Dr. Canady, who retired in 1968, was a faculty member and chairman of the psychology department at West Virginia State College for forty years. He was an active participant in the struggle for equal rights. He received Northwestern University's Alumni Merit Award and an honorary doctor's degree from West Virginia State College.

In 1934, Herman Canady married the former Julia Witten of Tip Top, Virginia, and was the father of Joyce A. and Herman G. Canady.

FREDERICK PAYNE WATTS (1904–   )

Frederick Watts was born in Staunton, Virginia. His father, Charles H., an avid reader, was at one time a farmer and later performed house maintenance services; his mother, Harriett, was intensely interested in rearing her five children. His parents instilled high ideals in all their children and encouraged them to become college educated—with the result that one became a physician, one a dentist, and one a psychologist.

Frederick Watts completed elementary and high school in Washington, D.C. His early professional goal was to become an ophthalmologist, and to this end he enrolled at Howard University with the intention of becoming a physician. To help finance his education, he worked at many odd jobs. The Army ROTC program at Howard was financially helpful. Watts's intense interest in "why people misbehave" led him to enroll in several psychology courses, and his psychology professor, the dynamic Albert S. Beckham, inspired him to major in psychology.

After graduating from college in 1926, with a double major in French and psychology, he received a teaching fellowship in psychology which provided him with the financial assistance needed to complete his master's degree at Howard. After a brief year of teaching at Kittrell College in North Carolina, he returned to Howard University to teach in the summer of 1928. By this time Beckham had left Howard, and Francis Sumner joined Watts forming a two-man department of psychology. Watts remained at Howard until 1942, teaching psychology with Sumner and another colleague, Max Meenes, who joined the department in 1930. During this period Watts published with Sumner a scholarly investigation of the "Rivalry Between Uniocular Negative After-Images and the Vision of the Other Eye" and his own research on "A Comparative and Clinical Study of Delinquent and Non-Delinquent Negro Boys."

In 1941, Watts received his Ph.D. in clinical psychology from the University of Pennsylvania, the first black person to receive this degree from that institution. While at Pennsylvania, he studied under L. Witmer, M. Viteles, and S. Fernberger.

In October 1942, Dr. Watts was called to serve in the army as a preinduction classification officer and personnel consultant during World War II. In this capacity, he assisted in setting up psychological testing facilities for the Baltimore induction station and supervised in the assignment and counseling of enlisted personnel in various military installations. Upon his discharge, as a captain in the adjutant general's department, he was appointed as-

sistant chief clinical psychologist for the Veterans Administration regional office in Philadelphia.

In 1948, Dr. Watts returned to Howard to establish the Liberal Arts Counseling Service, which was later expanded to encompass the total student body (and renamed the University Counseling Service). Watts conducted a number of institutional studies at Howard, including "Initial Group Counseling of Freshmen" and "A Study of the College Environment." Other studies accomplished at this time included "The Development of a Behavior Judgment Scale" and "Developmental Counseling."

Dr. Watts is affiliated with a number of professional organizations and is a Diplomate in Clinical Psychology (ABEPP). He was director of the University Counseling Service and taught psychology part-time until his retirement from Howard University in 1970.

He was married to the late Louise Armstead Watts and is the father of four daughters. Today he resides in Washington, D.C., and his current interests continue to be in counseling and clinical psychology.

JAMES ARTHUR BAYTON (1912–   )

James Bayton, born in Whitestone, Virginia, is the son of George and Helen Bayton; his father was a physician and a graduate of Howard University's medical school. Bayton graduated from Temple University's high school in 1931, and he then enrolled at Howard University as a chemistry major with the intent of eventually entering medical school. But Bayton enjoyed his psychology courses, taught by Francis Sumner, Max Meenes, and Frederick Watts, and it was not long before he had taken enough of them to declare psychology a major subject. After graduation with a B.A. in 1935, and with the assistance of a graduate scholarship, Bayton began studies for the M.S. degree in psychology.

When he was awarded the graduate degree at Howard, it was clear that the medical profession had lost out to his desire to become a professional psychologist. Bayton entered Columbia University in 1936, studying under R. S. Woodworth and A. T. Poffenberger; however, at the death of his father, Bayton transferred his graduate studies to the University of Pennsylvania in order to be nearer his home. At Pennsylvania, he studied under L. Witmer, S. W. Fernberger, M. G. Preston and M. Viteles. (It is interesting to note that Fernberger had also taught Francis Sumner and Max Meenes at Clark University and Frederick Watts at Pennsylvania.)

With his dissertation research under way, Bayton was offered a teaching position at Virginia State College. The prestige of VSC and the financial depression of the late 1930s together led Bayton to interrupt his studies to become an associate professor of psychology. He remained in this position from 1939 to 1943, during which time he performed research and published journal articles. Among his students at Virginia State was an enthusiastic young man who later became chairman of the psychology department at Florida A & M University, Dr. Joseph Cyrus Awkard. In 1943, with the aid of the prestigious Harrison fellowship at the University of Pennsylvania, Bayton was awarded his Ph.D. in psychology.

During the war years 1943–1945, Dr. Bayton was a social science analyst with the U.S. Department of Agriculture, working with R. Likert, D. Cartwright and A. Campbell. In 1945, he was appointed professor of psychology at Southern University in Louisiana. In 1946, Bayton moved to Morgan State College in Maryland as professor of psychology. In 1947, he returned to his alma mater, Howard University, as a professor of psychology. In 1948, Bayton answered a request to rejoin the Department of Agriculture, on a part-time basis, to provide assistance in their consumer behavior studies. His work with the Department of Agri-

culture was recognized by a Superior Service Award for "superior accomplishments in the development and application of psychological concepts and techniques in the field of commodity market research and for outstanding ability and leadership. . . ."

Dr. Bayton has since held a number of positions concurrent with his teaching duties. He was vice-president of National

Analysts, 1953–1962 and again 1966–1967; vice-president of Universal Marketing Research, 1962–1966; senior fellow at the Brookings Institution, 1967–1968; and senior staff psychologist at Chilton Research Services, 1968 to the present.

He has served on several advisory committees, including the Research Advisory Committee, Social Security Administration, HEW (1962–1964), and the Advisory Committee on Agricultural Science, Department of Agriculture (1965–1968). He was chairman of the committee appointed to study equal employment opportunity policies in the National Aeronautics and Space Administration. He has conducted lectures and seminars in many of America's leading universities.

Dr. Bayton's skill in directing marketing research has been of national record; his projects have included research for: DuPont, IBM, Armstrong Cork, Chrysler, Eli Lilly, Curtis Publishing, Johnson and Johnson, Schick, Pet Milk, American Dairy Association, Federal Reserve Board, Smith Kline, French, Proctor and Gamble, and the Office of Naval Research. He was responsible for another series of research projects over a period of thirty years dealing with the self-concept of black people. He has also served as an expert witness for the NAACP Legal Defense Fund in cases dealing with legal aspects of school desegregation and discrimination in employment.

His current interests are in government and corporate policy research, motivation, and consumer behavior. Dr. Bayton is the author of *Tension in the Cities—Three Programs for Survival* and a host of professional journal articles, including "Single Stimulus Versus Comparative Methods in Determining Taste Preferences," "Method of Single Stimulus Determinations of Taste Preferences," "Interrelations Between Levels of Aspiration, Performance, and Estimates of Past Performance," and "Intervening Variables in the Perception of Racial Personality Traits." A major project of his deals with the identification of factors related to racial tension in military settings.

Dr. Bayton was chairman of the psychology department at Howard from 1966 to 1969. He is a member of Phi Beta Kappa, Sigma Xi, and Omega Psi Phi fraternities. At present, he is a professor of psychology at Howard.

JAMES THOMAS MORTON, JR. (1911–1974)

Born in Greenwood, South Carolina, James Morton was taken to Evanston, Illinois, by his parents when he was eighteen months old. As an active, civic-minded youngster growing up in Evanston, Morton found mathematics and French easy subjects and reading an enjoyable but insatiable habit. He was athletically inclined and won numerous awards from the city recreational department for his athletic ability. Much of his time was spent with youth groups in attempts to open in them an awareness of the possibilities for a better intellectual and economic life for the youth of that day. On a voluntary basis, he taught classes in Negro history to members of the Evanston community and various church groups. His involvement in the Ebenezar Methodist Church of Evanston led to still more community activities.

After graduation from Evanston Township High School in 1931, Morton matriculated at the University of Illinois at Champaign. His desire to major in psychology was discouraged by one university counselor who informed him that "psychology was no career for the Negro and it was best for him to go into law or medicine." Nevertheless, he graduated with a B.A. in psychology in 1934.

With an accumulation of courses in both psychology and sociology, Morton enrolled at Northwestern University and received his M.A. in 1935. He began his teaching career at Bennett College in North Carolina, but he returned to Northwestern to earn his Ph.D. in psychology in 1942. Returning to Bennett, he was appointed Dean of Instruction.

Then Dr. Morton was drafted into the army as a private. His military career was uneventful; however, near the end, he was given a direct commission as a psychologist, the only black American to receive such an appointment during World War II.

Upon his discharge, he accepted a position at Dillard University in Louisiana as a professor and counselor. In 1946, he accepted an appointment at Tuskegee Veterans' Hospital in Alabama, becoming the first black chief psychologist for the VA. While in Alabama, he produced a study (unpublished) of black psychologists, hoping to use the data to assist in the recruitment of young black scholars in psychology. He also compiled an immense data-bank relating to the intelligence of black Americans as measured by the Wechsler-Bellevue Intelligence Test. In 1948, Dr. Morton was designated Diplomate in Clinical Psychology in the APA's first listing of Diplomate status awards. Morton was later elected to Fellow status in the APA.

164

In 1953, Dr. Morton returned to Evanston, Illinois, entered private practice, and subsequently became employed at the VA Hospital at Downey, Illinois. He also affiliated with other hospitals and educational institutions in the Chicago area. At the time of his death, in 1974, he was coordinator of training for psychology Ph.D. candidates at the VA Hospital at Downey.

For many years, Dr. Morton was a pioneer for blacks in clinical psychology and a strong advocate for equal education and employment opportunities for minority youth. His chief professional interests were in clinical and social psychology. He was married to the former Lorraine Hairston and the father of one child, Elizabeth.

MAMIE PHIPPS CLARK (1917–   )

Mamie Phipps Clark was born in Hot Springs, Arkansas, the daughter of Harold H. and Katie F. Phipps. Her father was a physician in Hot Springs, where she attended public schools from elementary to high school. Upon graduation from Langston High School in 1934, she enrolled at Howard University with the intent of majoring in mathematics; while at Howard she met her future husband, Kenneth B. Clark, and through his influence decided to major in psychology. In 1938, she was awarded the B.A. degree, magna cum laude, in psychology. With University Fellow status, she remained at Howard and subsequently earned her M.A. in psychology in 1939. In 1944, as a Rosenwald fellow at Columbia University, Mamie Clark received her Ph.D. in psychology.

Dr. Clark's professional experiences have included duties as a research psychologist for the American Public Health Association from 1944 to 1945; from 1945 to 1946, she assumed duties as a research psychologist for the United States Armed Forces Institute, New York Examination Center at Teachers College, Columbia University. In 1946, Dr. Clark became executive director of the Northside Center for Child Development in New York City, a position she presently holds.

Dr. Clark has at the same time held many other positions; she was a psychologist for the Riverdale Children's Association (1945–1946) and a visiting professor of experimental methods and research design at Yeshiva University (1958–1960). She has been a member of the board of directors for the New York Mission Society, Teachers College at Columbia University, New York City Public Library, American Broadcasting Company, Museum of Modern Art, and the Phelps Stokes Fund. Dr. Clark has served with several advisory groups including the Harlem Youth Opportunities Unlimited (HARYOU) and the National Headstart Planning Committee. In 1957, she received the Alumni Achievement Award of Howard University for outstanding post-graduate service in psychological research. In 1972, Dr. Clark received the honorary Doctor of Humane Letters degree from Williams College.

She holds membership in the American Psychological Association and Phi Beta Kappa, and she is a fellow of the American Association of Orthopsychiatry. She is the author of numerous monographs and research studies. Her publications, "Segregation as a Factor in the Racial Identification of Negro Pre-school Children," "The Development of Consciousness of Self and the Emergence of Racial Identification in Negro Pre-school Children," and

"Skin Color as a Factor in Racial Identification of Negro Pre-
school Children" (all with K. B. Clark) have become classics in the
field of psychology.

Dr. Mamie Clark is the mother of a son and a daughter.

SHEARLEY OLIVER ROBERTS (1910–   )

S. O. Roberts, born in Alexandria, Virginia, was the son of George and Esther (Ragland) Roberts. He graduated from Howard High School in Wilmington, Delaware, in 1928. His B.A. and M.A. degrees (with honors) were granted at Brown University in June 1932 and June 1933, respectively. His major was psychology and his minor work was in education and economics; his principal teachers at Brown were L. Carmichael and H. Schlosberg.

The University of Minnesota in 1944 conferred on Roberts a Ph.D. in child welfare (child development) and psychology. He had studied there with J. E. Anderson, F. Goodenough, B. F. Skinner and D. G. Paterson, under a George Davis Bivin grant in mental hygiene. Special work in human development on a General Education Board fellowship was done at the University of Chicago with R. J. Havighurst and E. W. Burgess.

Past and present experiences of Dr. Roberts include teaching, serving as dean of students, individual and group psychological testing and interviewing, and research in child development. He has held positions at Atlanta University (instructor, 1933–1936), Dunbar Junior College (acting dean, 1942–1943), and at Arkansas AM&N College (teacher and Dean of Students, 1939–1942 and 1944–1945). The psychology department at Fisk was established under his chairmanship in 1951–1952.

Dr. Roberts has been the recipient of numerous federal and private foundation grants. His areas of special interest are child development, mental health principles, testing, cultural differences, and personality adjustment.

He was a delegate to the White House Conference on Youth in 1950; he has participated in a number of other organizations and special meetings (the Thayer Conference on Psychology and Schools was one of these). He was editor of the Fisk-Meharry Local Preparatory Commission's Report on "Negro American Youth, Mental Health and World Citizenship." He is a Fellow of the Society for Research in Child Development and of the Division of Developmental Psychology of the American Psychological Association. He is a member of the American Educational Research Association and of Sigma Xi and Psi Chi societies. He has served on the Council of Psychological Resources in the South, the Governor's Committee on Training and Research in Tennessee, the board of the Mental Health Center of Middle Tennessee, the Nashville Metropolitan Action Commission (as member and vice-chairman), and other scientific and professional groups. Dr. Roberts is a professor of psychology and of education and the chairman of

Fisk University's psychology department. He is lecturer in psychology at Meharry Medical College. At Fisk, he inaugurated the Program in Child Life and Development in 1950.

He is married to Marion Pearl Taylor of Little Rock, Arkansas; they have three daughters, Esther Pearl Ashley, Barbara Taylor Stone, and Kay George.

ROGER KENTON WILLIAMS (1914–   )

Roger Williams was born in Harrisburg, Pennsylvania, where his father, James H. Williams, was a public school teacher and his mother, Carrie Williams, was busy rearing him, his two brothers, and a sister. After his graduation from Harris Senior High School in 1932, he attended Claflin College in South Carolina, where he earned his B.A. degree, magna cum laude, in sociology. While an undergraduate, Williams was president of the Student Government Association and class president, and he held other campus leadership positions.

Following his graduation in 1936, he remained at Claflin College as an Assistant to the Dean in charge of student personnel. During that time Williams realized the need to learn more about human behavior and the behavioral sciences. A decision to attend graduate school resulted in his enrollment at Pennsylvania State University in College Park in 1940.

In 1941, Williams accepted an appointment as associate professor of education and psychology at North Carolina Agricultural and Technical College, remaining there until his career was interrupted by military duty during World War II. For more than three years, Williams served in the U.S. Coast Guard as a Chief Yeoman in Recruitment and Morale. After his discharge in 1945, and with the financial assistance of the G.I. Bill of Rights, he returned to PSU and completed his Ph.D. studies in psychology in 1946. His dissertation focused upon "A Comparison of College Students Classified by a Psychological Clinic as Personality Maladjustment Cases and as Vocational Guidance Cases." While at Pennsylvania State University, he studied under C. C. Peters, E. B. Ormer, and R. G. Bernreuter.

In 1946, Dr. Williams returned to North Carolina A&T College as a professor of psychology and Director of the Veterans Administration Guidance Center. He remained in these positions until 1948, when he accepted appointments as professor of education and Director of Student Personnel at Morgan State College. From 1949 to 1972, he was professor of psychology and chairman of the psychology department. From July 1968 to January 1969, he was in addition acting dean of the graduate school at Morgan. From February 1972 to June 1973, he held the position of Vice-President for Academic Affairs. At present, Dr. Williams is Vice-President for Planning and Operations Analysis at Morgan State University.

He has also held a number of concurrent positions. From 1957 to 1968, Dr. Williams was director of Morgan's Independent

Study Project, and for several years he was a consultant to the Ford Foundation. In 1972, he was named chairman of the Maryland State Board of Examiners of Psychologists. His research publications include "Creating Institutional Opportunities for Producing More Black Ph.D.'s in Psychology" (with Bayton and Roberts), "Appearance, Features and the Concept of Black Militancy" (with Gregory Shannon), and a number of academic placement tests. His current research interests include student research supervision, independent study designs, and statistical application of qualitative data.

Dr. Williams is married to the former Beryl E. Warner and is the father of one son.

HOWARD EMERY WRIGHT (1908–   )

Howard Wright, the son of William H. and Evelyn (Ferguson) Wright, was born in Philadelphia. He attended elementary school in Washington, D.C., and Atlantic City High School in New Jersey. He entered Lincoln University in Pennsylvania in 1928 and received his B.A. degree in 1932. He then enrolled in the graduate school at Ohio State University and, in 1933, Wright was awarded the M.A. degree in psychology. His thesis research, "An Analysis of Results with Certain Tests of Interests and Attitudes," indicated his early interest in social psychology.

At twenty-five years of age, Wright became principal of the Campus Laboratory School at Albany State College in Georgia, a position he held until 1934. From 1936 to 1939, he was principal of Aracoma High School in Logan, West Virginia, and from 1940 to 1945, he was principal of the Campus Laboratory School at Prairie View College in Texas. At Prairie View he was also associate professor of education and director of teacher training. Wright then returned to Ohio State in 1945 as a graduate teaching assistant; he completed his Ph.D. in psychology in 1946.

From 1945 to 1948, Dr. Wright was chairman of the psychology department at North Carolina College in Durham. In the fall of 1948, he became chairman of the division of education and psychology at Texas Southern University, remaining in this position until 1953, when he returned to North Carolina to reassume the charimanship of the psychology department.

In 1961, Dr. Wright was appointed President of Allen University in South Carolina. In 1965, he was regional director of Community Action Programs for the Office of Economic Opportunity in Washington, D.C. From 1966 to 1967, he was branch chief of the Division of College Support for the U.S. Office of Education. Wright accepted the academic deanship at Maryland State College in Princess Anne in 1967; three years later he became acting chancellor at the University of Maryland.

In 1972, Dr. Wright became Director, Division of Social Sciences at Hampton Institute in Virginia, and in September 1974, he became professor of psychology at Salisbury State College in Maryland. He presently holds this position.

Dr. Wright has been a board member of: Home for Dependent Children (Houston, Texas), Child Guidance Clinic (Durham, North Carolina), and Advisory Committee to the Civil Rights Commission and Vice-President of Victory Savings Bank (Columbia, South Carolina). His fraternal memberships include the Elks, the Masons, and Omega Psi Phi. His professional affiliations in-

172

clude the American Association of University Professors and the American Psychological Association. His research interests remain in the areas of social psychology and attitudinal testing.

In 1936, he married the former Anne M. Nelson of Walkertown, North Carolina; they are the parents of Beverly and Howard Wright.

Notes

1. C. R. Drew, "Negro Scholars in Scientific Research," *Journal of Negro Education*, 35 (1950), pp. 135–136; part of an address delivered before the Annual Meeting of the Association for the Study of Negro Life and History, New York City, October 30, 1949.
2. J. Henry Alston, "Psychophysics of the Spatial Condition of the Fusion of Warmth and Cold in Heat," *American Journal of Psychology* (July 1920), pp. 303–312.
3. Personal correspondence with the author, September 4, 1974.
4. Arthur P. Davis, "The Negro Professor," *The Crisis* (April 1936), p. 103.
5. Ibid., p. 104.
6. A. M. Carter, "An Assessment of Quality in Graduate Education," *American Council on Education*, Washington, D.C., 1966. The ten prestigious departments of psychology, according to this report, were: Harvard, Stanford, Michigan, Berkeley, Yale, Illinois, Minnesota, Wisconsin, Brown, and Iowa.
7. Lauren Wispe et al., "The Negro Psychologist in America," *American Psychologist*, 24:2 (1969), pp. 142–150.

7

Francis Cecil Sumner –Father of black American psychologists

It was 1920, eleven years after the Department of Psychology at the small, prestigious Clark University in Worcester, Massachusetts, had propelled the seclusive psychoanalytic movement to consequence by inviting Sigmund Freud to America. Freedom from slavery was scarcely fifty years old and nearly one quarter of America's black people were designated as illiterate. History at that time had recorded a total of 239 lynchings of black people in the United States. Overt racial discrimination was the order of the day; racist views were not only accepted among America's masses but were significantly present in scholarly journals, textbooks, and medical reports.

Between 1876 and 1920 only eleven blacks, out of a total of ten thousand recipients, had earned Ph.D. degrees in America.

Francis C. Sumner

Edward S. Bouchet, who received the doctor of philosophy degree in physics at Yale in 1876, was the first black to receive a doctorate degree in America. The first American to receive a doctorate in *psychology* was Joseph Jastrow at Johns Hopkins in 1886, but it was not until thirty-four years later that a black American accomplished the same goal. In 1920, a twenty-five-year-old black, World War I veteran successfully defended his doctoral dissertation before a group of prominent scholars and psychologists at Clark University. Francis Cecil Sumner thus became the first black man in the western hemisphere to receive the doctor of philosophy degree in psychology, a feat accomplished in spite of innumerable social and physical factors mitigating against such achievements by black people in America.

Francis C. Sumner was born in Pine Bluff, Arkansas, on December 7, 1895. He had one brother, Eugene. His parents, David Alexander and Ellen Lillian Sumner, adopted their last name "in token of respect for the one time Massachusetts Senator, Charles Sumner."[1] Francis Sumner received his early education in the elementary schools of Norfolk, Virginia, and Plainfield, New Jersey; since secondary education for blacks during the early 1900s was rare, he did not have a formal high school education. Instead, as his father had done, young Sumner advanced his own education through intense reading and discussion of a wide variety of subjects. His parents provided guidance in his quest for knowledge by securing for him old textbooks and other reading materials. Reading was not only an early habit with Sumner; it proved to be a major contributor to his academic success and a lifelong pattern of behavior.

Lincoln University: 1911–1915

In the fall of 1911, at the age of sixteen, Sumner was permitted to enroll as a freshman at Lincoln University in Pennsylvania after passing a written examination (since he had no high school diploma). His parents worked to pay their son's fees and tuition at Lincoln, and Sumner himself worked, part-time and during the summer breaks, at many odd jobs to contribute to his college expenses. In 1915, at the age of twenty, Sumner was nominated valedictorian of his class, earning his B.A. degree in philosophy, magna cum laude.

During his senior year at Lincoln, Sumner began a series of correspondences with James P. Porter, a professor of psychology and Dean of the College at Clark University, concerning his possible enrollment in Clark College. It was Porter who subsequently notified Sumner of his acceptance to the undergraduate college for the fall semester of 1915[2] and later arranged for Sumner to live with a "fine colored family in Worcester."[3]

Perhaps it was Sumner's fondness for reading that led him to want to become a great writer. There was little doubt of his ability to succeed in this, for his talent had been recognized by most of his teachers. G. Stanley Hall later noted that Sumner "has a real literary interest (and) is an extraordinarily voracious reader."[4] In 1914, Sumner forthrightly expressed his desire to be a writer to a Clark official: "My sole ambition is to write. Yet I shall have to fall back on something—teaching—or government employ as an immediate means of livelihood."[5] He went on: "Many have endeavored to discourage me in my projected career and yet a few old heads have advised me to follow my own bent rather than in the least to be dissuaded by anyone."[6]

Clark College: 1915–1916

When Sumner enrolled at Clark College in 1915, he pursued his literary interests by enrolling in English courses (The Novel; Advanced Composition; Versification) and taking electives in foreign languages and psychology. This combination of studies led him to be described a year later by his fellow students as "more or less of a psychologist, and you can usually find him at the last table at the further end of the library reading something in the line of 'psychological' novels."[7] In June 1916, Sumner received his second B.A. degree.

Lincoln University: 1916–1917

In the fall of 1916, he returned to Lincoln University as graduate student and instructor of psychology and German. During the year at Lincoln he studied religious psychology, philosophy, and German. Teaching, which was part of his graduate course assignment, constituted the bulk of his program; he taught Psychology of Religion, Mysticism, and Rationalism; Experimental Psychology; Social Psychology; and Intermediate and Advanced German.

Near the end of his first semester of work at Lincoln, Sumner recognized a desire to continue in the field of psychology and a need for further advanced training. He began to investigate graduate schools, including the American University and the University of Illinois, for possible admission and financial assistance. Early in 1917, he again sought the advice and assistance of Dean Porter at Clark:

> The old problem of getting situated or of finding one's level is again before me. I am convinced that I can't do the work I want to do without further study. The chief hindrance to carrying out the latter is financial backing.[8]

While Sumner was strongly interested in psychology, he vacillated between psychology and German as his possible major, for he felt that graduate programs in German offered the best chances for financial assistance. Nevertheless, his leanings toward psychology were evident:

> Psychology appears the most vital subject in which I would specialize. Many have tried to discourage me from that subject, saying that it was not much in demand among colored people. However, I seem to see a great latent demand for it.[9]

Dean Porter's reply reinforced Sumner's bias toward psychology:

> I would not say one word to dissuade you from the study of German if you feel that that is your strongest interest. I thoroly (sic) believe that if you make of your study of psychology a practical matter you can be of the greatest service to your own people.[10]

Porter continued to spell out occupational possibilities in psychology:

> This need not to be confined to teaching, for the reason that many opportunities are more and more in evidence in which the knowledge of psychology may be turned to practical account for those in whom you may be interested.[11]

Finally, on March 28, 1917, after discouraging responses from American University and the University of Illinois, Sumner wrote G. Stanley Hall, president of Clark University, to ask his consideration for a junior fellowship in psychology award "to study race psychology."[12] Since Sumner's teaching and graduate study arrangement at Lincoln University was without pay, he further impressed upon Hall his need for financial assistance and his inability to find a teaching position: "I would drop out of school and teach for awhile if I could get an appointment but so far none has appeared."[13]

Shortly after Sumner received his M.A. degree from Lincoln in June 1917, he received word that he had been accepted at Clark and awarded a fellowship as a senior scholar in psychology.

Clark University: 1917–1918

As Sumner prepared to return to Massachusetts to enter the Ph.D. program at Clark, the American Expeditionary Forces began landings in France; America had entered World War I. Sumner was immediately classified 1-A for military service, and he was well aware that he might be drafted in spite of the government's intention "to limit the number of colored troops in the Army."[14] Nevertheless, Sumner began his graduate studies, and on October 15, 1917, G. Stanley Hall, Sumner's chief instructor, approved his application for candidacy for the Ph.D. in psychology. The following week, Sumner passed his French and German language qualifying examinations and was well into his course studies.

Sumner's acute awareness of social injustice toward black people in America led him to recognize the inconsistencies of popular accusations against World War I German *kultur* as being "symbolic of barbarity, immorality, and irreligiousness."[15] The ensuing conflict in his mind resulted in his writing several letters to the local newspaper expressing what was to become an unpopular view to several of Worcester's leading white citizens. Sumner's first letter to the editor said, in part:

> Within the soul of each member of my race the conscious self is saying, Serve your country, while the unconscious from the depths is thundering, You have a poor cause to serve. On the one side the martial music and the tramp of soldiers exhort to arms and patriotism; on the other side in movements of sweet, silent thought the words 'God punish America' ring of salvation.[16]

Several months later, as the fighting in Europe increased, Sumner wrote another lengthy letter criticizing the claim that America was "a self-appointed paragon of virtue."[17] In this letter, Sumner made an interesting psychoanalytic analysis of racism in America —which inflamed the local citizenry.

Sumner's statements, with their detailed arguments, resulted in several verbal attacks against the "Fellow in Psychology who has raised a traitor's voice in defamation of American ideals and of the spirit of American people."[18] The reaction to Sumner's letters reached such proportions that he was summoned to the U.S. Post Office in Worcester to give reason why he should not be listed as an enemy alien and his mail held up. (The case was referred to the Boston regional post office; Sumner convinced the postal authorities of his good intentions and his loyalty to America, and no further action was initiated by the post office.) On May 28, 1918, Sumner formally apologized, in a letter to the newspaper, for the circumstances of his "disloyalty to my native country."[19] A later memorandum, undoubtedly written by G. Stanley Hall, cleared the air by suggesting further explanations for Sumner's actions:

> Having lived in the South, he has taken a great interest, under the influence of the colored leader Du Bois, who was Booker Washington's chief rival, in lynchings, of which he has a ghastly collection of newspaper accounts, and some of which have come pretty near to him. . . . He was also smarting under the fact that by a rearrangement of the tables at the dining-hall, there happened to be at least some one at each table who preferred not to eat with a negro, so that a special table had been arranged for him and others who had befriended him.[20]

As the spring semester drew to a close, so did much of the discussion of Sumner's letters to the newspaper.

During this time, Sumner had finished a study, "Psychoanalysis of Freud and Adler," and was attempting to have it published by Badger Publishing Company. In the summer of 1918, he wrote Dr. Hall to ask him to consider the merits of this work as a potential doctoral dissertation.[21] Before he was able to elicit a response from Hall, Sumner was drafted into the army.

Military Service: 1918–1919

As soon as he had completed his basic training with the 48th Company, 154th Depot Brigade at Camp Meade, Maryland, Sumner wrote Hall to bring him "up-to-date." He expressed disappointment over the interruption of his graduate studies and commented that he was "trying hard to take my medicine with the courage befitting a regular soldier." Sumner found time to humor his mentor in the same letter by drawing a parallel between army food and one of Hall's theoretical postulates:

> I noticed here at camp that they feed one such much of raw onion to give one long wind. I find that it does have something of that effect upon me and that the fact has caused me to associate it with the "second breath" phenomena.[22]

Sumner felt he had a good chance of attending the army officer training camp and in another letter asked Hall to write his commanding officer to recommend him for such training.[23] Hall promptly responded with a recommendation for officer training, but it was too late: Sumner had been transferred to Company M, 808th Pioneer Infantry, and he was on his way to the battlefields of France as a twenty-two-year-old company sergeant.

Recalling his overseas experiences several years later, Sumner described the horrifying effects of the war:

> The greatest fear I have ever experienced was that which I experienced when first introduced to the cannonade of German artillery. I did not fear submarines in crossing the Atlantic against which so many precautions were being taken; I did not fear exposure to the elements, to sleeping on the frozen ground or in rain-drenched fields; I did not fear the ravages of influenza, but my resistances broke when quartered in a little shell-raked town upon which enemy artillery was trained. The man-sized projectiles would burst with the fury of a gigantic explosion, causing to shudder within me every fibre.[24]

Though the Armistice was signed on November 11, 1918, Sumner's unit remained in France until mid-1919. But he began to prepare for his return to the United States and to Clark University. A letter to Hall early in 1919 asked for consideration for reappointment as a senior fellow in psychology and readmission for the 1919–1920 school year.[25] On May 2, 1919, Hall approved Sumner's appointment as a senior fellow for the academic year, 1919–1920. Writing from the Pontanezen Barracks at Brest, Sumner expressed his appreciation to Hall and spoke of his travels in France, telling how much he enjoyed that country and expressing a desire to live there.[26]

Clark University: 1919–1920

After his discharge, Sumner returned to Clark in the fall of 1919. With the assistance of a YMCA Scholarship for Veterans and the money he had saved during the war, he enrolled in psychology courses taught by Hall, E. G. Boring, S. W. Fernberger, and K. J. Karlson. On June 11, 1920, at 3:00 p.m., Francis Sumner defended his doctoral dissertation, "Psychoanalysis of Freud and Adler." Sumner's defense was approved and his thesis was "accepted" on the same day (Figure 7.1). The following day, the *Action of the Faculty* labeled his doctoral candidacy as "passed." On June 14, 1920, Francis Cecil Sumner became the first black American to receive the Ph.D. degree in psychology.

Sumner's dissertation, published in the *Pedagogical Seminary* (later renamed *The Journal of Genetic Psychology*), was called an outstanding interpretation of psychoanalytic theories. Hall commented on Sumner's work:

> [He] has made what I think a remarkable compilation of opinions, with a genuinely new contribution, for his Doctor's thesis on the Freudian psychanalysis (*sic*) . . . Sumner had a strong penchant for it [psychoanalysis] and really has shown unusual facility in mastering and even pointing out the limitations and defects of the great authorities in that field.[27]

The one journalistic account of Sumner's graduation was in *Crisis Magazine* in its annual article, "The Year in Negro Education." The article noted that two Doctor of Philosophy degrees and twelve Master of Arts degrees had been awarded to black graduate students during 1920:

> Since the cessation of the war many Negroes who ordinarily would have continued their education, instead have entered into industry. This is inevitable; however, we are especially proud of those of our race who keep the ranks in education. . . . PhD, Francis C. Sumner in psychology.[28]

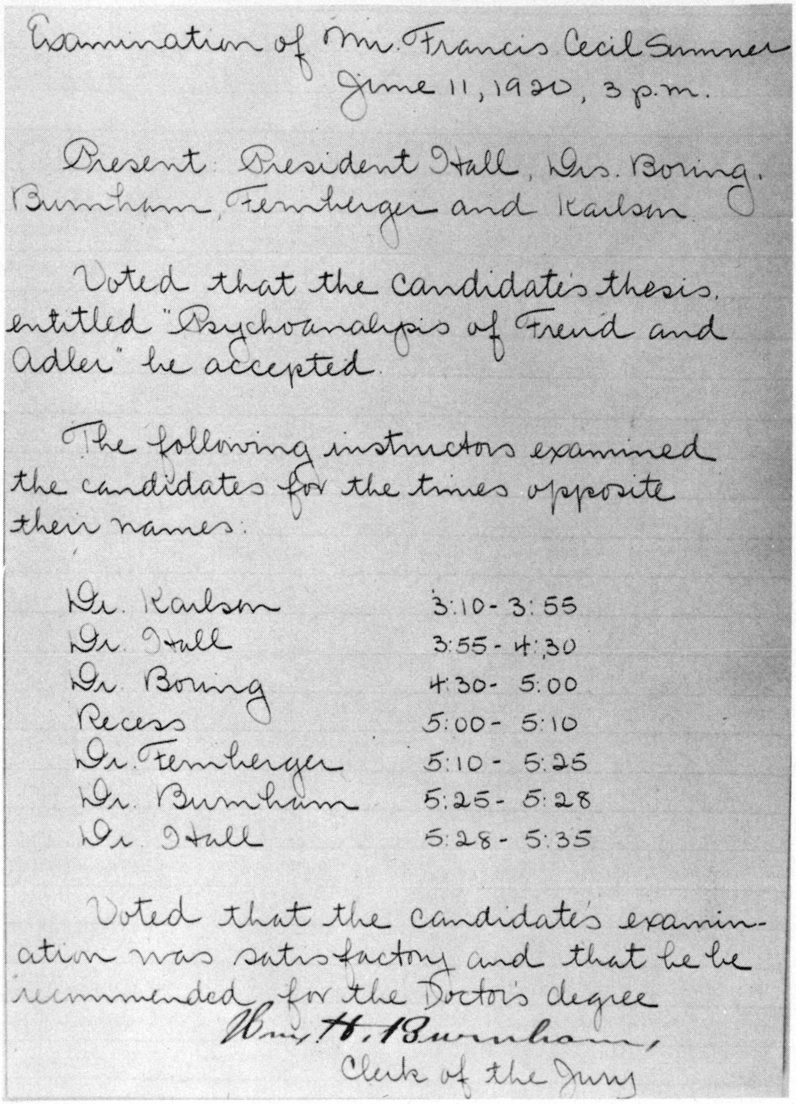

Examination of Mr. Francis Cecil Sumner
June 11, 1920, 3 p.m.

Present: President Hall, Drs. Boring, Burnham, Fernberger and Karlson.

Voted that the Candidate's thesis, entitled "Psychoanalysis of Freud and Adler" be accepted.

The following instructors examined the candidates for the times opposite their names:

Dr. Karlson	3:10 - 3:55
Dr. Hall	3:55 - 4:30
Dr. Boring	4:30 - 5:00
Recess	5:00 - 5:10
Dr. Fernberger	5:10 - 5:25
Dr. Burnham	5:25 - 5:28
Dr. Hall	5:28 - 5:35

Voted that the candidate's examination was satisfactory and that he be recommended for the Doctor's degree

Wm. H. Burnham,
Clerk of the Jury

Figure 7.1 (*Source:* University Archives, Goddard Library, Clark University, Worcester, Mass.)

West Virginia Collegiate Institute: 1921–1928

Dr. Sumner's first teaching position was as a professor of psychology and philosophy at Wilberforce University in Ohio during the 1920–1921 school year. In the summer of 1921, he taught at Southern University in Louisiana. In the fall of 1921, Sumner accepted an appointment as instructor of psychology and philosophy in the college department at West Virginia Collegiate Institute (now West Virginia State College). In a letter to Dean Porter at Clark, Sumner proudly told of the beauty of the campus, his salary, and plans by the state of West Virginia to make the Collegiate Institute a first class college.[29]

Shortly after his arrival at West Virginia, his lifelong emotional reaction to lightning and fire inspired him to make a contribution to the *American Journal of Psychology* upon being awakened one morning by a spring thunderstorm. Sumner's description of the "Core and Context in the Drowsy State"[30] was the first of a number of significant journal articles during his seven-year tenure at West Virginia (1924a, 1924b, 1925, 1926a, 1926b, 1927).

In one of his most timely articles, he attacked the classic heredity and environment dispute of the 1920s:

> In the current struggle between the respective protagonists of heredity and environment, the bone of contention has not been whether heredity or environment contributes all but rather whether heredity or environment contributes more in the determination of an individual's achievement. The proponents of the above mentioned explanations in their eagerness to defend the myth of Nordic superiority have intentionally or unintentionally assumed that which is to be proved, namely, that heredity counts all.[31]

All of Sumner's research studies while at West Virginia were done without outside financial assistance. He complained bitterly of the refusals he received when applying to white agencies for funds for research projects. His own field of psychology had to be neglected because of what he referred to as the *factor of race-prejudice,* which barred him from positions in northern universities, isolated him from his white colleagues, and, worst of all, exerted a peculiar effect upon his scholarship. He referred to this effect as the *obsession of race-persecution* and observed its attendant pathological symptoms, which forced him to engage most of his mental energies in contending with race-prejudice. Moreover, he called attention to the many black intellectuals who were forced to teach in rural environments because so many black institutions of higher learning were located in out-of-the-way sections of the country that were generally difficult to get to. In Sumner's words:

The intellectual Negro is often deprived by reason of the fact that Negro Universities and colleges are more frequently located in almost inaccessible rural districts. . . . In order to increase one's income that was at best half that of a white professor, he is forced to seek ways and means of increasing the family income. These side occupations run from preaching to common labor.[32]

In a series of controversial articles in 1926 and 1927, Sumner strongly endorsed some of the fundamentalist reforms of Booker T. Washington. Sumner declared: "Negro education is cryingly in need of a new dispensation. It needs awakening to the serious responsibility of morally redeeming the soul of black folk."[33] To accomplish this "new dispensation," he suggested that certain virtues be instilled in black students:

"Physical Well-Being; Simplicity in Living; Belief in God; Fondness for Literature, Art, and Music; Industry; A Contempt for Loud and Indiscreet Laughing and Talking; Thrift; Honesty; Courteousness; Respect; Race Pride; and Punctuality."[34]

Sumner believed that their acceptance as a part of western culture would clear the path for black people to enter the mainstream of American society. He also believed that there were far too many substandard black colleges and universities; he proposed "a drastic reduction in the number of Negro colleges from 40 to about five."[35] He wrote:

With only four or five large colleges advantageously located, with the resources of [the existing] forty institutions merged into the support of the smaller number and with salaries placed on a standardized basis, the teaching personnel [would] be rigorously selected on the basis of academic and professional qualifications. . . .[36]

And thus would he create first class institutions of higher learning. He further suggested a

division of labor among the five colleges of the new order. Two, at least, should be technical, that is, devoted to applied sciences such as home economics, business administration, electrical, chemical, civil, and mechanical engineering, social service, education, library science and agriculture. One college should specialize in the fine arts and literature, giving thorough training in music, painting, architecture, commercial art, sculpture, the histrionic art, and the writing of poetry and fiction. Two colleges should specialize in the liberal arts and sciences and should also have added to them professional schools of medicine, dentistry, law, and religion.[37]

Finally, Sumner criticized the practice of the semester system of instruction. He believed that the semester division of the school year did not allow adequate time for content mastery: "It is far more important for a student to learn thoroughly and in all their

ramifications three subjects a year (rather) than in isolated frag-
ments ten or twelve subjects."[38]

One of his final articles at West Virginia, Sumner's treatise on
"The Nature of Emotions," systematically evaluated several concepts of emotion from a behavioristic stance. In this evaluation,
Sumner called for the importance of understanding and training
the emotions of children. He criticized the "great evil of undisci-
plined emotions in the home" and illustrated how this resulted in
an "unfortunate augmentation of the conflict of the individual
with the social milieu."[39]

Howard University: 1928–1954

When Sumner left West Virginia State College for Howard
University in Washington, D.C., in 1928, he assumed the acting
chairmanship of the department of psychology.[40] He was convinced that in order to develop a strong program to train black
psychologists adequately, psychology departments needed to be
autonomous units divorced from departments and schools of
education. (The scheme then current in most black schools left
psychology to be taught as an ancillary subject to education.)
With the aid of Howard's relatively new president, Mordecai W.
Johnson, a separate department of psychology was permanently
established at Howard, and Sumner was appointed full professor
and head of the department in 1930.

A young graduate assistant, Frederick P. Watts, was at Howard
when Sumner arrived in 1928, and he assisted Sumner during the
early days; but it was clear that more help was needed to carry
out Sumner's plans for an expanding department. With the recommendation of E. G. Boring, one of his former professors at
Clark University, Sumner sought thirty-year-old Max Meenes at
Lehigh University in Pennsylvania as a new colleague. Meenes, a
white man holding a Ph.D. from Clark who had been trained as a
"brass instrument psychologist," had the desired specializations
and credentials. Meenes elected to join Sumner at Howard in
1930:

> I was teaching at Lehigh from 1926 to 1930 and I had received a
> promotion from instructor to assistant professor and it seemed clear
> that the next step to associate professor might take quite many
> years, and in the meantime I had received a letter in early 1929
> from Dr. Sumner at Howard University. He wanted another psy-
> chologist . . . he made me an offer that was attractive, so I said
> good-bye to Lehigh and came down here. I knew that Dr. Sumner
> was black and that Howard was a black school, but I was a teacher
> of psychology and I wanted to teach students in psychology wher-

ever they were. Dr. Sumner had an excellent reputation and was a brilliant scholar, so I joined him.[41]

A lifelong association was formed between Sumner, Meenes, and Watts in the creation of a three-man psychology department for training black students.

During World War II, Sumner stressed the need for Howard to train more psychologists:

> The demand for Negroes trained in psychology has been larger during the present emergency than heretofore, in fact larger than the supply. It is believed that the greatest immediate need . . . is the . . . training of specialized personnel particularly in the case of the better grade student.[42]

By 1946, as the program produced more psychologists, Sumner declared that "the enrollment at the graduate and undergraduate level was the highest in the history of the Psychology Department. The scholastic ability . . . (was) higher than usual."[43] It was clear, as the 1940s came to an end, that Sumner's plan for a "first-class department of psychology" had reached fruition.

Sumner's interest in the psychology of religion, a result of his teaching experiences at Lincoln, was renewed at Howard during the late 1940s, when he offered courses in the subject. He was also responsible for instigating studies and other research dealing with the relationship between psychology and the law. Several important studies were conducted in the late 1930s and the mid-1940s assessing the attitudes of blacks and whites toward the administration of justice.[44] Sumner and his graduate students surveyed more than two thousand college students and suggested in several studies procedures which might be used to administer justice on a more democratic basis.

Sumner was described by several of his former students as a "low-keyed and very dedicated psychologist"; as a "very quiet and very unassuming individual who was brilliant with a tremendous capacity to make an analysis of an individual's gestalt"; and as "Howard's most stimulating scholar."

His colleagues spoke of his deep interest in his students and recalled "the mimeographed newsletter he prepared and issued periodically, giving items of interest about graduates from his department."[45] His enjoyment of reading and his constant quest for knowledge led Sumner to write many reviews of a wide variety of books. He became an official abstractor for the *Psychological Bulletin* and the *Journal of Social Psychology*. In this capacity, he translated more than three thousand articles from German, French, and Spanish.

He was a fellow of the American Psychological Association

and held memberships in the American Association for the Advancement of Science, American Educational Research Association, Eastern Psychological Association, Southern Society for Philosophy and Psychology, and the District of Columbia Psychological Association. His fraternal memberships included Psi Chi, Pi Gamma Mu, and Kappa Alpha Psi. His first marriage was to Francees H. Hughston in 1922, and his second marriage was to Nettie M. Brooker in 1946. He had no children.

On January 12, 1954, Dr. Francis Cecil Sumner suffered a fatal heart attack while shovelling snow at his home in Washington, D.C. President Mordecai W. Johnson of Howard University delivered the eulogy at the University Chapel and a tribute was paid by J. St. Clair Price, Dean of the College of Liberal Arts at Howard. There was a military honor guard, in memory of Sumner's service in World War I, as he was buried at Arlington Cemetery in Virginia.

Notes

1. Personal correspondence from G. Stanley Hall, 1918, University Archives, Goddard Library, Clark University, Worcester, Massachusetts.
2. Personal correspondence, James P. Porter, 1915, University Archives, Clark University.
3. Personal correspondence, F. C. Sumner, June 16, 1915, University Archives, Clark University.
4. Personal correspondence, G. Stanley Hall, 1918, University Archives, Clark University.
5. Personal correspondence, F. C. Sumner, 1915, University Archives, Clark University.
6. Ibid.
7. "Who's Who, 1916," *Clark College Yearbook,* Clark University, Worcester, Massachusetts.
8. Personal correspondence, F. C. Sumner, June 1917, University Archives, Clark University.
9. Ibid.
10. Personal correspondence, James P. Porter, 1917, University Archives, Goddard Library, Clark University.
11. Ibid.
12. Personal correspondence, F. C. Sumner, June 1917, University Archives, Goddard Library, Clark University.
13. Ibid.
14. Personal correspondence, G. Stanley Hall, 1918, University Archives, Clark University.
15. F. C. Sumner in "The Forum of the People," *Worcester Gazette,* May 25, 1918, Worcester, Massachusetts.

16. Ibid., February 15, 1918.
17. Ibid., May 25, 1918.
18. H. Chamberlin in "The Forum of the People," *Worcester Gazette*, May 27, 1918.
19. F. C. Sumner in "The Forum of the People," *Worcester Gazette*, May 29, 1918.
20. Personal correspondence, G. Stanley Hall, 1918, University Archives, Clark University.
21. Personal correspondence, F. C. Sumner, June 1918, University Archives, Clark University.
22. Ibid.
23. Ibid.
24. Ibid.
25. Personal correspondence, F. C. Sumner, 1919, University Archives, Clark University.
26. Ibid.
27. Personal correspondence, G. Stanley Hall, 1920, University Archives, Clark University.
28. M. G. Allison, "The Year in Negro Education," *The Crisis*, July 1920, p. 126.
29. Personal correspondence, F. C. Sumner, June 1919, University Archives, Clark University.
30. F. C. Sumner, "Core and Context in the Drowsy State," *American Journal of Psychology* (April 1924).
31. F. C. Sumner, "Environic Factors which Prohibit Creative Scholarship Among Negroes," *School and Society*, 22 (1928).
32. Ibid.
33. F. C. Sumner, "The Philosophy of Negro Educating," *Educational Review* (June 1926).
34. Ibid.
35. F. C. Sumner, "Morale and the Negro College," *Educational Review* (March 1927).
36. Ibid.
37. Ibid.
38. Ibid.
39. F. C. Sumner, "The Nature of Emotion," *Howard Review*, 1 (June 1924).
40. Many of Howard's early faculty members previously taught at West Virginia State College.
41. From a taped interview conducted by the author with Max Meenes at Howard University on November 28, 1972.
42. F. C. Sumner, "The Nature of Emotion," *Howard Review*, 1 (June 1924).
43. Ibid.
44. Ibid.
45. "Funeral at Howard for Dr. F. Sumner," *The Washington Afro-American*, January 16, 1954, p. 5.

three
Conclusion

8
The past is prologue

In many ways we have come full circle in less than a hundred years of "scientific" psychology. Some of the dubious research of the 1920s has lingered nearly fifty years as a phantomlike apparition of pseudointellectualism. Present-day proclamations purporting to present evidence of limited intellectual capacities in black Americans resemble the claims of biased 1920 educational psychologists; race-betterment policies and recommendations for genetic control of the "socially unacceptable" reemerge with the same bigotry of a half-century ago. These theories recur with an appearance of "newness" enough to obscure the cobwebs of antiquity and actually encourage a repeat of the same defenses utilized decades ago. This is occurring today in the arguments against the continued use of IQ tests and the allegations of inherited mental deficits in black and brown children. The atmosphere that created the formation of minority professional caucuses in order to provide specialized agendas and unified forces are reminiscent of earlier attempts to organize black professionals.

A major section of Part One of this book focused on selected research activities of physical anthropology and psychology and their attempts to detect and measure minute variations in humans. While the activities of the two disciplines appear to be discrete, it is important to note that they shared similar philosophical biases, strongly influenced one another, and contributed heavily to the belief that one race was inherently superior to another. One could dismiss the early anthropometric findings as quaint examples of pseudoscience were it not for the fact that the results of these views molded the psyches of many Americans in various mixtures of arrogance and fear. And anthropometric quantifications of physical attributes encouraged the belief that psychological traits, too, could be measured. While the quantification of physical differences has now lost much of its credibility and acceptance, the profound impact of mental measurement still lingers.

The Myth of Mental Measurement

Over the past seventy years, attempts to measure and report individual and group intellectual capabilities in the form of a single score have failed. (These efforts represent one of the Waterloos of psychology.) A much deeper tragedy has been the basic assumption that a generalized, broad-based definition of intelligence could be created. Above all, the propriety of assigning blanket terms to all problem-solving behaviors is highly debatable in a multicultural society with wide variations in the cognitive and life styles of its citizens. And factorial studies have shown that a number of elements, normally ignored by conventional IQ tests, underlie the problem-solving behaviors of individuals regardless of cultural differences. The often quoted statement that "intelligence is whatever it is that intelligence tests test" not only sums up the existing state of past efforts, but becomes a sad recommendation for the continual use of such tests.

If it is deemed desirable to pursue this illusive hypothetical construct, let it be without the penalty of indelibly labeling those individuals who are the unwilling participants in such exercises. Most Americans, black and white, realize that IQ tests are not valid; but they are helpless in a system that has constructed and perpetuated the myth of mental measurement. Billions of dollars have been poured into the psychometric profession, making it difficult for those directly or indirectly involved in the industry to agree that the IQ concept is null and void. Just as the Binet test was legally contested in 1916 when institutionalization was the issue (see Chapter 3), it will necessitate similar challenges to achieve limits on the use of IQ test results in educational settings. And when this happens, no doubt, the old heredity-environment debate will resurface and the same arguments will be heard all over again.

Psychology and Politics

The 1954 Supreme Court decision, which required the public schools to integrate their classrooms "with all deliberate speed," rekindled the issue of inherited intellectual differences between racial groups. Former APA president Henry Garrett became a states' rights and segregationalist's "in-house psychologist" who provided a host of "reasons" why black children could not compete intellectually with white children. (It should be recalled that Garrett was involved in the early mental measurements of World War I and strongly supported the hereditarian point of view of that time.) Garrett's most vociferous attack against school integration was in a widely distributed twenty-four-page booklet, *How Classroom Desegregation Will Work,* which drew heavily upon selected IQ test results and anthropological data. The booklet was blatantly racist in content and remindful of the early studies of Ferguson and Mayo (see Chapter 2).

During the 1960s, individuals who supported the importance of heredity over environment voiced strong objections to President Lyndon Johnson's Great Society programs. Important elements of Johnson's War on Poverty proposals deemphasized hereditarian views and designed programs which would reduce the environmental differences between black and white Americans. A notable example, Project Head Start, the comprehensive preschool program for the children of the poor, was based on a recognition of the importance of environmental factors in learning; Head Start supported the notion that intelligence was malleable and not strongly deterministic. Two significant studies provided the intellectual bases for this point of view: J. McV. Hunt's influential attack on the prevailing notion of genetically determined and fixed intelligence, *Intelligence and Experience,* and Benjamin Bloom's *Stability and Change in Human Characteristics,* which argued that intelligence was plastic in the preschool and early elementary years and did not reach stability until about age twelve.[1]

Between 1964 and 1970, several studies directly or indirectly criticized the efforts of the federal government's compensatory programs. These criticisms shifted the blame for the declared scholastic failures of the programs to the problems of the students or their parents. Leaders in these analyses were Daniel Moynihan, James Coleman, William Schockley, and Arthur Jensen.

Old Wine, New Bottles

In 1965, *The Negro Family: The Case for National Action* (The Moynihan Report) concentrated almost solely on what was termed "negative" in the black existence. The report's findings proclaimed that "deep-seated structural distortions in the life of the Negro-American" existed and concluded that "the present tangle of pathology" would continue unless white intervention occurred. Moynihan reached his conclusions by comparing the absenteeism of the black male in the household with crime and delinquency data; as in earlier cases, the black family was viewed from a white middle-class perspective and the assumptions drawn from this bias resulted in gross oversimplifications of the data compiled. (The use of the white middle-class family as a "norm" insinuated that the white family was the ideal model for stability.) The major problem that Moynihan failed to comprehend was that of the practical adaptation to a racist environment confronting the average black family.

The following year (1966) The Coleman Report, *Equality of Educational Opportunity,* reinforced Moynihan's findings by declaring that the principal sources of scholastic failure of black children stemmed not from the schools but rather from the student's home environment and family background. This report concluded that "schools bring little influence to bear on the child's achievement that is independent of his background and general social context." This finding was suspect on two counts: first, a number of the schools sampled in the survey failed to return the lengthy questionnaires (this raised doubts of the representativeness of the sample); second, the questionnaire items themselves reflected a strong middle-class bias.[2]

Eugenics Revisited

Physicist William Schockley's entry into the hereditarian arena of human affairs created a resurgence of eugenic views when his paper, "Population Control or Eugenics" was made public.[3] His eugenic philosophy became further explicit when he spoke at a symposium sponsored by Gustavus Adolphus College in Minnesota on "Genetics and the Future of Man" in 1965. Even though Schockley possesses no credentials in the fields of genetics or psychology, his status as a former Nobel Prize Winner (co-inventor of the transistor, 1956) increased his acceptance and attracted audiences that would otherwise have been indifferent to him. Schockley advocates a national genetics control program to counteract what he terms as "*dysgenics,* a retroactive evolution through the disproportionate reproduction of the genetically disadvantaged." According to this view, the reported lower IQ scores of black Americans are due to inheritance rather than to environmental factors.

Schockley extends his dysgenic notion to explain that many of the "large improvident families with social problems have constitutional deficiencies in those parts of the brain which enable a person to plan and carry out plans."[4] (He localizes this deficiency in the brain's frontal lobe.) In order to halt the dysgenic trend, he calls for a bonus plan in which cash payments would be paid to black people with IQs below 100 who voluntarily submit to sterilization operations. Schockley's suggestions differ very little from the Laughlin Report of 1914, which discussed the "best practical means of cutting off the defective germ-plasm in Americans."

To support his genetic attribution theory of intelligence and social problems, Schockley draws upon studies comparing the intelligence quotients of identical white twins separated at birth and subsequently reared in different environments. These studies reported that the measured IQs were similar in identical twins regardless of environmental differences. Schockley interprets this data as conclusive evidence of the importance of heredity.

Fellow eugenicist Arthur Jensen lends support to this conjecture. Jensen, a University of California educational psychologist, attracted national attention in 1969 with his article, "How Much Can We Boost IQ and Scholastic Achievement?" This lengthy study drew on the author's analysis of the IQ heritability among 122 pairs of white twins—which he extrapolated to account for differences in IQ scores among black and white children. Both Schockley and Jensen conclude that inheritance accounts for 80 percent of the variability in intelligence, with environment accounting for the remaining 20 percent. These percentages are identical to Edward Thorndike's calculations in 1920 (see Chapter 3). And these views resemble the old rationale for separate educational curricula for black children (see Chapter 2). It is impossible to justify the Jensen-Schockley positions on the basis of the studies cited; selective factors in adoption (children were placed in homes of friends and relatives), questions of validity of the IQ test scores, and a number of contradictory findings suggesting the importance of environment were not discussed.[5]

Part Two of this book made an effort to recount events which led to the establishment of black higher education in hopes that the reader would develop an appreciation for the problems facing black colleges and the enormous difficulties that black graduates faced in securing postgraduate training. Biographical articles were included to provide brief personal and career histories of black psychologists, a close analysis of which should reveal that most of the work of these early psychologists was in the mainstream, more or less, of traditional psychological work in the area of racial differences. For this reason, the work of these black psychologists, in countering the biases of white psychologists, utilized the same paradigms of the profession.

At present there exists a scientific community of black scholars whose daily lives are affected by racism. This has brought about unified concerns on a number of issues within the discipline of psychology. Concern over inappropriate research stances (deficit modeling) and applied programs (urban and community psychology) are among the major priorities of black psychologists. While at present it is difficult to justify the existence of a black psychology, there is a theoretical basis for its creation. The chapters of this book are a testament to its prehistory.

Notes

1. M. S. Smith and J. S. Bissell, "Report Analysis: The Impact of Head Start," *Harvard Educational Review*, 40:1 (February 1970), p. 55.
2. Subjects were asked whether encyclopedias were in the home, inferring that a *yes* answer indicated parental concern and a *no* answer meant no parental concern for the child's education.
3. "Is Quality of U. S. Population Declining?" *U. S. News & World Report* (November 22, 1965), pp. 68–71.
4. Ibid., p. 69.
5. J. S. Kagan, "Inadequate Evidence and Illogical Conclusions," *Harvard Educational Review*, 39:2 (Spring 1969), pp. 126–129.

Appendix

Statement on Racial Psychology
by the Society for the Psychological
Study of Social Issues (SPSSI), 1938

Text of the Protest

The current emphasis upon "racial differences" in Germany
and Italy, and the indications that such an emphasis may be on
the increase in the United States and elsewhere, make it important to know what psychologists and other social scientists have
to say in this connection.

The fascists and many others have grossly misused the term
"race." According to anthropologists, the term "race" may legiti-
mately be used only for such groups as possess in common certain physical or bodily characteristics which distinguish them from
other groups. It is impossible to speak correctly of a "German
race" or of an "Italian race," since both of these groups have
highly diversified physical characteristics.

A South German may resemble a Frenchman from Auvergne
or an Italian from Piedmont more closely than he does a German
from Hanover. North Italians are markedly dissimilar from those
living in Sicily or Naples.

More important still, the emphasis on the existence of an
"Aryan race" has no scientific basis, since the word "Aryan" refers
to a family of language and not at all to race or to physical
appearance.

As far as the Jews are concerned, scientific investigations have
shown them to be tall or short, blond or dark, round-headed or
long-headed, according to the particular community studied. In

the light of this wide variation in physical characteristics, almost all anthropologists outside of Germany and Italy would agree that it is scientifically impossible to speak of a "Jewish race," much less of an "Aryan race."

In the experiments which psychologists have made upon different peoples, no characteristic, inherent psychological differences which fundamentally distinguish so-called "races" have been disclosed. This statement is supported by the careful surveys of these experiments in such books as "Race Psychology" by Professor T. R. Garth, of the University of Denver; "Individual Differences" by Professor Frank S. Freeman, of Cornell University; "Race Differences" by Professor Otto Klineberg, of Columbia University; and "Differential Psychology" by Dr. Anne Anastasi, of Barnard College.

There is no evidence for the existence of an inborn Jewish or German or Italian mentality. Furthermore, there is no indication that the members of any group are rendered incapable by their biological heredity of completely acquiring the culture of the community in which they live. This is true not only of the Jews in Germany, but also of groups that actually are physically different from one another. The Nazi theory that people must be related by blood in order to participate in the same cultural or intellectual heritage has absolutely no support from scientific findings.

Members of the SPSSI Council for the Statement on Racial Psychology

Members of the council were: Dr. F. H. Allport, Syracuse University; Dr. Gordon Allport, Harvard University; Dr. J. F. Brown, University of Kansas; Dr. Hadley Cantril, Princeton University; Dr. L. W. Doob, Yale University; Dr. H. B. English, Ohio State University; Dr. Franklin Fearing, University of California at Los Angeles; Dr. George W. Hartmann, Columbia University; Dr. I. Krechevsky, University of Colorado; Dr. Gardner Murphy, Columbia University; Dr. T. C. Schneirla, New York University; and Dr. E. C. Tolman, University of California.

List of Respondents to the 1930 Questionnaire Concerning the Validity of the Mulatto Hypotheses (Chapter 3).

Psychologists

1. Floyd H. Allport (Syracuse)
2. Gordon W. Allport (Dartmouth)
3. J. E. Anderson (Minnesota)
4. Ada H. Arlitt (Cincinnati)
5. F. A. Aveling (Univ. of London)
6. C. H. Bean (La. State)
7. C. E. Benson (New York)
8. Madison Bentley (Cornell)
9. Edwin G. Boring (Harvard)
10. J. W. Bridges (McGill)
11. Carl C. Brigham (Princeton)
12. Mary W. Calkins (Wellesley)
13. E. H. Cameron (Illinois)
14. Harvey A. Carr (Chicago)
15. J. E. Coover (Stanford)
16. S. A. Courtis (Michigan)
17. Elmer Culler (Illinois)
18. K. M. Dallenback (Cornell)
19. J. F. Dashiell (North Carolina)
20. C. B. Davenport (Carnegie Institute)
21. Walter F. Dearborn (Harvard)
22. Raymond Dodge (Yale)
23. Knight Dunlap (Johns Hopkins)
24. U. Ebbecke (Bonn)
25. Beatrice Edsell (Univ. of London)
26. H. B. English (Antioch)
27. S. W. Fernberger (Pennsylvania)
28. F. S. Freeman (Cornell)
29. T. R. Garth (Denver)
30. A. I. Gates (Columbia)
31. A. R. Gilliland (Northwestern)
32. Kate Gordon (Univ. of Calif., Los Angeles)
33. C. T. Gray (Texas)
34. W. T. Heron (Minnesota)
35. N. D. M. Hirsch (Duke)
36. H. G. Hotz (Arkansas)
37. W. S. Hunter (Clark)
38. A. M. Jordan (North Carolina)
39. D. Katz (Rostock)
40. T. L. Kelley (Stanford)
41. F. A. Kingsbury (Chicago)
42. H. L. Koch (Texas)
43. D. A. Laird (Colgate)
44. H. S. Langfeld (Princeton)
45. L. N. Lanier (Vanderbilt)
46. Mark A. May (Yale)
47. William McDougall (Duke)
48. H. Meltzer (Psychiatric Clinic, St. Louis)
49. F. A. Moss (Geo. Washington)
50. R. M. Ogden (Cornell)
51. Jean Piaget (Geneva)
52. D. S. Patterson (Minnesota)
53. F. A. C. Perrin (Texas)
54. Joseph Peterson (Geo. Peabody)
55. Henri Pieron (Sorbonne)
56. Rudolph Pintner (Columbia)
57. S. L. Pressey (Ohio State)
58. C. M. Reinhoel (Arkansas)
59. M. L. Reymert (Wittenberg)
60. Peter Sandiford (Toronto)
61. C. E. Seashore (Iowa)
62. Mandel Sherman (Child Research Center, Washington, D. C.)
63. L. M. Terman (Stanford)
64. R. H. Thouless (Glasgow)
65. L. L. Thurstone (Chicago)
66. H. A. Toops (Ohio State)
67. M. R. Trabue (North Carolina)
68. M. S. Viteles (Pennsylvania)
69. H. C. Warren (Princeton)
70. Margaret Washburn (Vassar)

Psychologists (Continued)

71. Paul V. West (New York)
72. H. H. Woodrow (Illinois)
73. R. S. Woodworth (Columbia)
74. Helen T. Woolley (Columbia)

75. R. M. Yerkes (Yale)
76. C. S. Yoakum (Michigan)
77. P. C. Young (La. State)

Sociologists and Anthropologists

1. Franz Boas (Columbia)
2. E. S. Bogardus (Southern California)
3. E. W. Burgess (Chicago)
4. Fay Cooper-Cole (Chicago)
5. Jerome Dowd (Oklahoma)
6. Ellsworth Faris (Chicago)
7. Ross L. Finney (Minnesota)
8. Loomis Havemeyer (Yale)
9. E. A. Hooton (Harvard)
10. Carl Kelsey (Pennsylvania)
11. J. M. Mechlin (Dartmouth)

12. R. D. McKenzie (Univ. of Washington)
13. Howard W. Odum (North Carolina)
14. H. A. Miller (Ohio State)
15. Wm. F. Ogburn (Chicago)
16. Robert Redfield (Chicago)
17. E. B. Reuter (Iowa)
18. J. H. Sellin (Pennsylvania)
19. F. G. Speck (Pennsylvania)
20. A. M. Tozzer
21. Donald Young (Pennsylvania)
22. Kimball Young (Wisconsin)

Educationists

1. W. C. Bagley (Columbia)
2. J. F. Bobbitt (Chicago)
3. F. G. Bonser (Columbia)
4. W. H. Burnham (Clark)
5. W. H. Burton (Chicago)
6. H. E. Burtt (Ohio State)
7. C. E. Chadsey (Illinois)
8. W. W. Charters (Ohio State)
9. G. S. Counts (Columbia)
10. J. O. Creager (New York)
11. E. P. Cubberley (Stanford)
12. John Dewey (Columbia)
13. J. J. Doster (Alabama)
14. I. N. Edwards (Chicago)
15. F. C. Ensign (Iowa)

16. F. N. Freeman (Chicago)
17. M. E. Haggerty (Minnesota)
18. C. H. Judd (Chicago)
19. Wm. H. Kilpatrick (Columbia)
20. H. D. Kitson (Columbia)
21. F. O. Kreager (La. State)
22. E. A. Lincoln (Harvard)
23. E. L. Morphet (Alabama)
24. L. A. Pechstein (Cincinnati)
25. C. C. Peters (Penn State)
26. B. F. Pittinger (Texas)
27. F. W. Reeves (Kentucky)
28. V. M. Sims (Alabama)
29. David Snedden (Columbia)
30. P. W. Terry (Alabama)

Miscegenation Laws in the United States

State	Year Passed	Groups Prohibited from Marrying White Persons
Alabama	1923	"Negro or descendent of a Negro to the 3rd generation inclusive."
Arizona	1928	"Negroes, Mongolians, Indians, Hindus or members of the Malay race."
Arkansas	Unknown	"Negroes and Mulattoes."
California	1929	"Negroes, Mongolians, Mulattoes or Members of the Malay race."
Delaware	1915	"Negro or Mulattoes."
Florida	1920	"Any Negro (person having one-eighth or more of Negro blood)."
Georgia	1926	"Persons with African descent;" "all Negroes, Mulattoes, Mestozos and their descendants having any ascertainable trace of either Negro or African West Indian or Asiatic Indian blood in their veins," "Mongolians."
Idaho	1919	"Mongolians, Negroes or Mulattoes"
Indiana	1926	"Persons having one-eighth or more of Negro blood."
Kentucky	1922	"Negro or Mulatto."
Louisiana	1926	"Persons of color."
Maryland	1924	"Negro or person of Negro descent to the third generation or a member of the Malay race."
Mississippi	1930	"Negro or Mulatto or Mongolian."
Missouri	1929	"Persons having one-eighth or more Negro blood," "Mongolian."
Montana	1921	"Negro or a person of Negro blood or in part negro," "Chinese person," "Japanese person."
Nebraska	1922	"Person having one-eighth or more Negro, Japanese or Chinese blood."
Nevada	1929	"Any person of the Ethiopian or black race, Malay or brown race, Mongolian or yellow race."
North Carolina	1919	"Negro or Indian," "or person of Negro or Indian descent to the third generation inclusive."
North Dakota	1913	"Negro."
Oklahoma	1921	"Any person of African descent."
Oregon	1930	"Any Negro, Chinese or any person having one-fourth or more Negro, Chinese or Kanaka blood, or more than one-half Indian."
South Carolina	1929	"Any Indian or Negro."
South Dakota	1929	"Any person belonging to the African, Corean, Malayan or Mongolian race."
Tennessee	1917	"African or the descendants of Africans to the third generation inclusive."
Texas	1925	"Negro or Mongolian."
Utah	1927	"Negro or Mongolian."
Virginia	1930	"Colored persons."
West Virginia	1923	"Negro."
Wyoming	1920	"Negroes, Mulattoes, Mongolians or Malays."

Selected Bibliography
of Psychological Studies, 1920–1946

1920
J. Henry Alston, "The Spatial Condition of the Fusion of Warmth and Cold in Heat," *American Journal of Psychology*, July.

1922
Francis C. Sumner, "Psychoanalysis of Freud and Adler or Sex-Determinism and Character Formation," *Pedagogical Seminary*, June.

1924
Francis C. Sumner, "Core and Context in the Drowsy State," *American Journal of Psychology*, April.
———, "The Nature of Emotion," *Howard Review*, 1, June.
———, "Environic Factors Which Prohibit Creative Scholarship Among Negroes," *School and Society*, 22, 558.

1925
Francis C. Sumner, "The Fear of Death and the Belief in a Future Life," *Kappa Alpha Psi Journal*, 12, December.

1926
Francis C. Sumner, "The Philosophy of Negro Education," *Educational Review*, January.

1927
Howard H. Long, "Educational Research, *Washington, D.C. Board of Education Reports*.
Francis C. Sumner, "Morale and the Negro College," *Educational Review*, March.

1929
Albert S. Beckham, "Is the Negro Happy?" *Journal of Abnormal and Social Psychology*, 24.
Howard H. Long, "Individual Differences Among Children," *Washington, D.C. Board of Education Reports*.

1934
Albert S. Beckham, "A Study of Race Attitudes in Negro Children of Adolescent Age," *Journal of Abnormal and Social Psychology*, 39, 1, April-June.
Horace M. Bond, "Investigation of Racial Differences Prior to 1910," *Journal of Negro Education*, 3, July.
Herman G. Canady, "The Motive of Human Behavior and Personality Adjustment," *Kappa Alpha Psi Journal*, 21.

Paul A. Witty and Martin D. Jenkins, "The Educational Achievement of a Group of Gifted Negro Children," *The Journal of Educational Psychology,* November.

1935

Paul A. Witty and Martin D. Jenkins, "The Case of 'B'—A Gifted Negro Child," *Journal of Social Psychology,* 6.

1936

Herman G. Canady, "Individual Differences Among Freshman at West Virginia State College and Their Educational Bearings, *West Virginia State College Bulletin, 23,* 2.

———, "The Intelligence of Negro College Students and Parental Occupation," *American Journal of Sociology,* 42.

———, "The Effect of Rapport on the IQ—A New Approach to the Problem of Racial Psychology, *Journal of Negro Education,* 5.

———, *Behavior Adjustment,* West Virginia State College Press.

Martin D. Jenkins, "Socio-Psychological Study of Negro Children of Superior Intelligence," *Journal of Negro Education,* 5.

Martin D. Jenkins, "Gifted Negro Children, *The Crisis,* 48, November.

Francis C. Sumner and Frederick P. Watts, "Rivalry Between Uniocular Negative After-Images and the Vision of the Other Eye," *The American Journal of Psychology,* 48.

1937

Herman G. Canady, "Individual Differences and Their Educational Significance in Guidance of the Gifted and Talented Child," *The Quarterly Review of Higher Education Among Negroes,* 5.

———, "Adjusting Education to the Abilities, Needs and Interests of Negro College Students, *School and Society,* 46.

1938

———, "Sex Differences in Intelligence Among Negro College Freshmen," *Journal of Applied Psychology,* 4.

1939

Herman G. Canady, "Psychology in Negro Institutions," *West Virginia State College Bulletin, 26,* 3.

Kenneth B. Clark and Mamie P. Clark, "The Development of Consciousness of Self and the Emergence of Racial Identification in Negro Pre-School Children, *Journal of Social Psychology,* 10.

Kenneth B. Clark and Mamie P. Clark, "Segregation as a Factor in the Racial Identification of Negro Pre-School Children," *Journal of Experimental Education,* 8.

Carlton B. Goodlett, "Negro Youth and Educational System," *School and Society,* 50.

Martin D. Jenkins, "Intelligence of Negro Children," *Educational Method,* 19.

———, "Mental Ability of the American Negro," *Journal of Negro Education,* 8.

Francis C. Sumner, "Measurement of the Relevancy of Picture to Copy in Advertisements, *The Journal of Psychology*, 7.

―――, "Attitudes Toward the Administration of Justice," *The Journal of Psychology*, 8.

1940

Kenneth B. Clark and Mamie P. Clark, "Skin Color as a Factor in Racial Identification of Negro Pre-School Children, *Journal of Social Psychology*, 11.

Kenneth B. Clark, "Some Factors Influencing the Remembering of Prose Material," *Archives of Psychology*, 253.

Carlton B. Goodlett, "The Educational Problems of Minority Youth," *School and Society*, 52.

Martin D. Jenkins, "Racial Differences and Intelligence," *American Teacher Magazine*.

1941

James A. Bayton, "Racial Stereotypes," *Journal of Abnormal and Social Psychology*, 30.

――― and M. G. Preston, "Differential Effect of a Social Variable Upon Three Levels of Aspiration," *Journal of Experimental Psychology*, 29.

Daniel P. Clarke, "Role of Psychology in Race Survival," *Journal of Negro Education*, 10.

―――, "Stanford-Binet "L" Response Patterns in Matched Racial Groups," *Journal of Negro Education*, 10.

Frederick P. Watts, "A Comparative Clinical Study of Delinquent and Non-Delinquent Negro Boys," *Journal of Negro Education*, 10.

1942

James A. Bayton, "Psychology of Racial Morale," *Journal of Negro Education*, 11.

―――, "Correlations Between Levels of Aspiration, *Journal of Negro Education*, 13.

Herman G. Canady, "The American Caste System and the Question of Negro Intelligence," *Journal of Educational Psychology*, 2.

Herman G. Canady et al., "A Scale for the Measurement of the Social Environment of Negro Youth," *Journal of Negro Education*, 11.

Herman G. Canady, "The Methodology and Interpretation of Negro-White Mental Testing," *School and Society*, 55.

―――, "The Question of Negro Intelligence and Our Defense Program, *Opportunity*, 20.

Kenneth B. Clark and Francis C. Sumner, "Some Factors Influencing a Group of Negroes in Their Estimation of the Intelligence and Personality Wholesomeness of Negro Subjects," Howard University unpublished Manuscript.

Kenneth B. Clark, "Morale Among Negroes," A chapter in Goodwin Watson's *Civilian Morale*, 1942 Yearbook of the Society for the Psychological Study of Social Issues.

1943

Herman G. Canady, "The Problem of Equating the Environment of Negro-White Groups for Intelligence Testing in Comparative Studies," *Journal of Social Psychology*, 17.

———, "A Study of Sex Differences in Intelligence Test Scores Among 1,306 Negro College Freshmen," *Journal of Negro Education*, 12.

Herman G. Canady, "Interrelations Between Levels of Aspiration, Performance and Estimates of Past Performance," *Journal of Experimental Psychology*, 33.

Roderick W. Pugh, "Comparative Study of the Adjustment of Negro Students in Mixed and Separate High Schools," *Journal of Negro Education*, 12.

1944

Kenneth B. Clark, "Group Violence; A Preliminary Study of the Attitudinal Pattern of its Acceptance and Rejection: A Study of the 1943 Harlem Riot," *Journal of Social Psychology*, 19.

Mamie P. Clark, "Changes in Primary Mental Abilities with Age," *Archives of Psychology*.

Ruth W. Howard, "Fantasy and the Play Interview," *Character and Personality*, 13.

Martin D. Jenkins et al., *The Black and White Rejections for Military Service*, The American Teachers Association.

Francis C. Sumner, "The Newer Negro and His Education," *West Virginia State College Bulletin*, 2.

Francis C. Sumner and Nettie M. Brooker, "Prognostic and Other Values of Daily Tests," *Journal of Applied Psychology*, 28.

1945

Herman G. Canady, "Differences Among the Peoples of the World," (Chapter 23) *Psychology for the Armed Forces*, E. G. Boring (Ed.), The Infantry Journal.

Kenneth B. Clark, "Zoot Effect on Personality: A Race Riot Participant," *Journal of Abnormal and Social Psychology*, 40.

Francis C. Sumner and Dorothy L. Shaed, "Negro-White Attitudes Towards the Administration of Justice as Affecting Negroes," *Journal of Applied Psychology*, 29.

1946

Herman G. Canady, "The Psychology of the Negro," In Encyclopedia of Psychology, P. L. Harriman (Ed.), Philosophical Library.

Kenneth B. Clark et al., "Variations in the Angioscotoma in Response to Prolonged Mild Anoxia," *Journal of Aviation Medicine*.

Ruth W. Howard, "Intellectual and Personality Traits of a Group of Triplets," *The Journal of Psychology*, 21.

Francis C. Sumner and Luis Andres Wheatley, "Measurement of Neurotic Tendency in Negro Students of Music, *Journal of Psychology*, 22.

Bibliography

Alston, J. Henry. "Psychophysics of the Spatial Condition of the Fusion of Warm and Cold in Heat," *American Journal of Psychology,* July 1920.

American Anthropological Association. "The New York Meeting of the American Anthropological Association," *Science* (New Series), 1939. Vol. 89, pp. 29–30.

Anonymous. "Some Suggestions Relative to a Study of the Mental Attitude of the Negro," *Pedagogical Seminary,* 1916. Vol. 23, pp. 199–203.

Arber, E. and A. G. Bradley, eds. *Travels and Works of Captain John Smith.* London, Wilson, 1910.

Armstrong, M. F. and H. W. Ludlow. *Hampton and Its Students.* New York, Putnam, 1875.

Bache, M. "Reaction Time with Reference to Race," *Psychological Review,* 1895. Vol. 2, pp. 475–586.

Barzun, J. *A Study in Superstition: Race.* New York, Harper and Row, 1935.

Bayton, James A. "Correlations Between Levels of Aspiration," *Journal of Negro Education,* 1942. Vol. 13.

Bayton, James A. "Differential Effect of a Social Variable Upon Three Levels of Aspiration," *Journal of Experimental Psychology,* 1941. Vol. 29.

"The Binet Test in Court," *Eugenical News,* August 1916. Vol. 1.

Bayton, James A. "Psychology of Racial Morale," *Journal of Negro Education,* 1942. Vol. 11.

Bayton, James A. "Racial Stereotypes," *Journal of Abnormal and Social Psychology,* 1940. Vol. 30.

Beckham, Albert S. "Is the Negro Happy?" *Journal of Abnormal and Social Psychology,* 1929. Vol. 24.

Beckham, Albert S. "A Study of the Intelligence of Colored Adolescents of Different Socio-Economic Status in Typical Metropolitan Areas," *Journal of Social Psychology,* 1933. Vol. 4, pp. 70–91.

Beckham, Albert S. "A Study of Race Attitudes in Negro Children of Adolescent Age," *Journal of Abnormal and Social Psychology*, April-June 1935. Vol. 29, part 1.

Bellamy, R. "Measuring Hair Color," *American Journal of Physical Anthropology*, January-March 1930. Vol. 14, Part 1, pp. 75–77.

Berstein, M. and S. Robertson. "Racial and Sexual Differences in Hair Weight," *Journal of Physical Anthropology*, July 1927. Vol. 10, Part 3, pp. 379–385.

Bey, P. As quoted by J. C. Prichard in *Natural History of Man*, ed. E. Norris. London, Wilson and Ogilvy, 1855.

Blackwood, B. "A Study of Mental Testing in Relation to Anthropology," *Mental Measurement Monographs*, December 1927. Vol. 4, p. 113.

Bond, Horace M. "Intelligence Tests and Propaganda," *The Crisis*, June 1924. Vol. 28, Part 2.

Bond, Horace M. "Some Exceptional Negro Children," *The Crisis*, October 1927. Vol. 34, pp. 257–280.

Borman, H. A. "The Color-Top Method of Estimating Skin Pigmentation," *American Journal of Physical Anthropology*, January-March 1930. Vol. 14, Part 1, pp. 59–70.

Broca, P. *Instructions generales pour les recherches anthropologiques a faire sur le vivant*. 2nd ed. Paris, 1879.

Brunschwig, L. "Opportunities for Negroes in the Field of Psychology," *Journal of Negro Education*, October 1941.

Buck v. Bell, Superintendent. United States Supreme Court, 1927. 274 US 200.

Burmeister, Hermann. *The Black Man: The Comparative Anatomy and Psychology of the African Negro*. New York, W. C. Bryant, 1853.

Burlingame, M. and C. P. Stone. "Family Resemblance in Maze-Learning Ability in White Rats," in National Society for the Study of Education, *Nature and Nuture, Their Influence upon Intelligence*. Bloomington, Illinois, Public School Publishing Company, 1928. Twenty-Seventh Yearbook, Part 1, pp. 89–99.

Canady, Herman G. "Adjusting Education to the Abilities, Needs and Interests of Negro College Students," *School and Society*, 1937. Vol. 46.

Canady, Herman G. "The American Caste System and the Question of Negro Intelligence," *Journal of Educational Psychology*, 1942. Vol. 2.

Canady, Herman G. *Behavior Adjustment*. West Virginia State College Press, 1936.

Canady, Herman G. "Differences Among the Peoples of the World," *Psychology for the Armed Forces*. Chapter 23. E. G. Boring, ed. *The Infantry Journal*, 1945.

Canady, Herman G. "The Effect of 'Rapport' on the IQ: A New Approach to the Problem of Racial Psychology," *Journal of Negro Education*, 1936. Vol. 5, pp. 209–219.

Canady, Herman G. "Individual Differences Among Freshman at West Virginia State College and Their Educational Bearings," *West Virginia State College Bulletin*, 1936. Vol. 23, Part 2.

Canady, Herman G. "Individual Differences and Their Educational Significance in Guidance of the Gifted and Talented Child," *The Quarterly Review of Higher Education Among Negroes,* 1937. Vol. 5.

Canady, Herman G. "The Intelligence of Negro College Students and Parental Occupation," *American Journal of Sociology,* 1936, Vol. 42.

Canady, Herman G. "Interrelations Between Levels of Aspiration, Performance and Estimates of Past Performance," *Journal of Experimental Psychology,* 1943. Vol. 33.

Canady, Herman G. "The Methodology and Interpretation of Negro-White Mental Testing," *School and Society,* 1942, Vol. 55.

Canady, Herman G. "The Motive of Human Behavior and Personality Adjustment," *Kappa Alpha Psi Journal,* 1934. Vol. 21.

Canady, Herman G. "The Problem of Equating the Environment of Negro-White Groups for Intelligence Testing in Comparative Studies," *Journal of Social Psychology,* 1943. Vol. 17.

Canady, Herman G. "Psychology in Negro Institutions," *West Virginia State Bulletin,* June 1939. Vol. 3.

Canady, Herman G. "The Psychology of the Negro," in P. L. Harriman, ed. *Encyclopedia of Psychology.* New York, Philosophical Library, 1946.

Canady, Herman G. "The Question of Negro Intelligence and Our Defense Program," *Opportunity,* 1942. Vol. 20.

Canady, Herman G. "A Scale for the Measurement of the Social Environment of Negro Youth," *Journal of Negro Education,* 1942. Vol. 11.

Canady, Herman G. "Sex Differences in Intelligence Among Negro College Freshmen," *Journal of Applied Psychology,* 1938. Vol. 4.

Canady, Herman G. "A Study of Sex Differences in Intelligence Test Scores Among 1,306 Negro College Freshmen," *Journal of Negro Education,* 1943. Vol. 12.

Carter, A. M. "An Assessment of Quality in Graduate Education," *American Council on Education,* Washington, D.C., 1966.

Clark, Kenneth B. "Group Violence: A Preliminary Study of the Attitudinal Pattern of its Acceptance and Rejection: A Study of the 1943 Harlem Riot," *Journal of Social Psychology,* 1944. Vol. 19.

Clark, Kenneth B. "Morale Among Negroes," in Goodwin Watson, *Civilian Morale.* Yearbook of the Society for the Psychological Study of Social Issues, 1942.

Clark, Kenneth B. and Mamie P. Clark. "Segregation as a Factor in the Racial Identification of Negro Pre-School Children," *Journal of Experimental Education,* 1939. Vol. 8.

Clark, Kenneth B. and Mamie P. Clark. "Skin Color as a Factor in Racial Identification of Negro Pre-School Children, *Journal of Social Psychology,* 1940. Vol. 11.

Clark, Kenneth B. and Francis C. Sumner. "Some Factors Influencing a Group of Negroes in Their Estimation of the Intelligence and Personality Wholesomeness of Negro Subjects," Howard University unpublished manuscript, 1942.

Clark, Kenneth B. "Some Factors Influencing the Remembering of Prose Material," *Archives of Psychology,* 1950. Vol. 253.

Clark, Kenneth B. and Mamie P. Clark. "The Development of Consciousness of Self and Emergence of Racial Identification in Negro Pre-School Children," *Journal of Social Psychology,* 1939. Vol. 10.

Clark, Kenneth B. et al. "Variations in the Angioscotoma in Response to Prolonged Mild Anoxia," *Journal of Aviation Medicine,* 1946.

Clark, Kenneth B. "Zoot Effect on Personality: A Race Riot Participant," *Journal of Abnormal and Social Psychology,* 1945. Vol. 40.

Clark, Mamie P. "Changes in Primary Mental Abilities with Age," *Archives of Psychology,* 1944.

Clarke, Daniel. "Role of Psychology in Race Survival," *Journal of Negro Education,* 1941. Vol. 10.

Clarke, Daniel. "Stanford-Binet 'L' Response Patterns in Matched Racial Groups," *Journal of Negro Education,* 1941. Vol. 10.

Cooper, P. "Notes on Psychological Race Differences," *Social Forces,* 1919. Vol. 8, p. 426.

Crane, A. L. *Race Differences in Inhibition.* New York, The Science Press. Archives of Psychology, 1923. Vol. 63.

Cronbach, L. J. *Essentials of Psychological Testing.* New York, Harper and Row, 1949.

Davenport, C. B. *Guide to Physical Anthropology and Anthroposcopy.* Cold Spring Harbor, New York, Eugenics Research Association, 1927.

Davenport, C. B. *Heredity in Relation to Eugenics.* New York, Arno Press, 1972 (1911).

Davenport, C. B. and M. Steggerda. *Race Crossing in Jamaica.* Washington, D.C., Carnegie Institution, 1929. Vol. 395.

Davenport, C. B. *The Trait Book.* Cold Spring Harbor, New York, Eugenics Record Office, 1912. Vol. 6.

Davis, Arthur P. "The Negro Professor," *The Crisis,* April 1936. p. 103.

Deniker, J. *The Races of Man: An Outline of Anthropology and Ethnography.* Freeport, New York, Books for Library Press, 1900.

Dennett, R. E. *At the Back of the Black Man's Mind.* London, Macmillan, 1906.

Downey, J. E. *The Will-Temperament and Its Testing.* Yonkers, New York, World Book Company, 1924.

Drew, Charles R. "Negro Scholars in Scientific Research," *Journal of Negro Education,* 1950. Vol. 35.

Dugdale, R. L. *The Jukes: A Study in Crime, Pauperism, Disease, and Heredity.* New York, Putnam, 1910.

Estabrook, A. H. *The Jukes in 1915.* Washington, D.C., Carnegie Institution, 1916.

Estabrook, A. H. and I. E. McDougle. *Mongrel Virginians: The Win Tribe.* Baltimore, Williams and Wilkins, 1926.

Ferguson, G. O., Jr. *The Psychology of the Negro: An Experimental Study.* New York, The Science Press, 1916.

Fitzgerald, J. A. and W. W. Ludeman. "Intelligence of Indian Children," *Journal of Comparative Psychology,* 1926. Vol. 6.

Flugel, J. C. and D. J. West. *A Hundred Years of Psychology.* New York, Macmillan, 1964.

Folkmar, D. and E. C. Folkmar. "Dictionary of Races or Peoples." Document No. 662. Washington, D.C., The Immigration Commission, 1911. p. 150.

Franklin, J. H. *From Slavery to Freedom: A History of Negro Americans.* 3rd ed. New York, Knopf, 1967.

Fritsch, G. "Bermerkungen zu der Hautfarbentafel," *Mitt Anthrop Ges Wien,* Berlin, 1916. Vol. 16, pp. 183–185.

Galton, F. "Annals of Eugenics," *Galton Laboratory for National Eugenics,* October 1925. Vol. 1, Part 1, p. 3.

Garth, T. R. "The Will-Temperament of Indians," *Journal of Applied Psychology,* 1927. Vol. 11, pp. 512–518.

de Gobineau, A. *The Inequality of Human Races.* New York, Putnam, 1915.

Goddard, H. H. *The Kallikak Family: A Study in the Heredity of Feeblemindedness.* New York, Macmillan, 1912.

Goodlett, Carlton B. "Negro Youth and Educational System," *School and Society,* 1939. Vol. 50.

Goodlett, Carlton B. "The Educational Problems of Minority Youth," *School and Society,* 1940. Vol. 52.

Gray, J. "A New Instrument for Determining the Colour of the Hair, Eyes, and Skin," *Man,* 1908. No. 27, pp. 54–58.

Haddon, A. C. *History of Anthropology.* London, Watts, 1934.

Haeckel, E. H. *Generelle Morphologie der Organismen.* Berlin, G. Reimer, 1866.

Hall, G. S. "The Negro in Africa and America," *Pedagogical Seminary,* 1912.

Hakluyt, R. "The First Voyage of Robert Baker to Guinie," in *Principall Navigations, Voiages and Discoveries of the English Nation.* London, 1589. p. 132.

Herskovits, Melville J. "A Critical Discussion of the 'Mulatto Hypotheses'," *Journal of Negro Education,* July 1934. p. 401.

Herskovits, Melville J. "Age Changes in Pigmentation of American Negroes," *American Journal of Physical Anthropology,* 1926. Vol. 9, Part 3, p. 323.

Herskovits, Melville J. *The Anthropometry of the American Negro.* New York, Columbia University Press, 1930.

Howard, Ruth W. "Fantasy and the Play Interview," *Character and Personality,* 1944. Vol. 13.

Hrdlicka, Ales. *Anthropometry.* Philadelphia, Wistar Institute of Anatomy and Biology, 1939.

Hrdlicka, Ales. "Directions for Collecting Information and Specimens for Physical Anthropology." Washington, D.C., United States National Museum, 1904. No. 39, Part R, p. 25.

Hunter, W. S. "Indian Blood and Otis Intelligence Test," *Journal of Comparative Psychology,* 1922. Vol. 2.

Hunter, W. S. and E. Sommermier. "The Relation of Degree of Indian Blood to Score on the Otis Intelligence Test," *Journal of Comparative Psychology,* 1922. Vol. 2, pp. 257–277.

Hurlock, E. B. "The Will-Temperament of White and Negro Children," *Pedagogical Seminary,* 1930. Vol. 38, pp. 91–99.

Jamieson, E. and P. Standiford. "The Mental Capacity of Southern Ontario Indians," *Journal of Educational Psychology,* 1928. Vol. 19, pp. 536–551.

Jenkins, Martin D. "A Socio-Psychological Study of Negro Children of Superior Intelligence," *Journal of Negro Education,* 1936. Vol. 5, pp. 175–190.

Jenkins, Martin D. "Gifted Negro Children," *The Crisis,* November 1936. Vol. 48.

Jenkins, Martin D. "Intelligence of Negro Children," *Educational Method,* 1939. Vol. 19.

Jenkins, Martin D. "Mental Ability of the American Negro," *Journal of Negro Education,* 1939. Vol. 8.

Jenkins, Martin D. "Racial Differences and Intelligence," *American Teacher Magazine,* 1940.

Jenkins, Martin D. et al. *The Black and White Rejections for Military Service.* The American Teachers Association, 1944.

Joncich, G. *The Sane Positivist: A Biography of Edward L. Thorndike.* Middletown, Connecticut, Wesleyan University Press, 1968.

Jordon, W. D. *White Over Black.* Chapel Hill, The University of North Carolina Press, 1968.

Karier, Clarence J. "Testing for Order and Control in the Corporate Liberal State," *Educational Theory,* Spring 1972. Vol. 22.

Klineberg, O. "An Experimental Study of Speed and Other Factors in 'Racial' Differences," *Archives of Psychology,* 1928. Vol. 93, p. 111.

Klineberg, O. *Race Differences.* New York, Harper and Row, 1935.

LaRue, D. W. "Teaching Eugenics," *Eugenical News,* August 1917. p. 62.

Laughlin, H. H. *Eugenics Record Office.* Cold Spring Harbor, New York, June 1913. Vol. 1.

Laughlin, H. H. *Report of the Committee to Study and to Report on the Best Practical Means of Cutting Off the Defective Germ-Plasm in the American Population.* Cold Spring Harbor, New York, Eugenics Record Office, February 1914.

Linnaeus, C. von. *Systema Natura.* Lugduni, Batavorum, 1735.

Long, Howard H. "Analyses of Test Results from Third Grade Children Selected on the Basis of Socio-Economic Status." Unpublished Doctoral Dissertation, Harvard University, 1933.

Long, Howard H. "Educational Research," *Washington, D.C., Board of Education Reports,* 1927.

Long, Howard H. "Individual Differences Among Children," *Washington, D.C., Board of Education Reports,* 1929.

Malthus, T. R. "An Essay on the Principle of Population." London, 1803.

Mayo, M. J. *The Mental Capacity of the American Negro.* New York, The Science Press, 1913. Archives of Psychology, Vol. 28.

McCuistion, F. *Graduate Instruction for Negroes in the United States.* Nashville, Tennessee, George Peabody College for Teachers, 1939.

McFadden, J. H. and J. F. Dashiell. "Racial Differences as Measured by the Downey Will-Temperament Test," *Journal of Applied Psychology,* 1923. Vol. 7, pp. 30–53.

Miller, George A. *Psychology.* New York, Harper and Row, 1962.

Miller, Herbert. "Science, Pseudo-Science and the Race Question," *The Crisis,* October 1935. Vol. 30, Part 6.

Miller, Herbert. "Some Psychological Considerations on the Race Problem," in W. E. B. Du Bois, ed., *The Health and Physique of the Negro American.* Atlanta University Press, 1906. pp. 54–59.

Moore, H. and I. Steele, "Personality Tests," *Journal of Abnormal and Social Psychology,* 1934–1935. Vol. 29, pp. 45–52.

Morgan, D. C. and H. A. Murray, "A Method for Investigating Fantasies: The Thematic Apperception Test," *Archives of Neurological Psychiatry,* 1935. Vol. 34, pp. 289–306.

Morse, J. "A Comparison of White and Colored Children Measured by the Binet Scale of Intelligence," *The Popular Science Monthly,* January 1914. Vol. 84, Part 1, pp. 75–79.

Paschal, F. C. and L. R. Sullivan. "Racial Factors in the Mental and Physical Development of Mexican Children," *Comparative Psychology Monographs,* October 1925. Vol. 3, pp. 46–75.

Phillips, B. A. "The Binet Test Applied to Colored Children," *Psychological Clinic,* 1914. Vol. 8, pp. 190–196.

Plato. *Republic,* trans. Paul Shorey. Loeb Classical Library. New York, Putnam, 1935.

Popenoe, P. and R. Johnson. *Applied Eugenics.* New York, Macmillan, 1920.

Porteus, S. D. *The Psychology of a Primitive People.* New York, Longmans, Green, 1931.

Pugh, Roderick W. "Comparative Study of the Adjustment of Negro Students in Mixed and Separate High Schools," *Journal of Negro Education,* 1943. Vol. 12.

Pyle, W. H. "The Mind of the Negro Child," *School and Society,* 1915. Vol. 1, p. 358.

Reisman, J. M. *The Development of Clinical Psychology.* New York, Appleton, 1966.

Sanchez, G. I. "Group Differences and Spanish-Speaking Children—A Critical Review," *Journal of Applied Psychology,* 1932. Vol. 16, pp. 549–558.

Schultz, D. P. *A History of Modern Psychology.* New York, Academic Press, 1969.

Schwinfurth, J. *Heart of Africa.* Berlin, Junker and Dunnhaupt, 1938.

Searle, L. V. "The Organization of Hereditary Maze-Brightness and Maze-Dullness," *Genetic Psychology Monograph,* 1949. Vol. 39, pp. 279–325.

"Selection of Negroes," *Eugenical News*, March 1917. Vol. 2.

Shaxby, J. H. and H. E. Bonnell. "On Skin Colour," *Man*, April 1928. pp. 41–42, 60–64.

Spearman, Z. C. "General Intelligence Objectively Determined and Measured," *American Journal of Psychology*, 1904. Vol. 15. pp. 193–201.

Stanton, W. *The Leopard's Spots, Scientific Attitudes Toward Race in America 1815–1859*. Chicago, University of Chicago Press, 1960.

Stern, W. *Uber Psychologie der Individuellen Differenzen*. Leipzig, 1900.

Stetson, G. R. "Some Memory Tests of Whites and Blacks," *Psychological Review*, 1895. Vol. 4, pp. 285–289.

Sullivan, L. R. *Essentials of Anthropometry, A Handbook for Explorers and Museum Collectors*. rev. ed. H. L. Shapiro. New York, American Museum of Natural History, 1928.

Sumner, Francis C. *Annual Reports, 1938–1947*. Howard University, Department of Psychology.

Sumner, Francis C. "Attitudes Toward the Administration of Justice," *The Journal of Psychology*, 1939. Vol. 8.

Sumner, Francis C. "Core and Context in the Drowsy State," *American Journal of Psychology*, April 1924.

Sumner, Francis C. "Environic Factors Which Prohibit Creative Scholarship Among Negroes," *School and Society*, Vol. 22, p. 558.

Sumner, Francis C. "The Fear of Death and the Belief in a Future Life," *Kappa Alpha Psi Journal*, December 1925. Vol. 12.

Sumner, Francis C. and Luis Andres Wheatley. "Measurement of Neurotic Tendency in Negro Students of Music," *Journal of Psychology*, 1946. Vol. 22.

Sumner, Francis C. "Measurement of the Relevancy of Picture to Copy in Advertisements," *The Journal of Psychology*, 1939. Vol. 7.

Sumner, Francis C. "Morale and the Negro College," *Educational Review*, March 1927.

Sumner, Francis C. "The Nature of Emotion," *Howard Review*, June 1924. Vol. 2.

Sumner, Francis C. "Negro-White Attitudes Towards the Administration of Justice as Affecting Negroes," *Journal of Applied Psychology*, 1945. Vol. 29.

Sumner, Francis C. "The New Psychology Unit at Howard University," *Psychological Bulletin*, 1935. pp. 859–860.

Sumner, Francis C. "The Newer Negro and His Education," *West Virginia State College Bulletin*, 1944. Vol. 2.

Sumner, Francis C. "The Philosophy of Negro Education," *Educational Review*, January 1926.

Sumner, Francis C. and Nettie M. Brooker. "Prognostic and Other Values of Daily Tests," *Journal of Applied Psychology*, 1944. Vol. 28.

Sumner, Francis C. "Psychoanalysis of Freud and Adler or Sex-Determinism and Character Formation," *Pedagogical Seminary*, June 1922.

Sumner, Francis C. and Frederick P. Watts. "Rivalry Between Uniocular Negative After-Images and the Vision of the Other Eye," *The American Journal of Psychology*, 1936. Vol. 48.

Sunne, D. "Personality Tests—White and Negro Adolescents," *Journal of Applied Psychology*, 1925. Vol. 9, pp. 256–280.

"Survey of Negro Colleges and Universities," *Bureau of Education Bulletin*. United States Department of the Interior, 1928. Vol. 7.

Terman, L. *Intelligence Tests and School Reorganization*. New York, World, 1923.

Terman L. and M. A. Merrill. *Measuring Intelligence*. Boston, Houghton Mifflin, 1937.

Thompson, Charles H. "The Conclusion of Scientists Relative to Racial Differences," *The Journal of Negro Education*, July 1934. Vol. 3, pp. 494–512.

Thorndike, E. L. "Eugenics: With Special Reference to Intellect and Character," *The Popular Science Monthly*, 1913. Vol. 83, p. 126.

Thorndike, E. L. *Human Nature and the Social Order*. New York, Macmillan, 1940.

Todd, T. W., B. Blackwood, and H. Beecher. "Skin Pigmentation," *American Journal of Physical Anthropology*, 1928. Vol. 11, Part 2, pp. 187–205.

Todd, T. W. and L. Van Gorder. "The Quantitative Determination of Black Pigmentation in the Skin of the American Negro," *American Journal of Physical Anthropology*, 1921. Vol. 4, Part 3, pp. 239–260.

Tryon, R. C. "Genetic Differences in Maze Learning in Rats," in National Society for the Study of Education, *Intelligence: Its Nature and Nurture*. Bloomington, Illinois, Public School Publishing Company, 1940. Yearbook 39, Part 1, pp. 111–119.

Van de Water, M. "Racial Psychology," *Science-Supplement,* September 1938.

Virchow, Rudolf. *Zeitschrift für Ethnologie*. Berlin, Heft, 1895. Vol. 11.

Waitz, Theodor. *Introduction to Anthropology*. London, Longmans, 1863.

Watts, Frederick P. "A Comparative Clinical Study of Delinquent and Non-Delinquent Negro Boys," *Journal of Negro Education*, 1941. Vol. 10.

Welsing, F. As quoted in "Soul: The Sixth Sense," in *New Directions* by Genevieve E. Kaete. Washington, D.C., Howard University, Spring, 1974.

Wispe, L., P. Ash, J. Awkard, L. Hicks, M. Hoffman, and J. Porter, "The Negro Psychologist in America," *American Psychologist*, 1969. Vol. 24, Part 2, pp. 142–150.

Witty, P. and Martin D. Jenkins. "The Case of 'B'—A Gifted Negro Girl," *Journal of Social Psychology*, 1935. Vol. 6, pp. 117–124.

Witty, P. and Martin D. Jenkins. "The Educational Achievement of a Group of Gifted Negro Children," *Journal of Educational Psychology*, November 1934.

Woodworth, R. S. *History of Psychology in Autobiography*, Carl Murchison, ed. Worcester, Massachusetts, Clark University Press. 1932. Vol. 2.

Woodworth, R. S. "Racial Difference in Mental Traits," *Science*, February 1910, p. 171.

Index